Popularisation of Science and Technology Education: Some Case Studies from Africa

Edited by
Mike Savage and Prem Naidoo

COMMONWEALTH SECRETARIAT

African Forum for Children's Literacy
in Science and Technology (AFCLIST)

Commonwealth Secretariat
Marlborough House
Pall Mall
London SW1Y 5HX
United Kingdom

Published by the Commonwealth Secretariat
Designed by Wayzgoose
Printed by Formara Limited

Wherever possible, the Commonwealth Secretariat uses paper sourced from
sustainable forests or from sources that minimise a destructive impact on the
environment.

Price £13.90
ISBN: 0-85092-742-0

Web site:
http//www.thecommonwealth.org

The editors would like to thank the following for their assistance in compiling
this book

Jophus Anamuah-Mensah
Bongile Putsoa
Daya Gobind

Contents

Part III   113

Part IV   237

Prologue

The New Africa Partnership (NEPAD) heralds the dawn of the African century and renaissance – a rejuvenation and vigorous socio-economic development of the continent and its people so that they can compete as equal partners in the new global knowledge economy. Science and technology are key to making NEPAD a reality and all African governments, private and public institutions, and organisational forums need to be mobilised to deliver NEPAD.

Since our future depends on a popular understanding and application of science and technology, its popularisation is imperative. Human resource development in science and technology is crucial to build a critical mass of skilled people, whether such development takes place in educational institutions, in the workplace or through traditional and modern mass media. Africa needs scientifically and technologically literate citizens who can better promote development by:

♦ Better decision-making about the science and technology that impacts on everyday life, thus promoting an improved quality of life in a participatory democracy;

♦ Providing the workforce with appropriate skills for delivery of quality products for national and international markets, thereby promoting economic growth and social development;

♦ Producing scientists and technologists who generate and apply knowledge and technologists to solve local problems and create innovations that can be put to commercial use at national and international levels.

In South Africa we have radically changed our science and technology policy and restructured our network of science and technology institutions to meet the challenges of the new millennium. As chairperson of the Commonwealth Ministers of Science and Technology, I welcome the publication of this book by the African Forum for Children's Literacy in Science and Technology and the Commonwealth Secretariat. It could not be more timely in its analysis of the innovative ways that formal and informal mechanisms have been used in Africa to promote on a wide scale the scientific and technical understanding our peoples need to take the continent into the new millennium.

Dr B. S. Ngubane
Minister of Arts, Culture, Science and Technology
Republic of South Africa

Foreword

Science and technology, and science and technology education, play an important role in the development of a country's economy, environment, social relations and other sectors. African countries recognise this role and many have committed considerable resources to the development of science and technology and to their educational systems. In the early 1960s, immediately after independence, most African countries promoted capacity building in science and technology by sending scholars for training in universities in industrialised countries, while offering science and technology as subjects in their primary and secondary schools. Some invested heavily in the development of infrastructure such as national laboratories, and university and school science departments.

Despite such investment, the countries of sub-Saharan Africa continue to rely on the agrarian and extractive sectors and in some cases on tourism. The agrarian sector largely consists of subsistence farmers and pastoralists who often cannot produce sufficient excess to meet both national needs and exports of cash crops such as coffee, tea and horticultural products. Tourism is dependent on adequate infrastructure and stability, itself dependent on good governance. The extractive sector mines and exports resources such as chrome (97 per cent of world stocks) and platinum (50 per cent of world stocks), without adding value by processing them into manufactured and secondary products. The United Nations Economic Commission for Africa (UNECA) estimates that Africa contributes only 2 per cent of the world's industrial output. Most of the world's 97 least developed countries are in Africa.

In African countries, science and technology education stresses the memorising of facts rather than problem solving and concentrates on the teaching and learning of acultural and irrelevant science and technology. African countries must, therefore, recognise the need to promote, develop and sustain a relevant science and technology culture, which includes problem solving and indigenous aspects, in order to narrow the gap between them and the industrialised countries. Otherwise Africa will continue to be a source of cheap labour and raw materials, and a market for imported products, dependent on foreign technology and aid on dictated terms. African countries must reform policy, engage in programme development, reorganise institutions and reallocate resources to develop science and technology systems. However, such reform must be promoted with a sensitivity that learns from past failures, recognises the existing resource base and takes into account the developmental needs of the continent. South Africa has developed a new science and technology policy framework with appropriate institutional arrangements to deal with the challenges of the twenty-first century. Through such country case studies this book will, therefore, re-examine and revisit:

♦ Why science and technology should be popularised;

♦ What and whose science and technology systems should be introduced and promoted;

♦ How science and technology should be implemented and practised.

This book is a joint effort by the Commonwealth Secretariat and the African Forum for Children's Literacy in Science and Technology (AFCLIST).

AFCLIST is an informal association of African educators, scientists, technologists, media specialists and international resource persons. It is based at the University of Durban-Westville, South Africa and works jointly with Chancellor College, University of Malawi. The AFCLIST mission is to develop a base for a strong science and technology culture among young people in Africa. Involvement in this culture provides young people with opportunities to participate actively in democratising the educational process and society, as well as providing a base for the development of higher level human resources in science and technology. AFCLIST aims to generate popular understanding of the practical applications of science and technology among young people in Africa. It believes that this understanding must be based on interaction between learners and the environment, peers, teachers and other adults in the community, together with accepted views of science. AFCLIST achieves its mission through five interlocking programmes:

♦ **Grants programme:** Project proposals on innovations in science and technology education are scrutinised by an AFCLIST grants committee according to established criteria.

♦ **Networking:** The AFCLIST Secretariat constantly monitors and advises project leaders by means of workshops in their countries.

♦ **Publications programme:** A writing and dissemination programme to achieve maximum benefit from the outcome of projects.

♦ **Node programmes:** Nodes are centres of excellence implemented by educational institutions. These centres are specialist centres dealing with particular problems in science and technology education in Africa, such as the node on teaching science and technology in large under-resourced classrooms.

- **Innovation and change programme:** By means of workshops, AFCLIST brings about change and innovation on aspects of science and technology education. An example is the AFCLIST–FEMSA gender workshop to be held in Nairobi, Kenya in December 2001.

The different country case studies provide some critical insights that are crucial for the realisation of the New Africa Partnership programme. It is hoped that this will assist African policy-makers and practitioners to instill a vibrant and successful science and technology literacy among its people and help to make Africa prosper.

Professor M.F. Ramashala
Vice Chancellor
University of Durban-Westville
Durban, South Africa

Nancy Spence
Director
Social Transformation Programmes Division
Commonwealth Secretariat
London, UK

Preface

Popularisation of Science and Technology Education: Some Case Studies from Africa completes a series of publications sponsored by the Commonwealth Secretariat. The publication was developed jointly with the African Forum for Children's Literacy in Science and Technology, a pan-African organisation that, since 1989, has done much to promote a public understanding of science and technology throughout sub-Saharan Africa.

The vision of popularising science and technology is broader than using traditional and modern mass media to promote a better public understanding of their role in development. AFCLIST believes that:

◆ It is as much the creativity and problem-solving processes of science and technology that are needed by people at all levels of society, whether or not they are in science and technology-related occupations, as the knowledge produced by science. It further believes that such a mindset is a sound preparation for an active participation in the democratic process.

◆ The bulk of people in Africa hold non-scientific beliefs because these have worked for them for countless generations, just as people in industrialised countries believe in science and technology because science and technology have worked for them in their context. In neither case is the belief based on reasoned evidence or an understanding of the respective belief systems. AFCLIST argues that both are acts of faith. On this basis, AFCLIST contends that science-based projects that clearly demonstrate their immediate impact on the quality of people's lives do much to promote public support for, and an understanding of, science and technology.

◆ Since the countries of sub-Saharan Africa lack the extensive networks of modern mass media of industrialised countries, they must develop creative ways to use formal educational systems to target the general public as well as enrolled students.

Popularisation of Science and Technology Education: Some Case Studies from Africa is based on these beliefs.

Part I sets the context as it examines the history, present-day practices and challenges of science and technology, and of science and technology education, in the countries of sub-Saharan Africa. In Chapter 1, 'Issues and Realities', Prem Naidoo and Mike Savage provide an overview, arguing that science and technology have not yet realised the hopes that leaders and professionals throughout the continent have had for the disciplines; they propose a differently defined science and technology that is more orientated towards solving problems, together with a vigorous approach for its popularisation. In Chapter 2, 'The Contribution of Science and Technology', Naidoo and Savage examine what type of science and technology is needed by the countries of sub-Saharan Africa at both the popular and specialist levels, and argue that ways are needed to redirect their development. In Chapter 3, 'Choosing Good Science in a Developing Country', Robert Adams suggests ways in which African countries can develop research portfolios more relevant to Africa's needs.

Africa produces a significant percentage of the world's oil. Nigeria alone is the twelfth largest producer, and promisingly rich fields have recently been discovered in the Gulf of Guinea and off the coast of Angola. Africa's reserves of diamonds and other precious stones are well known, as is the richness of its gold deposits. Equally valuable, but less known, are Africa's deposits of other minerals. The continent produces 97 per cent of the world's stocks of chrome, 50 per cent of its platinum and many other minerals much needed by industrialised countries, without adding value by their processing into manufactured and secondary products. Indeed, UNECA estimates that Africa contributes only 2 per cent of the world's industrial output. Furthermore, the extraordinarily rich biodiversity of Africa's rain forests and ecosystems, such as those found in the southern Cape and Madagascar, has so far been exploited only for the benefit of multinationals and other interests outside the continent. Spirulina harvested by the peoples living on Lake Chad, and a new slimming drug based on the extensive knowledge of the peoples of the Kalahari that will soon be released by Pfizer, are but two of many examples. It is no secret that the bulk of the profits made from Africa's unique tourist opportunities never reach the continent.

Part II, therefore, focuses on how science and technology is being and can be used to exploit this rich resource base for economic and social transformation within the continent. In Chapter 4, 'University Science and Technology Education and Economic Development', Emmanuel Fabiano in Malawi, and Keto Mshigeni and Osmund Mwandemele in Namibia, describe university projects where research at the highest level has popularised science and technology by dramatically demonstrating how they can transform both local and national economies. In Chapter 5, 'Small-scale Industries in the Popularisation of Science and Technology in Ghana', Jesse Amuah examines the role of popularising science and technology in Ghana in transforming the small-scale industrial sector. In Chapter 6, 'The Suame Magazine', Henry Brown-Acquaye uses another Ghanaian example to show how university researchers have established a consultancy service on which the formal and informal sectors of the economy have become dependent. In Chapter 7, 'Indigenous Knowledge Systems and their Economic Potential in South Africa', Otsile Ntsoane examines the potential of indigenous knowledge systems for economic development. Michael Kahn discusses how regional co-operation could strengthen both science and technology and science and technology education in Chapter 8, 'Promoting Co-operation in Science and Technology in the SADC Region'. In Chapter 9, 'Regional Co-operation for Capacity Building in Science and Technology', J.G.M. Massaquoi and Mike Savage describe two effective research networks that have strengthened scientific culture in the eyes of the masses through work that demonstrably leads to improvements in their quality of life.

Part III uses case studies to examine current practices in popularising science and technology. Chapter 10, by Jane Mulemwa, and Chapter 11, by Mike Savage, address issues common to all African countries, namely women's participation and performance and the effective use of the media. Chapters 12–17 are case studies of projects in Malawi and Zanzibar (Mike Savage), Malawi (Matthew Chilambo), Swaziland (Bongile Putsoa), Ghana (Jophus Anamuah-Mensah), South Africa (Botlhale Tema, Kebogile Dilotsotlhe and Jaap Kuiper) and Sierra Leone (Sonia Spencer). In Chapter 18 Marian Addy uses an example from Ghana to show how television can be used to popularise an understanding of science and technology.

In Part IV, Chapter 19, 'A Synthesis', Prem Naidoo summarises the ideas put forward in the previous chapters about ways of popularising science and technology and a way forward is discussed. Finally, in Chapter 20, 'Towards a Theory of Change: A Postscript for Policy-makers', Mike Savage summarises the AFCLIST experience and develops tentative policy guidelines for consideration by those responsible for developing and implementing effective ways of popularising an understanding of science and technology.

Introduction

A large number of Commonwealth countries are making efforts to popularise science and technology to achieve scientific and technological literacy amongst the public at large. A number of strategies are being employed to reach different target groups. In order to assist member countries in their efforts, the Commonwealth Secretariat has started a project on popularisation of the culture of science and technology.

Regional Expert Group Meetings were organised to identify the efforts which have already been made by different countries, problem being faced by them, ways forward and strategies that could be employed in the popularisation of science and technology programmes. The Regional Expert Group Meetings made a number of recommendations, which are being followed by the Commonwealth Secretariat and individual countries. A number of case studies from Asia have been published. The present booklet is a further contribution to existing Commonwealth countries in their efforts to popularise science and technology and contains a set of case studies from Africa. In the same series a book on Using Museums to Popularise Science and Technology has also been published.

There is a growing worldwide concern about pragmatic strategies for initiating entire populations into the important form of human understanding enshrined in science and technology. It is now widely acknowledged that science and technology exert a profound influence on such diverse areas as our interaction with the physical world; patterns of production and distribution of goods and services; socio-economic life styles of communities; and even the value systems of some nations. An understanding of science and technology can therefore be regarded, as one of the most essential pre-requisites for coping with facts, principles, forces, gadgets and practices, which shape the human world. It is now a globally accepted reality that science and technology are indispensable components of modern society and can be used as potent means for development. It is largely because of their capacity to meet our unending quest for social and economic prosperity besides comfort and security. The achievement in genetic engineering and medicine, information technology and space science are indeed mind-boggling. But in the wake of the existing economic divide and the knowledge gap between the `haves' and the `have-nots', science and technology assume an added significance for developing countries. And in this perspective, science and technology education becomes imperative for societal development. Undoubtedly this is an extremely formidable task, particularly, because the developing nations are facing tremendous resource crunch in providing even `basic education for all'. The efforts made so far in this direction have fallen woefully short of societal needs and expectations.

We have had rich and poor nations, people in each village/society, and that we still continue to have, but a whole group of nations being reckoned as rich and another as poor is a relatively new phenomenon. It is unfortunate situation that a little over 23 per cent of the world living in developed countries have access to nearly 80 per cent of the resources, and the remaining about 77 per cent have access to only 20 per cent of the resources – an imbalance that has vast potential for unrest and instability. What has contributed to this imbalance? Is it language, religion or race, the economic organization of the political systems, or the area of the land and natural resources that have generated this inequality? The rich nations are what they are because of their mastery over science and technology (S&T), ability to create new knowledge in S&T, and capacity to apply the knowledge so generated for the social and economic uplift of their people. The capacity of a nation to create, master and apply knowledge in a discipline depends on the level of higher education and research. Moreover, the capacity to absorb new tools and processes that may be generated depends on the level and spread of education.

Even to be able to buy or borrow knowledge in science and technology and to put it to appropriate use, a nation has to adapt it to suit its special requirements and it is believed that for one to be able to make use of an innovation with necessary modification and adaptation, one should have very nearly the capacity for making the innovation itself. Further, any new tool or process can be used only if disseminated among and absorbed by the people. This requires that science and technology must be rooted in the cultural ethos and values of the respective societies. Further, to build bridge and minimize inequitable distribution of resources requires collaboration and learning from each other. It is in this context that Commonwealth Secretariat sponsored this volume and it is heartening to note that several indigenous technologies/experiences have been presented that should benefit the practioners of science and technology.

Dr Ved Goel
Acting Deputy Director and Head
Education Section
Social Transformation Programmes Division

PART I

Chapters 1 and 2 review the role of science and technology in individual, community and national development. Despite high hopes and a substantial allocation of scarce funds, science and technology have not fulfilled the expectations of countries of sub-Saharan Africa. Part I argues that most of what has been and is currently being practised is not truly science and technology. Rather than participating in knowledge production, Africa consumes the products of science and technology. Only when African countries break with tradition and popularise an inquiring, problem-solving science and technology can her peoples solve pressing problems of development and participate actively in the democratic process. Chapter 3 suggests ways to reprioritise the research portfolios of the countries of sub-Saharan Africa to better meet the continent's development needs.

1. Issues and Realities

Prem Naidoo and Mike Savage
African Forum for Children's Literacy in Science and Technology
University of Durban-Westville, South Africa

The Role of Science and Technology

Science and technology, and science and technology education, play an important role in the development of a country's economy, environment and social relations. African countries recognise this role and many have committed considerable resources to the development of their science and technology, and educational systems. In the early 1960s, immediately after independence, most African countries promoted capacity building in science and technology by sending scholars for training in universities in industrialised countries, while offering science and technology as subjects in their primary and secondary schools. Some invested heavily in the development of infrastructure such as national laboratories, and university and school science departments.

Despite such investment, the countries of sub-Saharan Africa continue to rely on the agrarian and extractive sectors and, in some cases, tourism. The agrarian sector largely consists of subsistence farmers and pastoralists who often cannot produce sufficient excess to meet both national needs and provide exports of cash crops such as coffee, tea and horticultural products. Tourism is dependent on adequate infrastructures and stability, which itself depends on good governance. The extractive sector mines and exports resources such as chrome (97 per cent of world stocks) and platinum (50 per cent of world stocks), without adding value by processing them into manufactured and secondary products. UNECA estimates that Africa contributes only 2 per cent of the world's industrial output. Most of the world's 97 least developed countries are in Africa.

Facing Realities

In much of sub-Saharan Africa, to borrow from the Chinese saying, people live in interesting times. Many countries, for example Sierra Leone, Somalia and the Sudan are ravaged by civil war, while others are scourged by HIV. Some countries suffer from long-established, increasingly despotic leaderships. Others are riddled with corruption, and the international press features violence and crime throughout the continent. Lest we despair as science educators that there is little we can do in the path of what appears to be the horsemen of the apocalypse, we should look at other changes taking place. Uganda and Ghana, both countries that have experienced extraordinary hardships during the past, are for the most part peaceful, economically thriving and, just as important, full of hope for the future. In Nigeria, which has been plundered for some 30 years, there are signs that a more democratic, less corrupt era may emerge. A newly democratic South Africa is contributing to the development of the region with increasing confidence, despite the legacy of its troubled past. It is against this varied and complex background that we consider the role of science and technology, and science and technology education.

Despite its wealth and diversity of resources, Makhurane and Kahn (1998) report a UNECA estimate that '... Africa's contribution to the world's industrial output is only 2 per cent'. It has been estimated that the rich countries of the world together account for about three-quarters of global product, though their residents add up to only a fifth of all humans. Most countries of sub-Saharan Africa continue to earn foreign exchange through exporting cash crops and minerals or from tourism. Debt repayment on loans plunge many further into debt since their debts are larger than their meagre foreign exchange earnings. In some ways, the peoples of Africa are fortunate in having economies based on subsistence level farming, pastoralism and thriving informal sectors where a bewildering variety of goods and services are sold. Rural communities in Africa can survive, though as Cheru, quoted by Naidoo and Savage (1998), states, 'In 1981, according to the World Bank, 29 of the 36 countries with the lowest Gross National Product (GDP) were in Africa. Seventy out of every 100 Africans are either destitute or on the verge of poverty'.

In most countries of sub-Saharan Africa, the manufacturing and industrial sectors, usually dominated by an in-country, multinational presence, account for at most 20–30 per cent of GDP. South Africa is the only industrialised country in sub-Saharan Africa, but this has been achieved at a price. To power the mines and factories, black Africans were driven from the land and deprived of their means of survival. There is little or no subsistence level farming in the country. Ironically, this has contributed to a higher wage structure than in other parts of the continent where bachelor wages are paid, since it is assumed there is a wife back home on the farm to feed the children. Apartheid also ensured that the South African workforce had few skills. The combination of relatively high wages and a low level of skills resulted in a situation that suited the small white elite, but which has left the new South Africa uncompetitive in world markets.

Despite high levels of investment in education – in Kenya some 40 per cent of the recurrent government budget goes to education and some estimate that rural households spend over 75 per cent of their cash incomes on schooling – weak local currencies and bad governance render even these sacrifices inadequate. The peoples of rural Africa do survive despite central government and most of Africa is rural. However, most, especially the young, have higher aspirations. People have hopes that their children will live past the age of five and that they themselves will find healing when they are sick. People, especially women, hope for less drudgery. They hope for good sources of water closer to home and for energy that they can switch on rather than having to walk miles for firewood. Parents invest heavily in schooling hoping for better lives for their children who will look after them when they are old. In short, people in Africa hope for development and know that development only comes with good governance.

Numerous theories are used to explain this underdevelopment of Africa, including a lack of science and technology infrastructures. We argue that much science and technology, and science and technology education, is irrelevant or dysfunctional to developmental needs in Africa, and that this failing can be ascribed to a lack of understanding of what and whose science and technology system has been introduced and promoted. The first assumption made when science and technology was 'introduced' to Africa was that no science and technology was practised, and that the knowledge base and tools for science and technology had to be imported and transplanted. Most African scientists were trained in developed countries with rich resource infrastructures for research that focused largely on fundamental problems within the scientific disciplines. As a result many could not continue their research in Africa, while most could not contextualise their research within the continent's development needs. Within the industrial sector, little scientific research is conducted in Africa because most industries are multinationals that conduct research in the parent companies located in the mother country. Thus, the development and practice of science and technology is the state's responsibility, and is largely confined to education and training. Over the past decades, economic decline has contributed to a deterioration of government infrastructures for science and technology, promoting a flight of many of the best African scientists to developed countries. Furthermore, training of scientists at school and university levels is based on irrelevant curricula that are decontextualised from societal problems and indigenous informal and formal sector science and technology practices. Such science is alien tŏ African society, an alienation that is further promoted by rote learning that does not embed science and technology in everyday practice and culture. Thus science and technology are seen as alien, Western bodies of facts that must be memorised and that have no bearing on the improvement of the everyday existence of African people.

For such reasons, we argue, science and technology have not realised their full potential for improving the quality of life for most people in Africa, though they have contributed, for example, to reducing the incidence of infectious disease, improving agricultural production and have led to better communication and transportation. However, these and other benefits have been better capitalised on in developed countries and will continue to contribute to an accelerated pace of development, hence widening the gap between rich and poor countries. Indeed, developed countries have launched major programmes on 'Science for All' to popularise science in their countries. They have recognised that scientific and technological literacy is a major precondition for continued modernisation, wealth generation and the development of a democratic society. They argue that a science and technology culture addresses the need for innovation and problem solving, acquisition of transferable skills, a capacity to think and act rationally in response to new experiences and to appreciate new technological developments, as well as the ethical issues involved in active participation in modern democracies. This renewed interest in science and technology in developed countries recognises the role of the local community, state and private sectors in promoting, developing and sustaining a science and technology culture, as well as the comparative edge it gives in the global economy.

Although science and technology, and science and technology education, have so far failed African countries, we emphasise that this has been a science and technology that stresses memorising rather than problem solving. African countries must also, therefore, recognise the need to promote, develop and sustain a culturally sympathetic problem-solving science and technology culture if they are to narrow the gap between them and the industrialised countries. Otherwise Africa will continue to be a site for cheap labour and raw materials, a market for imported products and dependent on foreign technology and aid on dictated terms. African countries must reform policy, engage in programme development, reorganise institutions and reallocate resources to develop science and technology systems. However, such reform must be promoted with a sensitivity that learns from past failures, recognises the existing resource base and takes into account the developmental needs of the continent. This book will, therefore, re-examine and revisit:

- Why science and technology should be popularised;

- What and whose science and technology systems should be introduced and promoted;

◆ How science and technology should be implemented and practised.

Although science and technology, and science and technology education, have failed in most parts of sub-Saharan Africa, there are pockets of excellence that have made an impact on improving the quality of life in some communities. We need to learn from these pockets to widen their implementation throughout the continent. To help do so therefore, we will present analytical case studies of selected successful pockets.

Room for Cautious Optimism

Good governance has been lacking in most of Africa where civil war, tribalism, nepotism and corruption on an unimaginable scale have been the rule. Yet we tend to forget the recentness and fragility of the economic vigour and democracy of the industrialised world. *Dark Continent* by Mark Mazower is not about Africa, but Europe. Mazower reminds us that if Europe stood for civilisation, in 1945 civilisation ground to a bloody halt. How different are the Hitlers, Mussolinis, Stalins and Milosevics from the Amins, Bokassas and Mobutus of this world? How different was the economic collapse of Germany between the Great War and the emergence of the Third Reich, to that of Ghana or Tanzania? We forget so quickly that the economic recovery in Europe after 1945 was due as much to a mix of state intervention and social services as to market-force capitalism. We forget the centrality of US assistance to Europe in the form of the Marshall Plan, or to Taiwan and South Korea in the Orient. A mere 50 years on and we feel gloomy about Africa! An Africa whose starting point was so different, thanks to slavery, colonialism and economic exploitation. The USA still bears scars from the period of its history when its economy depended on that dehumanising brutality. Is it any wonder that countries such as Zaire remain haunted by King Leopold's Ghost?

In *Why the American Century?* (1999), Olivier Zunz, Professor of History at the University of Virginia, emphasises the role of mass consumption in America's economic success in the twentieth century. Unlike in Europe, Zunz argues, university academics created a vast 'institutional matrix of inquiry'. Business financed research, graduate programmes manned industry, social scientists worked with advertisers and intellectuals stressed the importance of material abundance to promoting equity. Africa, the last to pass the peak, saw its rate of population growth decline just before 1990, but is still the fastest growing continent and potential market (Morrison and Tsipis, 1998). Development and national responsibility grow together, since only with economic development can networks emerge based on class rather than tribal loyalties. Arguably, countries such as Kenya maintain some form of stability only because of a significant urban middle class that transcends tribe, and has more in common with each other than with their relatives in the village. In many countries, rural subsistence farming communities are rapidly becoming enriched with a new resource, namely retired, experienced, well educated and skillful people. The very breakdown of central government is pushing local communities to better marshal their own resources to improve schooling, health and the local economy. On a macroeconomic scale, South African manufactured goods, services and investment are spreading throughout a continent that is one of the few large remaining potential markets. Over the last decade, pressures from within and without are, in some countries of sub-Saharan Africa, providing cautious optimism for a better twenty-first century. We see reason for hope.

2. The Contribution of Science and Technology

Prem Naidoo and Mike Savage
African Forum for Children's Literacy in Science and Technology
University of Durban-Westville, South Africa

Technological dependence lies at the heart of all dependencies. Therefore, we in the developing countries should evolve a technological capacity appropriate for our own conditions; select technologies and adapt them to our own economic and social infrastructures in the context of our own culture and way of life.

Dr Rodrigo Borja, former President of Equador

What Science and Technology?

Before the 1300s, Europe was not and had never been the most powerful and advanced society in the world. Two centuries later, Europe's dominance was firmly established – a dominance largely due to the rise of science and technology. Since then, by comparison with the non-industrialised countries, developed countries have enjoyed unprecedented levels of socio-economic growth, recently accelerated by the development of information technology. At a time of talk of the global village, despite being blessed with natural resources, most of Africa remains entrenched in millions of isolated rural villages scattered throughout the continent, and the gap between industrial and non-industrial countries widens increasingly rapidly. Many external factors have contributed to this crisis, such as slavery, colonialism and economic imperialism. However, some factors are internal, such as corruption and poor governance. Though poverty is the most visible symptom of such societies, another major underlying cause of poverty is the mindset that has characterised village societies throughout history. Common attributes of the village mindset include:

- A deep-rooted conservatism that clings firmly to the traditional ways that by definition have enabled the village to survive;

- A similarly deep-rooted suspicion of external influences that so often have destabilised the status quo;

- A strong commitment to the authoritarian, patriarchal power structures that maintain village cultures.

AFCLIST believes that modernisation in Africa must be viewed through the lens of this rural village mindset, and must be based on development of the continent's human as well as its natural resources. Only when Africa institutionalises innovation can the countries of sub-Saharan Africa join the global rather than the rural village mindset that for aeons has absorbed outside influences as the body absorbs food that in some cases is digested to make the body stronger and at other times makes the body sick, but never changes it in any basic way. The rural village is sustainable in a physical, though undoubtedly basic, sense and consumes outside influences, be it Coca-Cola, modern drugs, Kalashnikovs or schooling, in the same way as it absorbs its food. But there is a critical difference. The food eaten in the rural village is prepared by cooks from the village, but the Coke, Panado, arms and knowledge are always prepared far from the village and even from the nation. It has been argued that information technology is the 'magic bullet' that will transform rural Africa. But unless the basic village mindset also changes, the 'magic bullet' will turn out to be as effective a tool as the 'magic water' that 'protected' Africa's warriors from the real bullets of the Lee Enfield and Maxim guns of the colonial powers. AFCLIST strongly believes that appropriate science and technology education can play a significant role in fundamentally changing this village mindset. AFCLIST believes science and technology education can do so because the disciplines:

◆ Constantly innovate, and use tradition only as a stepping stone to new knowledge and not to preserve the status quo;

◆ Welcome, rather than suspect, outside influences because they can lead to new understanding;

◆ Favour an open and questioning mindset that is committed to developing, rather than maintaining, society and that has strong implications for better governance than that to which Africa and the world are accustomed.

The science and technology that AFCLIST promotes is not the knowledge or products of the disciplines that are currently taught for students to consume. AFCLIST is emphatic that it is inquiry science, or the mindset of the knowledge production processes of science and technology, that the young people of the continent must learn if Africa is to leapfrog from the rural village into the global village. In making this jump, information technology becomes an additional intellectual tool to be used just like any other intellectual scientific tool rather than yet another gadget to be switched on like a television set.

There are several implications in adopting the knowledge production approach of science and technology education that AFCLIST promotes, with its implicit assumption of problem identification and solving. These include the assumption that the educational process involved is:

- Relevant since the problems are, for the most part, those in the learners' environment rather than those in the textbook;

- Economically feasible since the local problems identified are solved using locally available resources and not some unavailable (because of the expense) piece of equipment such as a Wheatsone Bridge;

- Culturally appropriate since the learning takes place within the learners' experience and not within the context of the textbook or standard laboratory.

That science and technology would bring development became a mantra in many countries of sub-Saharan Africa immediately after independence. As Yoloye (1998) and Reddy (1998) report, regional and national policy statements such as the Lagos Plan of Action (1980) and the African Priority Programme for Economic Recovery (1986) repeatedly stated government intentions to support science and technology. Despite such declarations, Ghana and Uganda, for example, in 1993 only spent 0.08 per cent and 0.06 per cent of government expenditure on research and development. Important as levels of funding are, what science and technology should Africa pursue? As Borja asks, what science and technologies are appropriate? Which should Africa select? And how should we adapt them to our own contexts?

Makhurane and Kahn (1998) and Naidoo and Savage (1998) suggest a need in Africa for a targeted practice of research science. Africa's comparative advantage is limited to a few fields such as cosmology where the University of Cape Town is a recognised authority on the southern sky. Africa, however, has pressing needs to which research science can contribute, such as the breakthroughs in root crops and pest control made by international research centres such as the International Institute for Tropical Agriculture (IITA) in Nigeria and the International Institute for Insect Physiology and Entomology (ICIPE) in Kenya. It is inappropriate for most individual countries in sub-Saharan Africa to support research science that is costly and that, for the most part, can only duplicate research elsewhere. The funding that is available for such research may be better used to support international centres that could become centres for high-level training and co-ordination of national research. Makhurane and Kahn (1998) recognise a need for some research in Africa '... that pushes back the frontiers of knowledge' for the inspiration that its intellectual integrity gives to those working in the more directly relevant fields of applied science. They also suggest subscribing to journals, attending specialised meetings and exchange programmes as alternative ways that scientists practising applied science can keep in contact with the cutting edge.

Chapter 5 provides examples of how top research scientists have popularised the practice of research science and technology by demonstrating their relevance to everyday problems. In Kumasi, Ghana, the University of Science and Technology supports workers in the agricultural, informal and formal sectors who are attempting to solve local problems. The work of Dr Emmanuel Fabiano extends over some six years in Malawi. His research, in collaboration with university and industrial scientists in Canada and industrialists and young university researchers in Malawi, has led to plans for a factory that will manufacture a variety of products from cassava (see Chapter 4). South Africa has mapped its future route for science and technology and has identified its basic strategic science and technology needs, such as research in biotechnology to support its wine and fruit juice industry. But Africa still has a need for basic as well as applied sciences.

Makhurane and Kahn (1998) define applied science as that which '...enables people to add value to their resources, is itself problem-solving in its execution, and blurs distinctions between science, technology and, on occasion, sociology'. They cite agricultural extension work with farmers, university consultancy centres and health extension work as good examples of the practice of applied science needed by Africa. Educational systems in countries of sub-Saharan Africa could learn from their style of work. Schools are the most widely distributed educational institutions in Africa, yet they rarely serve as resources for local communities. Chapters 2 and 3 describe examples of primary schools, secondary schools and tertiary institutions working to bridge school science and technology and that practised in the community.

There is considerable debate about the universality of science. Some, like Jegede (1998), take a constructivist view of knowledge and argue that there is a 'Western Science', an 'African Science', a 'Japanese Science' and so on arising from the different cultural contexts. Others, such as Makhurane and Kahn (1998), take '... a rationalistic view of science as a culture that may be superimposed on any culture since it is universal, and a culture of hope and undying optimism'. However, there is less debate about the universality of technology. Technology is practised in every community in Africa, ranging from the technology of the traditional herbalist whose knowledge of plants is extensive to that of the roadside mechanic whose tinkering genius keeps vehicles on the road long past the time they would have been scrapped in any industrialised society. It is, however, fruitless to encourage Africa to chose between indigenous technology and Western science. Only a judicious balance between the two can bring the economic development for which the peoples of sub-Saharan Africa hope.

We see little need to discuss the science and technology normally taught in schools. We are all only too familiar with a subject that bears no resemblance to research science, applied science or that practised in the community. Most school science has little relevance other than being necessary to pass examinations, and it is little wonder that it has failed to bring the hoped for economic and social benefits. Subsequent chapters will illustrate what science and technology we think should be popularised to achieve these goals.

Popularising Science and Technology

Yoloye (1998) reports on some of the many regional conferences that in the early 1960s stressed the importance of science and technology education to economic development in Africa. These include the 1961 Addis Ababa Conference of African States on the Development of Education in Africa, and the 1962 Conference of Ministers of Education on the Development of Higher Education in Africa, held in Tananarive, Madagascar. The recommendations of such meetings became a guideline for many countries of sub-Saharan Africa. Science and technology appear on primary school syllabuses of most Anglophone countries of English-speaking Africa. Yoloye quotes World Bank studies as claiming that in 1993 Nigeria spent 200 per cent of the subsidy to general secondary schools on agricultural schools and 125 per cent on industrial schools. Countries such as Nigeria have almost achieved the 60:40 ratio for science admissions to university recommended at Tananarive (Fabiano, 1998).

What science education?

Traditional science education has failed to make the contribution to development for which Africa hopes. Despite the overall bleakness, however, there is considerable evidence that more appropriate science education can not only develop the skilled human resources necessary for economic development, but also the critical skills and values needed for good governance. *not just through science.*

Jegede argues that '... the knowledge base for schooling should draw from traditional and current beliefs, taboos, superstitions, customs and traditions'. His position is strongly supported by constructivist theories of learning, as well as by good classroom practice in Africa and elsewhere. Harris (Commonwealth Secretariat) quotes studies in India by Passi that '... through a locally developed curriculum ... placed in a non-formal, learner friendly environment, girls, rural learners and members of scheduled castes and scheduled tribes performed at comparable levels to, and sometimes better than, their upper caste and urban counterparts'. Chapter 4 describes examples such as the

'Linking Community with School Science' project in Malawi that do so. This multimedia project has developed resource materials for teacher education. The opening videotape shows interviews with village craftspersons. Subsequent tapes show primary school pupils being taught in a way that uses that community knowledge. A project in Zimbabwe first interviewed primary school pupils about their understanding of syllabus topics before developing learning materials in mathematics and science. 'Thinking Science' in Malawi is a secondary school project based on the same assumption that students must actively reconstruct their own meanings for true learning to take place. Its effectiveness can be measured by the superior external examination results of students involved in the project, not only in the sciences, but also in languages and mathematics (Mbano, 1998).

There are other reasons for using community knowledge of science and technology as a base to teach school science. Fabiano (1998) pleads that, 'The immediate school environment and community are rich but often neglected resources for science and technology teaching. Ignoring them and ignoring the knowledge base of communities in Africa increases the costs of supporting learning.' Savage (1998) describes how in Kenya, the tutor of a teachers' advisory centre made extensive use of local resources. He helped pupils in one primary school to set up a community science museum from which teachers could borrow teaching aids. Pupils turned another school into a factory for producing tools. A third became a soil conservation centre that mapped friable soil sites. Parents could buy horticultural seeds, grasses, multipurpose trees and ornamental shrubs from the school-based centre. Using local resources can considerably reduce the costs of science teaching. Doing so also brings community knowledge of technology to the attempt to solve problems in schools and takes universal knowledge of technology from schools to solve problems in the community.

Rollnick (1998) argues '… in African classrooms, where science education is not only irrelevant … its very irrelevance is considered a virtue … Irrelevance affects quality of life and the ability of students to control their lives'. Use of the local environment and knowledge base to teach school science not only makes learning more accessible and meaningful, it can also add to community knowledge by helping solve local problems. Chapter 12 describes the work of Andrew Nchesi, a primary school teacher in Malawi, whose pupils have won many national and international awards, and whose teaching has the full support of parents and the community. Often his pupils' research is directly relevant to village life and has including designing fuel-conserving stoves, the use of alternative fuels from refuse such as maize cobs and charcoal water-evaporating cooling boxes. 'The Water Project' in South Africa has designed simple kits that enable children to monitor local water supplies and provides scientific evidence when they complain to the appropriate authorities.

Reddy (1998) reports that 'In the Sudan, 80 per cent of urban, but only 20 per cent of rural, children go to school'. She quotes International Council of Education Development estimates that only 50 per cent of school-going rural children in most countries complete four or more grades. Reddy reports Odaga and Henneveld (1995) as estimating that in Africa in 1990, girls made 45 per cent of primary, 40 per cent of the secondary school and only 31 per cent of the tertiary level population; participation rates in the sciences were even lower. In Zambia, a lack of school space denies access to formal education to 45 per cent of seven-year-olds, and only 38 per cent of the small secondary school population go to university. Secondary school enrolment in Malawi and Tanzania is less than 10 per cent.

Science education can do nothing to promote better access. However, to those in school, equity becomes a curriculum issue. Reddy reports a study by Obura (1991) showing that laboratory costs of teaching conventional science in secondary schools are US $20,000 in Nairobi, $32,000 in a rural area close to a tarred road and $40,000 off the tarred road. Not surprisingly, few rural schools offer science subjects, especially chemistry and physics which require specialised equipment. Of all candidates registered in Kenya for senior examinations in 1994, Reddy, quoting Wasanga (1995), claims that 22 per cent studied physics, 42 per cent chemistry and 58 per cent physical science. In Nigeria (Okebukola, 1995) claims that 93 per cent of senior secondary students studied biology, 30 per cent chemistry and 16 per cent physics. Clearly, a curriculum based on learning science through the local environment would be less costly, thus making the subject more accessible to all students. Furthermore, the content of traditional science often has a strong cultural bias that can deny intellectual access to groups such as villagers, pastoralists and girls. Textbook examples and illustrations are generally framed in urban, male settings. Classroom interactions favour boys, especially those with a good command of English. Again, these are professional issues that science educators can change by localising the curriculum.

In Africa, applied science is a tool for development. Its purpose is to improve the quality of life of the continent's people and to contribute to economic development. A characteristic of applied science is that it uses knowledge to solve problems in the immediate environment and community, whereas the characteristic of research science is to acquire new knowledge. Should school science curricula use community resources, doing so would be relevant to the bulk of school leavers and be a more appropriate preparation for the few who will engage in applied science as, for example, agriculturists, medical staff and industrialists.

Though preparing for research science should not be a goal of school science, for the most part in Africa today, the school knowledge base assumes that it is. Rollnick (1998) notes that Ogunniyi (1986) laments the isolation of African scientists from the debate on curriculum development. Most scientists complain that existing secondary science courses do not prepare students for research science in the university. Many think that a problem-solving approach based on learning from community resources is a better preparation for even future research scientists.

Whose science education?

Science education in countries of sub-Saharan Africa is accessible only to the few, particularly at post-primary levels of schooling. The Jomtiem Conference, making a call for education for all across the world, initiated a call for science education for all. Most African countries recognise the issues of increasing access to science education. The realities of doing so, however, include more human, physical and financial resources than most realise. Science for all can only become a reality at primary and lower secondary school levels if a single science subject is offered, rather than separate subjects such as agriculture, biology, chemistry and physics. Separate subjects do not make epistemological sense at these levels of schooling and are costly. Therefore science education that is rooted in the physical and human resource base of local communities better addresses the realities of Africa than education in the separate disciplines. It would be a more appropriate, accessible and cost-effective science education that African countries could deliver.

Social Impact of Science Education

Science and technology, and science and technology education, has not had the hoped for impacts, as Reddy, Fabiano and others repeatedly point out. 'Odhiambo, 1993, estimates that … most African countries have fewer than three scientists and engineers per 1000 graduates and that the industrial sector employs only 7 per cent of the workforce' (Fabiano, 1998). We recognise this unfortunate legacy of a hierarchical, academic and centralised science education system in our recommendation that science teaching in our schools should be inquiry based, using the resources and knowledge base of local communities.

Countries of sub-Saharan Africa cannot afford specialised secondary schools. Most pre-vocational courses offered in primary and secondary schools are unpopular and ineffective (Yoloye, 1998). Yet the decentralised economies of Africa desperately need the problem-solving, 'tinkering' ethos that contributed so much during the period when Europe and the USA industrialised. Teaching inquiry science using the community resources and knowledge base would develop such a spirit amongst those living in the agricultural and informal sectors. It is such people upon whom the economic future of Africa depends. It is they who will have to make decisions about how best to use the technologies needed to transform the quality of life such as improved crops and farming methods, alternative energy sources and best preventive health practices. It is the rural and urban dwellers who will have to evolve their own solutions to such everyday problems and whose purchasing power will drive the economies of Africa.

Employers, including government and universities, constantly complain of the lack of initiative, team spirit and complacency of their employees, and it is within these sectors that 'low' and 'high' science are practised. Initiative, team spirit and determination are precisely the qualities promoted by inquiry science. Inquiry science has a deep impact on classroom relationships since inquiry is motivated by students' interest and authority lies with whoever can best marshal and interpret evidence. In such a learning environment, teacher-dominated and often male-centred patterns of interaction become less predominant. A facility with language, familiarity with the so-called culturally neutral rules of the classroom and masculine interests promoted by the conventional syllabus and textbook all become less important. Presenting science as a discipline that is activity engaged in by people to solve problems they identify, shifts it to Phase 5 of the model developed by McIntosh and discussed by Harris (Commonwealth Secretariat, 1999). Harris argues, and we agree, that only by restructuring the subject and the accompanying pedagogy can we truly promote an equitable access to science and technology regardless of class, culture or gender, though she does not deny the importance of other programmes that promote equity.

An equally important goal of teaching inquiry science using community resources is the development of qualities of good citizenship and governance. As Greick argues:

Memorisation replaced understanding … Students learned names and abstract formulations … Words about words … Feynman despised this kind of knowledge … Rote learning drained away all that he valued in science: the inventive soul, the habit of seeking better ways to do anything. His kind of knowledge – knowledge by doing – gives a feeling of stability and reality about the world and drives out many fears and superstitions … Science is a way to teach how something gets to be known, what is not known, to what extent things are known (for nothing is known absolutely), how to handle doubt and uncertainty, what the rules of evidence are, how to think about things so that judgments can be made, how to distinguish truth from fraud, and from show.

Genius: The Life and Science of Richard Feynman, pp. 284–5

We believe that inquiry science will bring to the children and youth an Africa blessed with an environment rich in the phenomena of nature. This should be a science that '... permits the possibility that you do not have it exactly right...' and that educates young minds 'to deal with doubt and uncertainty', an experience the value of which Feynman believed '... extends beyond the sciences' (*New York Times*, 17 May 1998). Feynman believed in the deep connections that link science with democracy – Africa surely needs sceptical, reflective citizens. Africa also needs tinkering problem solvers at all levels who are prepared to suspend judgment when there is insufficient evidence. Liberal, rather than social, democracy, as Dahl (1998) argues, requires that all members of the community are equally entitled to, and are competent in, collective decision-making; that they have an 'enlightened understanding' of political issues. We believe that inquiry, rather than traditional science, best develops such qualities.

Delivery of Science Education

Subsequent chapters describe projects that use both formal and informal structures to implement the teaching of inquiry science. They demonstrate that with good planning and minimal support, the countries of sub-Saharan Africa can develop structures that promote quality science education. Chapter 12, 'Malawi and Zanzibar: Exemplars of Inquiry Science in School and Community', provides a rich description of how outstanding classroom teachers popularise the science and technology education we have advocated in this chapter. It identifies the impact of their work on the community, and analyses what inspires and sustains their work. Chapter 10 discusses how teacher development programmes can systematically provide such inspiration and support to enable teachers to popularise inquiry. Chapter 11, 'Using the Mass Media to Promote Science and Technology', shows how informal mechanisms can effectively popularise science and technology and Chapter 4, 'University Science and Technology Education and Economic Development', illustrates how research science can link with 'traditional science' to solve development problems. Chapter 16 briefly describes a government (that of South Africa) that effectively co-ordinates national popularisation programmes.

Those in positions to influence events should know what is possible. Ignorance of what has been achieved by some science educators in Africa should not be a reason to block change. And we know that African children and teachers are not the problem blocking the achievement of a vision of inquiry-based science and technology education.

3. Choosing Good Science in a Developing Country

Robert Adams

Department of Arts, Culture, Science and Technology, South Africa

Models for national systems of innovation generally involve the interaction of a strong science base with local industry. However, in developing countries the term 'science base' may be over-optimistic. Instead, at best we have isolated peaks of scientific excellence. Is it possible to optimise this configuration of peaks to support national development? Or is the useful coupling of scientific endeavour to developmental goals inevitably scale-dependent, with science in low GDP per capita countries linked only to global knowledge paradigms somewhat remote from the local concerns? This paper outlines a system for generating a research portfolio which uses local advantages to generate world class science.

Introduction

There are two basic principles underpinning government support for scientific programmes:

1. The programme can contribute towards addressing social or economic goals.

2. The programme is potentially world class and can contribute to leading edge global knowledge.

Increasingly, particularly in developed countries, these principles tend to overlap. Fiercer competition brought about by globalisation and the rapid growth of information technology and biotechnology has led to the shortening of the innovation cycle. The new global economy is more dependent on knowledge than ever before and it is obviously new knowledge that delivers competitive advantage. How should developing countries position themselves with respect to the knowledge economy, which depends critically on the national research portfolio, and on linkages between this portfolio and the national system of innovation?

I would like to introduce the central question addressed in this paper by quoting from a lecture given by Sir William Stewart, former Scientific Advisor to the British Prime Minister. According to Stewart 'Britain does 5 per cent of the world's research and tries to maintain sufficient competence in the other 95 per cent to be able to move into it if necessary'. Is this a viable strategy for

South Africa, which does about 0.5 per cent of the world's research, and for other catch-up nations? It seems unlikely that we will be able to cover all possibilities within the remaining 99.5 per cent from our much narrower base. This realisation has stimulated a discussion on whether government has a responsibility to optimise the national research portfolio and if so, what criteria should drive this optimisation. Should we choose, and if so, how?

I begin by discussing international trends in science-industry linkages and move on to depict the most serious constraint on South Africa's entry into the knowledge economy, namely human resources. Finally, I attempt to set out a framework for determining a national science portfolio and to show how it could be applied to South Africa.

Science-Industry Linkages

It is a widely held belief among both scientists and economists that public science is a driving force behind technological and economic growth. Recent research has shown that 73 per cent of the papers cited by US industry patents are public science, written at academic, governmental and other public institutions; only 27 per cent are written by industrial scientists. A strong national component of this linkage has also been found, with each country's inventors preferentially citing papers written in their own country by a factor of between two and four. The pronounced diagonal in Figure 3.1 depicts this clearly. The growth in linkage has been rapidly increasing (see Figure 3.2). In general, the cited papers are from the mainstream of modern science; they deal with basic issues, appear in influential journals, are written at top-flight research universities and laboratories, are relatively recent and supported by National Institutes of Health, National Science Forums and other public agencies.

Figure 3.1. Percentage Research Article Citations in US Patent Applications by Country

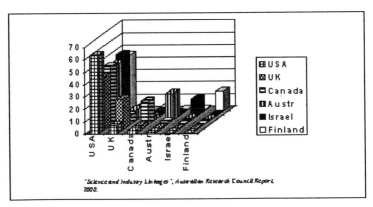

Figure 3.2. Citations from Patents to Papers versus Time (smoothed)

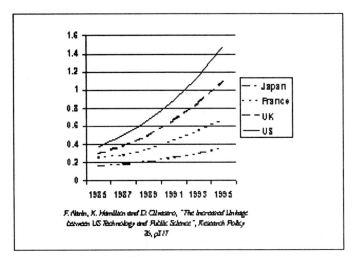

F. Narin, K. Hamilton and D. Olivastro, "The Increased Linkage between US Technology and Public Science", Research Policy, 26, p117

The linkages are much stronger in 'new economy' areas than in 'old economy' areas. For example, the average number of citations of research articles per US patent application differs by a factor of approximately 200 between the fields of biotechnology and machinery parts (see Figure 3.3). This indicates that basic science will play an increasingly important role in global competition. Unfortunately, the linkage between science and industry in what the OECD terms 'catch-up' countries, such as South Africa and Brazil, is much weaker. The rate of application for US patents is much lower to begin with and the national components are less significant. Where good science exists, it tends to be linked to programmes in developed countries. Local industries generally purchase technology and related know-how from abroad rather than connect to local scientific thrusts. Towards the lower end of the development spectrum there is an almost total disjuncture between science and industry. The only way that scientific programmes contribute is via human resource development; scientists leave science and join industry and the thinking processes they have acquired are of assistance in the new environment. The 'scale-dependence' of industry-science relationships is summarised pictorially in Figure 3.4. Given the increasing science-dependence of innovation, and consequently of economic development, three key issues facing developing nations are:

- How to increase the scale of scientific activity;

- How to optimise the portfolio of scientific activities;

- How to generate linkages between science and industry.

Figure 3.3. New Economy is Dependent on Basic Scientific Research

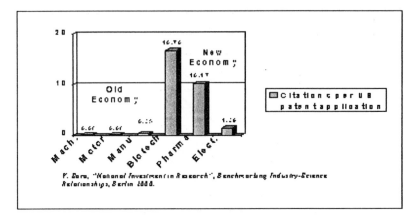

Figure 3.4. Scale-Dependence of Science/Industry Linkages

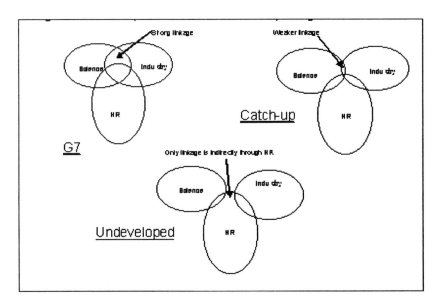

Human Resources Constraints

Science is a highly globalised activity. Even in advanced economies such as Germany and Canada there is a worrying trend of the best scientists being drawn towards the highly dynamic US system. To counteract this trend the affected countries are attempting a range of interventions. For example, Canada has set aside funds to create 2000 university chairs in science and engineering over the next five years. Both France and Germany are in the process of radically overhauling their legislation for the purpose of promoting science-industry linkages in line with the highly successful US Bayh-Dole Act. In South Africa recent studies show attrition rates of approximately 11 per cent per annum from government laboratories and 15 per cent per annum from universities for researchers. Of those who leave, about 5 per cent of the government laboratory scientists and about 22 per cent of the academics emigrate. Given the current fiscal environment and skills scarcity, the vacant posts are not automatically filled.

South Africa spends approximately 0.69 per cent of its GDP on research and development This figure does not compare well with the OECD average of 2.15 per cent. Nevertheless, it is interesting to note that the average expenditure per full-time equivalent researcher in South Africa is about $100,000 – more than the equivalent figures for Australia and New Zealand and about 70 per cent of those for Canada and Japan. The reason for this apparent contradiction is the extremely low number of full-time equivalent researchers in the labour force, approximately 0.72 per 1000, compared with 10.1 for Japan and 4.8 for Korea. The indicators for countries such as Turkey and Mexico are very similar to those for South Africa. This clearly implies that any strategy for improving research outputs from 'less developed countries is unlikely to succeed unless it incorporates a bold human resource acquisition, development and maintenance plan. Individual researchers in such countries suffer less from underfunding than they do from a dearth of colleagues'.

Choosing Niche Areas

It is often said that governments are bad at choosing research priorities. This is less a criticism of the acumen of government officials than a consequence of the fact that detailed planning can never capture the quicksilver nature of innovation. Nevertheless, technology foresight studies have become the norm rather than the exception over the past decade in developed countries. Japan has a regular five-year cycle and the UK is beginning its second exercise. Increasing interest is being shown in non-OECD countries too, with South Africa, Thailand and the Commonwealth Science Council taking the lead. The methodology underpinning these studies involves creating a shared vision among decision-makers and within key sectors regarding the threats and opportunities likely to be faced in the future and how to respond to these in terms of broad portfolio planning. It does not pretend to forecast the details of actual technologies.

In 1998 a review (somewhat similar to Britain's Forward Look) was conducted of the South African national system of innovation. From this review a set of criteria emerged for recognising what were termed 'core competence clusters'.

A core competence cluster is an effectively functioning set of infrastructure, technology, capabilities and platforms that provides outputs to clients and stakeholders which they can appropriate and evaluate. A nation's technological competitiveness rests on an appropriate portfolio of such clusters.

Criteria for recognising core competence clusters were also developed. In general they should:

♦ Provide a global competitive edge

♦ Be sustainable

♦ Be hard to emulate

♦ Have multiple applications

♦ Attract international collaboration and investment.

What type of core competence clusters should South Africa try to establish? The information society concept lies at the heart of the knowledge economy. Increasingly, biotechnology is being seen as equally critical. The South African Foresight study proposes that the country should invest in establishing platforms in research and development (R&D), training and technology transfer in base information and communication technologies such as: (i) access technologies, for example connectivity, low-cost satellites and stratospheric communication; (ii) spatial numeric environments; (iii) human language technologies; and (iv) security technologies. The Foresight study also recognises that biotechnology, the term given to the wide range of agriculture, industrial and medical technologies that make use of genetic manipulation of living organisms to create new products, will be a key factor in improving the quality and quantity of the world's supplies.

Clearly, we cannot afford to be on the wrong side of the information or the bio divide. The generic technologies underpinning rapid development in information technology and biotechnology are non-negotiable in the modern world. Are there other areas in which it is possible to achieve a world class standard? If so, how do we recognise them? In general we can define two additional broad features which are likely to underpin the more specific criteria for core competence clusters listed above.

♦ Scientific areas where there is an obvious geographic advantage. In the case of South Africa there are several of these which stand out. Examples are:

  • Astronomy where we have good access to the southern skies and the engineering capability to build telescopes locally;

- Human palaeontology where we have excellent sites in the Krugersdorp region dating from shortly after the bifurcation between apes and humans;

- Biodiversity where the Cape Floral Kingdom is the most diverse of all the seven floral kingdoms.

Other possible phenomena or systems on which it has been or would be possible to base good science include the Kaapvaal Kraton (geology) and the South Atlantic Magnetic Anomaly (geomagnetism and space science).

◆ Scientific areas where there is an obvious knowledge advantage. Important South African examples are:

- Indigenous knowledge where clearly the collective inherited and evolving knowledge systems of indigenous peoples constitute a national competitive advantage;

- Technology for deep mining where geological conditions and economic imperatives have pushed South Africa to the forefront;

- Microsatellite engineering – although large multinational consortia now dominate the communication satellite market, South Africa has retained a niche competence in microsatellites deriving from a fusion of defence spin-offs and university research;

- Encryption technology such as spin-offs from state investment in the defence sector that have recently generated significant foreign exchange;

- Fluorine technology where high entry barriers mean that the competence developed in the uranium enrichment programme could be turned to advantage.

These examples are intended to be illustrative rather than exhaustive. They illustrate a way of looking at science that attempts to prioritise in terms of likely outcomes, moderated by what is deemed necessary in terms of national competitiveness in the broadest sense of that term. Despite the fact that the motivations of individual scientists are generally fired by intellectual curiosity rather than by weighing potential outcomes, it is necessary for decisions to be made unsentimentally. Not to prioritise in a way that attempts to optimise impact is irresponsible and potentially wasteful. The public and their elected decision-makers respond positively to success. It is a sound strategy for scientists, science administrators and policy specialists to develop a common approach towards maximising the chances for success.

Conclusion

In this paper I have attempted to show three things:

- The evolution and the scale-dependence of industry-science relationships;
- The critical importance of human resources to the national research and development effort;
- An approach towards optimising the national science and technology portfolio.

The space available has dictated suggestive rather than rigorous arguments. Nevertheless, I believe that there are important lessons here for the nurturing of a healthy science base in a developing country.

PART II

The emphasis of Part II is on how a broader, more focused public understanding can lead the countries of sub-Saharan Africa to more effectively harness science and technology for the economic benefit of the individual, community and society. In one case, the selected examples demonstrate the countrywide economic benefits that have come through the problem-solving expertise of top research scientists through the establishment of a manufacturing industry in Malawi (Chapter 4). Other examples illustrate the effectiveness of problem-solving science and technology in the transformation of the informal sector of the economy in Ghana (Chapters 5 and 6). Chapter 7 eloquently presents a case for the economic value of the indigenous knowledge sectors of African societies, particularly of Southern Africa. Part II closes with a review of the economic benefits of sharing resources in science and technology in the southern region of the continent (Chapters 8 and 9).

4. University Science and Technology Education and Economic Development

Dr Emmanuel Fabiano
African Forum for Children's Literacy in Science and Technology,
Chancellor College, University of Malawi, Zomba, Malawi

Professor Osmund Mwandemele
University of Namibia

Keto Mshigeni
University of Namibia

Introduction

The centrality of the role of science in modern societies is unquestionable. Only the deep understanding of nature that the basic sciences provide explains the gap between the industrialised and non-industrialised worlds. This gap is increasingly widening as scientific knowledge in industrialised countries continues to grow. Though fundamental research is responsible for this ever-growing understanding, it is application of this understanding that brings the benefits that lead to an improved quality of life. That such benefits abound in industrialised countries, this chapter argues, is largely why people believe in science and technology rather than because they have an understanding of the subjects. Science and technology are a major belief system in such societies; a belief based on little evidence other than that it works. Similarly people in the countries of sub-Saharan Africa, we contend, believe in indigenous knowledge systems because they work for them, rather than because they have an understanding of the knowledge-generating processes and rules of evidence used by those systems. This chapter uses examples from Malawi and Namibia to show how the basic and applied sciences have and will lead to a demonstrably improved quality of life, and to demonstrate that such efforts are of major significance in popularising science and technology. Only when the evidence is overwhelming that science and technology are more effective in improving the quality of life will there be a popular belief in science and technology.

Examples from Malawi

ICRAF

As described below in Chapter 9, the International Centre for Research in Agroforestry (ICRAF), established in Nairobi in 1977 with sub-offices throughout the world including Malawi, is an autonomous, non-profit research body supported by the Consultative Group on International Agricultural Research. ICRAF aims to improve human welfare by alleviating poverty, improving food and nutritional security, and enhancing environmental resilience in the tropics. ICRAF conducts strategic and applied research, in partnership with national agricultural research systems, for more sustainable and productive land use.

ICRAF has five research and development themes, namely diversification and intensification of land use through domestication of agroforestry trees; soil fertility replenishment in nutrient-depleted lands with agroforestry and other nutrient inputs; socio-economic and policy research to allow policies that will benefit smallholder farmers; acceleration of impact on farms by ensuring that research results are used; and capacity and institutional strengthening through training and the dissemination of information. ICRAF's impact in Malawi is becoming highly visible, with many people in various parts of the country aware that it is this 'scientific' organisation that is leading to an improvement of crop yields, availability of wood-fuel, provision of animal feed and soil conservation.

The starch adhesives project

The project has a long history, going as far back as 1988 when the International Development Research Centre (IDRC), Nairobi, organised a meeting in Zimbabwe to discuss possible reasons why many good applied research projects that develop as far as pilot plant studies do not proceed to the stage of becoming commercialised. The meeting received reports from Botswana, Ethiopia, Kenya, Malawi, South Africa, Tanzania, Zambia and Zimbabwe which indicated that having completed their pilot plant studies, projects were unable to commercialise the processes or products developed. Project directors gave a variety of explanations, but a common thread was that scientists and engineers had implemented all the projects without close consultation with appropriate industrialists or potential investors with an interest in the processes or products concerned. In view of this, participants agreed that in future everybody seriously concerned with promoting their research projects beyond the laboratory and the pilot stage should involve potential users of the products or processes being developed.

As a follow up to this meeting, Fabiano applied for training in technology transfer and management and in 1991 was accepted by the Commonwealth

Secretariat to participate in a training workshop in New Zealand. The workshop required participants to identify the major constraints that prevented scientists and technologists in their countries from implementing their applied research beyond the laboratory or the pilot stage. Each participant took time to make their presentation to the other trainees and the resource persons, and discussion assisted in identifying the main constraint in each country that prevented commercialisation of research results in relation to specific projects cited in the presentations made. Presenters then developed and presented possible solutions to their country constraints. Presentations were discussed and major viable solutions were identified and prioritised. Each presenter then developed possible strategies to implement the solutions identified and presented these in turn to the group who assessed and prioritised available options. Thereafter, each participant was given an assignment to go back to his or her country and implement an applied research project that was capable of being implemented from the research laboratory, through pilot plant studies, to commercialisation of results.

Apart from the presentations made by each participant and the discussions that followed, there were lectures and visits to research institutions, universities, industries and government departments to learn how their projects developed to a point of being commercialised. One visit was to a government pilot plant used to assess the technical viability of research results from various research institutions and universities in the country. The plant has the human, material and financial resources to evaluate research results in engineering, biotechnology and chemistry. One lesson learned from the pilot plant was that on average out of every hundred research projects, about ten (10 per cent) produce results that justify the project being accepted for pilot plant studies. Similarly, out of every hundred projects accepted by the pilot plant for technical evaluation, only about ten (10 per cent) are found to be commercially viable. Thus, on average, only 1 per cent of basic or applied research projects succeed to the extent of being commercialised. The moral is that to increase the chances of a research project reaching the stage of commercialisation, there is need for careful planning in designing and implementing the project.

On returning to Malawi, Fabiano carried out a literature search at the Department of National Statistics to find out the different types of raw materials and products that could be manufactured locally using local raw materials. The intention was to develop a project that would lead to local production of one or more imported product. Among the many imported products that were bought in large quantities and could easily be produced locally were starch and some types of glues. The researcher compiled data on types of starch and glues imported, their quantities, countries of origin, unit prices and the users of these imports to Malawi. He then conducted a survey of industries to determine the quantities and types of starch and glues imported by the industries visited, as well as to identify for what the materials were used. The industries visited were also asked whether or not they would be willing to buy similar products if they were manufactured locally and sold at similar prices.

Having assessed the market for starch and glues in Malawi, a literature search was carried out to determine existing technologies, the raw materials used to produce starch and the different types of glues on the international market, with emphasis on the internal market as well as in neighbouring countries. Realising the importance of starch as a product and that of adhesives in the economy of the country, the University of Malawi initiated a project that was funded by IDRC and co-managed by the Forintek Canada Corporation (Canada) from 1993 onwards. The project was carefully designed so that it involved participation of industries and economists in its implementation to increase the chances of success beyond the laboratory. The main goal of the research project was to develop the technology needed to initiate production of adhesives in Malawi using cassava starch. It addressed the following specific objectives.

- Development of ten adhesive formulations (three hot-setting and seven cold-setting) using starch from bitter cassava varieties as a raw material;

- Demonstration of the technical and economic feasibility of production of adhesives through pilot operations;

- Dissemination of the research results for utilisation by local industry.

Major project activities included a market survey, starch analysis, adhesive formulation and evaluation, pilot plant operation, waste product handling, economic evaluation, transfer of technology and reports.

Anticipated project results and outputs included:

- ten formulations for making adhesives

- processes for manufacturing the developed adhesive formulations

- creation of a capability for producing adhesive raw materials in Malawi

- reduction of imports resulting in savings of foreign currency

- creation of rural income opportunities

- strengthening the research capabilities of the University of Malawi.

Achievements included:

- Four hot-setting adhesive formulations, two of which have been successfully tested in industrial plants;

- Four cold-setting adhesive formulations and product specifications which have been finalised, although none have been produced above pilot scale;

- Completed laboratory studies on waste product handling of the effluent, pulp and peel;

- Dissemination of research results at international and local conferences, at technology fairs and at a public lecture.

- Acceptance of project results for commercialisation. Negotiations are underway to establish an industry that will manufacture both the starch and some types of glues. For instance, four formulations for hot-setting adhesives have been developed for use by manufacturers of corrugated board, such as Packaging Industries Malawi (PI) Limited. Two of these formulations are based on a mixture of 50 per cent cassava starch and 50 per cent corn starch. Of the two, one formulation is based on a one-tank preparation (Formulation A) whereas the other is based on a two-tank preparation (Formulation B). Two other formulations are based on 100 per cent cassava starch using the principles of one-tank (Formulation C) and two-tank preparation (Formulation D).

What science has the starch project promoted?

In development of the starch adhesive project, aspects of indigenous science and modern technical practices were overridden by applied science. Being a continuum of sciences in practice, it is not always easy to draw a line from one type of science to another. Therefore, a selection of examples will help make this distinction.

The project has some practices that have become common among people, such as production of different grades of starch from cassava for domestic use. Technology for the extraction of starch from cassava and technology for making household-type cold setting cassava adhesives already exists. Therefore the large-scale production of high-quality cassava starch runs parallel to indigenous practices. However, the development of new formulations of adhesives to meet specific requirements makes use of applied research with high-technology equipment

Depending upon raw materials and the intended application, starch-based adhesives contain between 17 per cent and 40 per cent of solids by weight, the rest being water or another solvent. The solid portion is mostly made up of starch (at least 16 per cent by weight of the total adhesive) that is chemically modified during processing, as well as small amounts of sodium hydroxide (<1.0 per cent of the total) and borax (1.0 per cent of the total). Other substances, such as formaldehyde, tamanori, sodium silicate and clay, can be added in small amounts to increase the adhesive's stability or to improve binding properties. All the components are mixed and heated in different sequences, depending upon the desired adhesive properties (binding wood, paper, labels on glass, foil lining and so on). The type of starch, such as corn, potato or wheat, also affects the final properties of the adhesive because of the different initial chemical structure. The critical variables in adhesive chemistry are pH, viscosity, wet-strength, stability and setting time; all need adjustment for each application.

How can school science benefit from these examples?

Schools can benefit from these examples in that a number of activities are within the capabilities and capacities of schools as long as they select what to do based on human, material and financial resources available to them. For instance, some of the practices of artisans in their trade make use of many of the principles taught in standard technical schools and conventional schools that have technical subjects in their curriculum. The project leader enabled all schools in Malawi to obtain 1 kg of starch and 0.5 kg of dextrin free of charge. Schools were also sent a brief write-up on how they can produce their own high-quality starch from cassava and an address to write to should they need help. A problem in many African countries is that applied research results and principles do not trickle down to lower levels of education in a way that is useful to both teachers and pupils. As a result, such work does not contribute to popularising science and technology among those who are responsible for the future of science and technology in our countries.

The Cassava Starch Adhesives Project was implemented by first identifying a need and moving forward to satisfy that need. This is the principle of technology push. However, once development of the process or products exceeds the need, it is important to identify ways of implementing a component of technology push so that the initiative can go beyond what clients already know and accept. The beneficiaries will include existing industries that will provide services to the Starch Manufacturing Industry (SMC) and buy starch from SMC, as well as the people who will obtain productive employment at the industry. Since the SMC will depend on a sustainable supply of cassava, the employees at the farms will also be beneficiaries. Thus, many Malawians, industries as well as the government, will benefit from the establishment of the SMC. Similar arguments apply for future R&D in the expansion of the uses of starch This is because more cassava will be bought from small-scale farmers, industries will benefit from the new products and employment will come about as a result of increased or new agricultural and production industries. The country will save foreign exchange as a result of import substitution by cassava starch products. The project is expected to improve incomes of the rural cassava producing community, providing resources needed for local development. At the same time, introduction of advanced technologies, and especially mechanisation of cassava root production, may adversely affect gender balance in the community because technology-related jobs are often dominated by men, while cassava production is traditionally dominated by women.

Some Examples from Namibia

Africa is richly endowed with an enormous variety of natural resources in the form of industrial and other minerals, enviably rich biodiversity and a wide range of environmental regimes with a capacity for sustainable biomass production as well as unique scenic beauty, giving the continent an enormous potential for highly profitable ecotourism. Yet millions of Africans are classified as living in absolute poverty and many others die every day from diseases that could be prevented through society's enlightened use of Africa's rich indigenous knowledge of her natural resources.

Africa must significantly intensify her efforts in science and technology education and training if the poverty prevailing amongst its people is to be eradicated and if rapid socio-economic progress is to be brought about. Thus the innovations pioneered by the University of Namibia aim to:

◆ Promote awareness of the significance of science and technology as an engine for alleviating and eradicating poverty in the Southern African Development Community (SADC) region and on the continent, and of how universities can play a major role in promoting development by taking science and technology to the people;

◆ Remind ourselves that Africa is blessed with a rich endowment of natural resources, whose potential as economic assets has hardly been tapped;

◆ Promote sharing of information and expertise on unrealised wealth based on Africa's rich biodiversity and on Africa's mineral resources heritage;

◆ Demonstrate, by way of local examples, what African nations are likely to achieve in terms of human development through increased government investment in science and technology education at all levels.

We view increased expenditure in science and technology as a critical necessity for liberating Africa from the poverty trap.

As the Vice-Chancellor of the University of Namibia has often said, our vision of the future of Africa, and especially of our SADC region, should not be that of a warring or a war-torn continent. Our vision should be that of an enlightened, free, well-informed and healthy people, living as a harmonious, integrated and caring community, guided by a democratic culture of peace based on shared values, open to positive interaction with other cultures, with access to lifelong learning at all levels, in an economy that is productive, diversified and sustainable, and which provides meaningful employment. All this is only possible if we invest in science and technology education and training of our people, and demonstrate to them how the power of science and technology can bring about development and improvement of the quality of human life on our continent.

Knowledge of science and technology is the key

Good science and technology education will serve to enlighten our people that we need to treasure all categories of resources we have on our planet, since each is a potential source of wealth (Mshigeni, 2000). We must have profound knowledge of their chemistry and their biology, and this can only be unravelled through both basic and applied research.

That science and technology education is the engine that drives economic development and growth can be best realised by making reference to Japan. In the late nineteenth century, Japan developed a sharp, long-term vision directed towards the promotion of scientific and technological knowledge, which is both the key and the engine to industrial development. What should we do, as Africans, to achieve the same? What roles can universities and other institutions of higher learning and research play? What should be the role of African governments? These are questions and issues that need to be addressed so that solutions and recommendations can be made to deal with the problems facing Africa today.

Implementation of the ZERI Principles

The Zero Emission Research Initiative (ZERI) looks at a wide spectrum of materials that are normally discarded as wastes, often polluting the environment, with a view to transforming them into raw materials for new marketable, value-added products. The ZERI concept is driven by a global concern that society must respond to the world's growing needs for water, food, health care, shelter, energy, new jobs, sustainable productivity and wise environmental management.

Under the chairmanship of Gunter Pauli, the founder of ZERI, the ZERI Foundation based in Geneva co-ordinates all ZERI activities worldwide. The University of Namibia became involved with ZERI in 1994 and currently houses the UNESCO/UNU ZERI Chair, as well as the ZERI Africa Regional Project Co-ordinating office, with Professor Keto E. Mshigeni as Regional Co-ordinator, with financial support from the United Nations Development Programme (UNDP). As a concept, philosophy and new vision, ZERI made sense to us, and today we are proud to report a few success stories on the implementation of the ZERI concept in Namibia.

The ZERI Brewery in Tsumeb

ZERI activity in Tsumeb, Namibia:

◆ Was the first project selected for implementation in Namibia, and indeed Africa, to demonstrate that the ZERI concept to a large extent works and has great potential in creating job opportunities, thus contributing to poverty reduction;

◆ Was a pioneer example in Namibia demonstrating a functional university-industry partnership, between the University of Namibia and Namibia Breweries;

◆ Was directed towards addressing Africa's increasing energy needs with a view to demonstrating that if appropriate technologies are applied, renewable energies (in this case biogas energy) can be generated from the enormous quantities of organic biomass around us;

◆ Involved multidisciplinary teams of scientists, management experts, engineers, and technicians such as Professor George Chang, an expert on biogas digesters, Professor S.J. Chang, an expert on mushroom production, and the University of Namibia's experts in animal science, crop science, and biology who, working together, were able to generate a tangible impact;

◆ Serves as a demonstration to the Namibia public and Africa at large that with the application of the ZERI vision we can alleviate poverty, recreate new high-quality food and other products from what others conceive as waste, reduce overdependence on firewood as a source of fuel, create new jobs for the people and alleviate the problem of environmental degradation;

◆ Provides a framework for environmental education to our school communities.

The key inputs for any brewery industry are an organic source, in this case sorghum grain (microbial biota that catalyze the fermentation process) and water. (Figure 4.1 summarises the ZERI activity in Tsumeb.) Spent sorghum

Figure 4.1. A Simplified Schematic Representation of an Integrated Production System

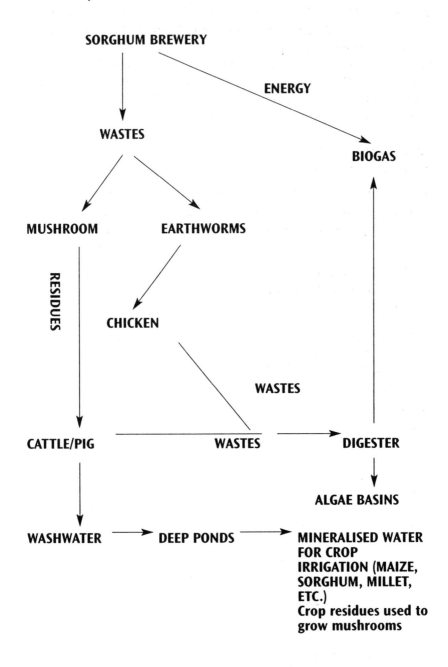

waste from the brewery is used to feed earthworms which are good feed for chicken, while the vermi-compost is good organic fertiliser for crops. The sorghum waste is also used to grow mushrooms, which is a very high value crop. Residues from mushroom farming that have improved nutritional quality are fed to pigs and cattle. Waste-water from the factory and all the wastes such as manure from the animal pans are flushed into a biogas digester where anaerobic digestion takes place eliminating most potential harmful pathogens. Biogas generated from the digester is used to provide heating energy, while solids are a good source of organic fertiliser. The effluents from the digester pass through a series of algae ponds, which further cleans and purifies the water that becomes rich in nutrients and stimulates growth of phytoplankton that is good food for fish before it flows to the deep ponds. If there is enough water, it can also be used to irrigate crops that provide food, while crop residues are a good source of the substrate for growing mushrooms. Thus value-added products are produced from wastes providing food and income as well as energy, and at the same time the problem of environmental pollution emanating from wastes generated by the brewery can be solved.

Today, the operation and maintenance of the system is fully managed by Namibia Breweries that generates 100 kg of tasty, nutritious and marketable oyster mushrooms per week from materials that would otherwise be discarded as waste. The University of Namibia is proud to be associated with this success, which has the potential to be replicated by many breweries on the continent.

ZERI peri-urban agriculture in Windhoek

From the experience acquired in Tsumeb, the University of Namibia, through its Faculty of Agriculture and Natural Resources, subsequently undertook to promote the application of ZERI principles towards generating value-added products such a vegetables, mushrooms, and biogas for cooking and general domestic use for the benefit of poverty stricken peri-urban communities at Goreangab in the vicinity of the city of Windhoek. The integrated bio-system at Goreangab makes use of household generated organic wastes for value addition (Figure 4.2). Through this innovation the communities involved in the project are no longer tempted to destroy the vegetation in their ecosystems to produce firewood, or to use their meagre financial resources to purchase charcoal. Thus the innovation, which is supported by the European Union, albeit modest, is successfully demonstrating that we can address both the problem of environmental degradation, and of peri-urban poverty, through the application of ZERI principles. Discussions are in progress with Government to promote this vision in other communities in Namibia.

Figure 4.2. A Typical Rural-Urban Household Integrated Biosystem Setting

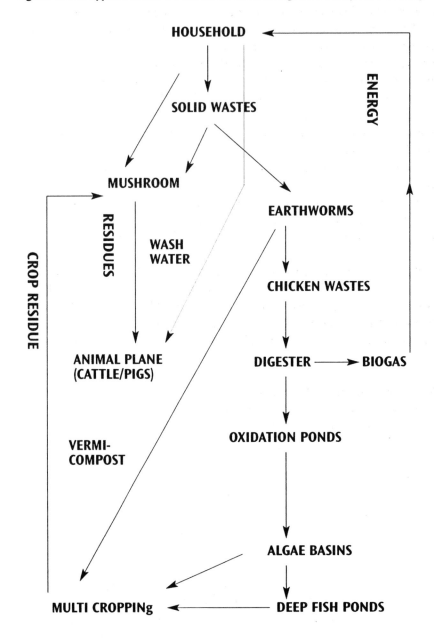

ZERI UJAMS project

Again building from the Tsumeb experience, with some inputs provided by UNDP, the University of Namibia, in partnership with various industrial establishments based in Windhoek, such as Namibia Breweries, MEATCO and Hartlief together with Windhoek Municipality, is planning to undertake a joint venture known as the ZERI UJAMS Project, which will involve the construction of large biogas digesters and replicate the Tsumeb vision on a larger scale to help transform Windhoek's urban wastes into renewable energies and other value-added products. MEATCO and Hartlief, for example, generate large quantities of livestock stomach contents in their slaughter houses every day, which could be used as vital components of substrates for mushroom cultivation. We believe that when successfully executed, this innovation will serve as a model for Africa's cities of the future. We are currently looking for additional funding to facilitate the implementation of the project vision.

Encouraged by these and other related achievements, UNDP Africa is supporting a Regional Africa-wide ZERI project, directed towards promoting sustainable human development from the continent's rich biodiversity, which, to a large extent, will also encompass many elements of the Tsumeb experience. This initiative is also based at the University of Namibia. We have already begun to implement the regional project and we have reason for a high level of optimism, since Africa has such rich biodiversity and such enormous quantities of biomass which are currently discarded as waste but which could be put to many sustainable uses. The rich biomass includes a wide range of agricultural crop residues, a huge tonnage of water hyacinth biomass and enormous quantities of marine resources that have to a large extent remained untapped. Our ZERI Tsumeb initiative has revealed the suitability of seaweeds such as *Laminaria* and *Ecklonia* as a component of mushroom cultivation ventures (Molloy *et al.*, 1999). It is in realisation of that fact that H.E. President Sam Nujoma has committed government resources to promote the development of a marine resources research centre of excellence in Henties Bay on the Namibian coast (Mshigeni *et al.*, 2000). We need additional donor funding support to promote the success of the envisaged ZERI research activities at the centre. Some of the identified projects focusing on Africa's biomass resources are:

♦ Production of value-added products from Africa's seaweed resources including their utilisation for goitre control, for the production of industrial hydrocolloids, livestock feed supplements, fertiliser and so on.

♦ Sustainable utilisation of the water hyacinth that is a challenge involving turning a regional environmental problem into a development-oriented opportunity.

♦ Production from organic wastes of edible and of marketable mushrooms, including those of medicinal value, and also production of earthworms for use as a high-quality protein-rich poultry feed. The production of iodized mushrooms will be attempted by using algae species that contain high levels of iodine as a substrate for growing mushrooms. This innovation is intended to produce iodized mushrooms that will not only provide valuable nutrients but also make available the iodine to consumers, thus helping to solve the problem of iodine deficiency which is said to affect at least 30 per cent of the African population south of the Sahara.

♦ Production of *Salicornia* in selected coastal village communities on the continent for industry and commerce, using technologies involving crop irrigation with seawater.

♦ Promotion of integrated biomass systems in Africa's grossly neglected marshlands.

♦ Research on harvesting fog along the Namibia coast, and on harnessing water condensation from the cold Benguela ecosytem. In doing this, we are attempting to mimic nature. Indeed, *Welwitschia mirabilis*, the wonder plant which is endemic to the Namib desert, and which deserves to be considered as a unique world heritage, has survived for millennia by harvesting the desert fog that condenses on its leaves.

♦ Sustainable development of Africa's bamboo resources for housing, construction, and various value-added products.

♦ Sustainable development of selected high value micro-algae abounding in Africa's aquatic ecosystems with special reference to *Spirulina* for its protein, and *Dunaliela* for its beta carotene. Here we are attempting to mimic the lesser flamingoes, which discovered that *Spirulina* was edible long before humans did so.

Back to Malawi

Everywhere one drives in Malawi, one sees guinea-fowl; they are not restricted to the 'bush' as they are in most of Africa, but wander around villages pecking away at the dirt in the way chickens do. Both the flesh and the eggs of these birds are delicious; people in some countries regard them as gourmet foods! Yet in Malawi, one of the poorest countries of the world, everybody seems to eat them. So they are a suitable bird for villagers in Africa to domesticate. Since Africa is their natural habitat they are much more resistant to diseases than chickens, and the species flourishes by foraging in the bush.

The wide-spread presence of guinea-fowl in Malawi is the result of a modest but persistent project of the Wildlife Society of Malawi and university staff that conducted the painstaking research needed to domesticate the bird, as well as their promotion through donations of breeding pairs and advice.

We close with this example to demonstrate that the sophisticated approaches and facilities of science are not always needed. It is the problem-solving ingenuity of science and technology that often leads to breakthroughs; this ingenuity can be practised anywhere and by almost anyone. Why then do our schools, universities and other educational institutions continue to teach as if they were located in some 'culture-free' zone similar to the 'tax-free' zones that some claim will transform the continent?

Conclusion

Science and technology can be popularised directly or indirectly. This chapter suggests the power of doing so indirectly; AFCLIST's contention is that throughout the world, including the industrialised world, people believe in and support disciplines because they so demonstrably work. But most of Africa has yet to experience the improved quality of life that science and the applied sciences can bring.

The examples in both Malawi and Namibia also highlight the power of well-focused and planned university co-operation with the private sector, indeed its necessity. Frequently in Africa, the research capacity of the private sector is based in the already industrialised world where priorities are different, and neither government nor the university has the financial and human resources necessary for large-scale implementation.

AFCLIST has supported a number of projects that attempt to link school science with community and industrial science and technology, yet the science curriculum in African universities rarely does so. These two examples of how universities have contributed to popularising science and technology show how, if the science curriculum in all educational institutions better addressed developmental needs, the continent might succeed more rapidly in the socio-economic transformation and achievement of improved quality of life that is a prerequisite to a belief in science as a world view.

5. Small-scale Industries in the Popularisation of Science and Technology in Ghana

Dr Jesse Amuah

Director, National Board for Small Scale Industries (NBSSI), Ghana

Introduction

The development of the technological knowledge and skills needed to effectively exploit available natural resources is an important factor for economic development and poverty alleviation. Whether this implies setting up industries or initiating technological development in areas such as health, agriculture and resource management, it is only by doing so that the countries of sub-Saharan Africa can become self-reliant. Self-reliance does not mean the development of every technology and every basic industry, but adding value to a country's agricultural and mineral resources by establishing basic industries to supply an internal market and earn foreign exchange from exports. Technology must, therefore, be adopted and adapted, but the risk entailed must also be accepted. Greater productivity calls for more scientific research and diversification of inputs such as seeds, pesticides and investment in tools and equipment, as well as facilities for storage and marketing.

Government support of the national science community as an instrument for development is a political decision that strengthens not only the scientists' role but also that of government, and subsequently of the entire nation. Most important of all, however, rapid industrialisation depends not on scientists and technologists, but on society's ability to absorb their findings, inventions and innovations.

The Role of Science and Technology in Development

The role and responsibility of science and technology (S&T) in society is heatedly discussed in every country in the world. Their impact on all spheres of life radically affect the disciplines themselves as well as their interrelationships with society. Social development is becoming ever more closely connected with S&T, especially in the era of information technology, so that today it is hardly possible to speak about social phenomena in isolation from scientific and technical endeavour.

The goal of any country is development, that is improvement of the standard of living and quality of life of its people. This can only be achieved through the mobilisation and utilisation of its natural and human resources. National development must bring sustained improvement of the well-being of the individual and all citizens, bringing transfer of surpluses and income to rural areas to correct historical inequities and imbalances. Such rural industrialisation must be based on mobilising, utilising and maximising the locally available physical and human resources. High population growth rates and rapid urbanisation require expansion of high-quality food processing activities and rural industrial growth to guarantee food security and facilitate the expansion of non-farm employment. Any effective strategy to accelerate the pace of industrialisation must focus on the promotion of agro-based industries.

Small-scale industries and development

Worldwide, micro and small-scale enterprises are increasingly regarded as indispensable components of national economics. Developed countries that in the past relied on large industries, now recognise small enterprises as viable economic activities for many high-tech ventures in terms of subcontracting made increasingly possible by information technology. Historically, micro and small-scale industries played a strategic role in industrialised countries. In Japan, for example, the contribution of a myriad of small entrepreneurs in the nineteenth century gave impetus to the mobilisation of domestic resources for industrialisation and today's industrial giants still subcontract extensively to small companies. As privatisation gathers momentum in Ghana, small enterprises will need to progressively take over industrial operations that are currently owned by the public sector.

Micro and small producers often operate more efficiently at competitive costs for relatively limited local markets. More often, they call for less energy utilisation, less capital intensive technology and less complicated production and marketing processes; they also tend to employ more labour than large industries. Their role must be recognised, defined and incorporated into national industrial policies and strategies to enhance the effective development of the sector.

Promotion of small-scale industries in Ghana

The Government of Ghana established the National Board for Small Scale Industries (NBSSI) to promote industrialisation through small-scale operations initiated and implemented through entrepreneurship development programmes. A major objective of NBSSI is to promote the adoption of suitable productivity-enhancing technologies. Illustration of some of its promotional activities in this direction will be considered below.

The NBSSI has advisory centres in all 10 regional and in some district capitals in Ghana. These centres serve as focal points for the promotion and development of rural entrepreneurship skills to enhance employment generation, adoption of improved technologies and effective utilisation of available natural, human and financial resources. To accelerate the development and growth of rural small-scale enterprises and to strengthen the capacity of existing enterprises in the districts, NBSSI focuses on training entrepreneurs in technical and managerial skills as well as technology transfer and introduction of new business opportunities. The main objective of the NBSSI programmes is to contribute to the alleviation of rural poverty by increasing productivity, employment and income in the rural economy through structured support for agriculture-related, small-scale rural enterprises. Target beneficiaries include artisans and craftspersons, owners and operators of rural small-scale enterprises, apprenticed youth, socially disadvantaged women, unemployed youth and the redeployed.

The purpose of training artisans is to upgrade their technical capacity and their management and training skills so that they can train their apprentices more effectively and thus meet consumer demand for a sufficient quantity of quality goods and services. The NBSSI uses local resources and disseminates suitable technologies in response to demands in the districts. The objective is to provide benefits to small-scale enterprise operators in drudgery reduction, labour saving and improvements in post-harvest operations. The support of NBSSI is also intended to improve the profitability of existing enterprises and promote self-employment. It creates the needed enabling environment for sustained business promotion through providing appropriate tools, support services and training. The Board helps groups form district level, entrepreneurial co-operatives to conscientise them to lobby for national recognition and support. The categories of small-scale enterprises being supported in districts include:

- Agribusiness and general processing

- Primary fabrication and repairs

- Traditional crafts such as pottery, weaving, and catering

- Service enterprises such as cobblers, chop-bar keepers

- Agricultural and forest products through support to off-farm activities, as well as to projects with linkages with agriculture such as bee-keeping and mushroom farming

- Infusing science and technology in small-scale industries.

The Ghana Regional Appropriate Technology Industrial Science (GRATIS), like the NBSSI, was established to support the promotion of small-scale industrialisation in Ghana. GRATIS does this by offering consulting services to small-scale industrialists so that they can upgrade their activities by introducing appropriate technologies, new manufacturing processes and equipment, technical advice and training. GRATIS operates through a network of nine regional Intermediate Technology Transfer Units (ITTUs) apart from the mother centre, namely the Suame Magazine, the first ITTU to be established by the Technology Consultancy Centre of the University of Science and Technology, Kumasi. Basically an ITTU is a production workshop operating and demonstrating activities such as metal machining, welding and fabrication, carpentry and foundry work. The ITTU demonstrates new products and manufacturing processes, trains master craftsmen and apprentices in new skills, promotes the marketing of products and implements a machine tool hire-purchase and working capital schemes.

Promoting S&T through Small-Scale Industries

The rest of this chapter will describe selected activities of the NBSSI in promoting science and technology and their application in Ghana.

The Aiyinase Coconut Development Project

The Aiyinase Coconut Development Project was established as a pilot project in 1995 to promote everyday small-scale technologies for the coconut sector in the Nzema East District, Western Region. An estimated 90 per cent of some 30,000 small holdings totalling 42,00 hectares lie in the Western and Central Regions, with the former alone reported to have over 30,000 hectares with six districts, namely Nzema East, Wassa East and West, Shama-Ahanta East, Twifo-Henan and Lower Denkyira, accounting for the bulk of production. The pilot project at Aiyinase popularises production and utilisation of coconut fibre using small-scale appropriate technologies developed in India and introduced into Ghana by the Commonwealth Secretariat's Industrial Development Unit. The objective is to create employment and improve the quality of life of people in the area.

The project made three retting tanks and installed a defibreing unit consisting of a husk opener, a coconut husk crusher, a sifting machine with a set of combs and sifter screens, a willowing machine and a bailing press. To further prepare trainees, the project made coir fibre spinning equipment for making twine and a unit for making doormats. Batches of trainees are taken through an induction and a hands-on training programme to produce coir fibre. Having acquired the necessary skills, the project provides a loan so that trainees can buy equipment and set up their own workshops and businesses.

In furtherance of its objective, the NBSSI collaborates with S&T institutions to prepare product profiles on manufacturing processes. Profiles have been completed on extraction of vegetable oil from soft seeds, extraction of palm oil and an intermediate technology for brick production.

The 'Expanded Markets for Cassava' project is an attempt by the NBSSI to facilitate access by micro and small enterprises to science and technology. The project is a collaborative undertaking between the NBSSI and Food Research Institute (FRI), Forestry Research Institute of Ghana (FORIG), Department of Nutrition and Food Science of the University of Ghana, the Ministry of Food and Agriculture and the Natural Resources Institute (NRI) of the UK. The Department for International Development (DFID) of the UK is sponsoring the project under its Crop Harvest Programme. The project seeks to address farmers' needs in finding new markets for cassava and to encourage the development of local products to reduce Ghana's reliance on imported materials. The science and technology institutions in the project are undertaking the following activities:

- The Food Research Institute is researching the production of high-quality cassava flour for bakery products. FRI is also developing recipes for cassava flour bakery products.

- The Forestry Research Institute of Ghana has successfully tested the use of high-quality cassava flour as a partial substitute (45 per cent) for imported wheat flour in making glue mixes for two plywood factories in Kumasi. A locally manufactured paperboard adhesive consisting of high-quality cassava flour mixed with a small amount of soluble borax has also been successfully tested as a complete substitute (100 per cent replacement) for imported adhesive.

- The Department of Nutrition and Food Science of the University of Ghana is researching into production of industrial alcohol and sugar syrups from high-quality cassava flour.

- The UK Natural Resources Institute co-ordinates all research activities.

The NBSSI is expected to disseminate research results to stakeholders, including policy-makers, businessmen, industrialists and professionals in the plywood, paperboard, bakery, confectionery and catering industries through:

- Holding awareness seminars in industrial and commercial centres in Ghana, such as Accra-Tema, Kumasi and Sekondi-Takoradi;

- Production and distribution of brochures based on research results;

- Organising training workshops for selected stakeholders on the technology of producing high-quality cassava flour and cassava flour-based adhesives for plywood and paperboard production.

The NBSSI also promotes institutions such as the Benlex School of Technology in Tema, established in 1993 to train students to use local raw materials to produce equipment such as hand sprayers and oil cans from empty oil gallons; mouse traps, kerosene stoves and gas cookers from scrap metals; solar stoves from broken pieces of mirrors; and sawdust from wood. The school generates hydrogen for balloons and other experiments, as well as preparing copper sulphate for electroplating. The school uses aluminium for cups, frying pans, plates, trophies, and charcoal and gas fuelled irons. Scrap metal becomes long and flat-nosed pliers, hacksaw and jigsaw frames, and bench vices. Students are trained with equipment for the most part designed and manufactured by the students themselves and graduates can acquire equipment on hire purchase arrangements to start up their own businesses.

Small-scale industries therefore play an important role in popularising science and technology in the country in ways that directly result in poverty alleviation and improve the quality of life of the rural and urban poor.

Conclusion

The development of appropriate technology is crucial for the development of the small-scale agricultural and informal sectors of the economy in the countries of sub-Saharan Africa. Stakeholders in small enterprise development need to research into existing technologies to identify those that need upgrading with innovative designs that will enhance productivity. Access to and dissemination of information about such technologies to the mass of people are essential components of the popularisation process of science and technology.

6. The Suame Magazine

Henry A. Brown-Acquaye
University College of Education of Winneba, Winneba, Ghana

Introduction

When Ghana gained its independence in 1957 from the British colonial government, there was already a corps of highly educated Ghanaians in all disciplines, including science and engineering. The colonial government recognised the contribution that higher education could make towards the general well-being of the nation. *[handwritten margin note: interesting!]*

In 1945 the Asquith Commission on Higher Education reported:

The immediate objective is to produce men and women who have the standards of public service and capacity for leadership which progress of self-government demands, and to assist in satisfying the need for persons with professional qualifications required for economic and social development of the colonies.

The 'Elliot Report' presented to the British Parliament by the Secretary of State for the Colonies in June 1945 cleared the way for the establishment of the University College of the Gold Coast and later the College of Technology, Science and Arts at Kumasi.

Indeed, the fundamental political character underlying the British colonial government's policy for the provision of education had already been established. In 1882 an education ordinance was enacted and was to be applied generally to British West Africa. The education system was to be modelled on the English pattern.

Following all the expressed motives inherent in the colonial government's promotion of higher education, it came as no surprise that the motto chosen for the University of Science and Technology, the successor to the College of Technology, Science and Arts, was, translated literally into English: 'The knot of wisdom can be untied only by the wise'. The ordinance promulgating the legal existence of the College of Technology, Science and Arts was passed by the Gold Coast Government on 6 October 1951. The role of the university was to produce the personnel needed for the technological development of the country and, in doing so, to attempt to solve some of the difficult problems that confronted the country.

By the time the College of Technology, Science and Arts achieved full university status in 1961, it had a list of highly-qualified Ghanaian academic staff members, including the late Dr R. P. Baffour OBE, M.I. Mech.E., M.I.Nucs.E, F.R.A.S., who became the first Vice-Chancellor. There was also a large number of internationally respected foreigners on the academic staff.

During the period 1971–85, most developing countries such as Ghana experienced the disastrous effects of the global economic recession after the crude oil price hikes of the early 1970s. This serious economic situation caused social problems that led to mass migrations. Many highly-qualified personnel left the country for Europe, particularly the UK, USA and neighbouring West African countries, especially Nigeria, which was then experiencing an oil boom. University lecturers joined the mass exodus.

However, it did not look too easy for highly-qualified university engineering lecturers to find suitable jobs outside the country. Hence a number remained but the situation at home was so bad that they had to find other ways and means to supplement their income by establishing their own small-scale businesses. The functions and activities of the dormant Technology Consultancy Centre that had been established to offer consultancy services to industries were activated by these engineering lecturers who remained in Ghana. The situation compelled them to innovate in problem solving to sustain the informal sector, from which they made extra earnings.

The formal sector was collapsing. While other non-engineering lecturers who had remained in the country supplemented their incomes by becoming involved with commerce, engineering lecturers worked more and more closely with the informal sector, and students' dissertations were based on it.

Suame Magazine

In the early 1970s the Technology Consultancy Centre (TCC) of the then University of Science and Technology, now called Kwame Nkrumah University of Science and Technology (KNUST), introduced the concept of the Intermediate Technology Transfer, after interacting with the many artisans working in the informal industrial sector, particularly with those at Suame Magazine, located in the north-western suburbs of Kumasi, the second largest city in Ghana.

At that time Suame Magazine was an informal first-generation engineering industrial centre, concerned mostly with the needs of the motor vehicle. The artisans were mostly engaged in some aspects of the repair of road transport vehicles such as general auto-fitting, engine overhauling, body straightening, vulcanising, auto-electrics, battery servicing and upholstery.

A survey conducted by the Department of Housing and Planning Research of the Faculty of Architecture, University of Science and Technology, in 1971 recorded a total population of 5485 artisans in the area. Of this number, 1615 were masters and 3870 were apprentices. The breakdown is given in Table 6.1.

Table 6.1. Composition of Artisans in Suame Magazine, Ghana in 1971

Number of Shops	1085
Number of Masters	1615
Number of Apprentices	3870
Total Population	5485
Shops by Trade	
General Fitters	287
Diesel Fitters	4
Land Rover Fitters	5
Tractor Fitters	4
Traders – General	101
General Spare Parts Dealers	99
Secondhand Spare Parts Dealers	16
Brand New Spare Parts Dealers	32
Secondhand Car Dealers	6
General Welding and Straightening	194
General Blacksmith	98
Block Machine Maker	1
General Electrical Works	48
Battery Charging	23
Lathe Turner	7
Spray painting	32
Printing Press	1
Carpenters	49
Tailoring	9
Car Lining	28
Vulcaniser	5
Others	566
Total	**1615**

In the same survey, the educational background of the masters was also established and is given in Table 6.2.

The artisans at Suame Magazine in those days were mostly engaged in the repair of imported machinery. However, there were some activities that bordered on innovative manufacturing processes such as the building and installation of new wood and steel bodies on old chassis. Examples of the innovative designs and products of the artisans at Suame Magazine included locally designed trailers used for agricultural tractors and the very popular pull-along trolleys with four car wheels found and used in Ghanaian markets to cart goods. These artisans also produced charcoal stoves using the steel sheeting of old car bodies. Later, products such as steel burglarproof screens and ornamental iron work gates were also produced at Suame Magazine.

A group of lecturers at the Faculty of Engineering of the University of Science and Technology, Kumasi, recognising the skills of these artisans at Suame Magazine, decided to assist them by forming the Suame Product Development Group. This was done to establish a link between the university and the local artisans in the informal industrial sector at Suame Magazine.

Table 6.2. Percentage of Masters having Education

Level of Education	Percentage
None	12
Primary	17
Middle School Leavers Certificate	42
City and Guilds Test	1
Private Trade Test	24
Other	4
Total	**100**

What kind of science has been promoted?

There are aspects of both indigenous science and modern technical practices at Suame Magazine. University authorities realised the important contribution the Suame Product Development Group was making towards the utilisation of research findings for the informal industrial sector and thus decided to integrate the group with the official (TCC). Through this integration the artisans at Suame Magazine gained access to the use of semi-automatic capstan lathes for the production of steel bolts and nuts of many different types. Initially there were different levels of operation. This was partly why, despite the attempt to attract and sustain the interest of the artisans in new production techniques to the extent of TCC establishing production and training units on the university campus, it was later realised that the proper location of the production and training units was the hub of the informal industrial area and thus the concepts of the Intermediate Technology Transfer Unit (ITTU) came into focus. If the training had continued to be based at the university campus, the curriculum and qualifications of the candidates would probably have risen to a point whereby the original target audience would have been eliminated.

The non-engineering or secondary industries, such as agricultural and craft industries, provided many opportunities for the ITTU to introduce new equipment. The involvement of a Rural and Women's Industries Extension Officer (RAWIEO) ensured sustenance of the non-engineering industries. This officer identifies new opportunities for the local manufacture of tools and equipment and also organises training programmes to ensure their effective use. The RAWIEO concentrates on promoting employment opportunities for women, even encroaching on traditional male enterprises such as cloth weaving and engineering.

The peculiarities of each region are highlighted by the ITTU through the programmes of rural and women's industries, depending on their local natural resources and basic traditional skills. For example, rice, cotton and bullock farming have influenced the work programmes of Tamale ITTU in contrast to Kumasi ITTU. The fishing industry in the southern parts of Ghana is taken care of by the Cape Coast and Tema ITTUs.

It is thus evident that while the ITTUs all possess essentially the same range of engineering capabilities, there is a bias in their secondary manufacturing activities. The ITTUs work with people at the grassroots and share the same economic and social environments. By design the ITTU promotes grassroots industrial development by means of technology transfer to the small-scale and informal sectors, and by so doing the informal sector gains some of the advantages of the large-scale formal sector industries such as consultancy services, training and access to imported plant and machinery. Information, advice and training are three basic services provided free of charge by the ITTUs.

The ITTUs are self-financing in terms of recurrent expenditure. An important aspect of the ITTUs is that they are not technical training institutes in any formal sense. They do not train beginners but rather provide an in-service training programme for the informal sector. All trainees have some practical skills acquired from a master artisan or some theoretical knowledge acquired at a technical school or polytechnic. The training programmes of ITTUs are designed to enable the trainee to find self-employment later. Trainees are afforded a range of services to help them establish new and sustainable enterprises and are also assisted to acquire the machinery and manufacturing equipment needed to establish their own workshop on cash and credit terms.

Who were the anticipated beneficiaries?

The Suame Magazine ITTU was formally commissioned on 23 February 1981. The success of the intervention by the university lecturers of the Faculty of Engineering in the early 1970s was demonstrated by the artisans who had received training at the Suame ITTU established by the Technology Consultancy Centre Clients Association in 1982 when they successfully mounted an exhibition of their products at the 'Ghana Can Make It' Exhibition held in October 1983.

The need to establish ITTUs in the other regions thus became apparent and in 1984 the Technology Consultancy Centre drew up plans for the establishment of ITTUs in all other regional capitals in the country and recommended the setting up of the Ghana Regional Appropriate Technology Industrial Service (GRATIS). This recommendation was accepted and in 1987 GRATIS was established and two new ITTUs were immediately commissioned at Tamale in the Northern Region and at Tema, the port city in the Greater Accra Region. These early commissions were possible because there were already existing facilities in those two towns. Further establishments were started from scratch. The European Community (EC) and the Canadian International Development Agency (CIDA) heavily supported the GRATIS project. All ten regions of Ghana now have ITTUs.

Owing to the success of the ITTUs in Ghana, GRATIS has now been converted into a non-profit making development organisation under the new name GRATIS Foundation. It is a company limited by guarantee with this mission statement: 'The corporate Mission of GRATIS Foundation is to support Ghana's vision to become a middle-level income country through the development of micro, small and medium enterprises'.

Following its positive results in the field of technological advance, the European Union (EU) in March 2000, at the request of the Ghana Government, agreed to give further financial support for the third phase of the GRATIS projects that will cover the enhancement of the development service programme at each ITTU, the restructuring and expansion of the technical apprentices training programme, and the establishment of a loan fund for GRATIS/ITTU registered clients and graduated apprentices.

The Intermediate Technology Transfer Unit (ITTU)

An ITTU is composed of a group of basic engineering workshops, physically placed in the centre of an informal industrial centre that offers:

- Metal machining

- Welding, steel fabrication and steel metal working

- Blacksmithing

- Ferrous and nonferrous metal casting

- Woodworking/pattern making.

Ideally, each section of the ITTU is designed to be a replica of an informal sector workshop. In each section a master is assisted by between four and six apprentices as is the case in the informal sector. Each section emphasises the promotion of new manufacturing activities in addition to offering repair services, and the ITTU searches for markets for the new products or services to ensure motivation. In a dynamic process the ITTU activities are passed over to the clients and as they become competent the ITTU continues to help them by identifying new products and manufacturing technology to meet future needs and market opportunities.

Can School Science Benefit from these Examples?

Schools can benefit from these examples in that a number of activities are not beyond the capabilities and capacities of schools as long as they select what to do based on the human, material and financial resources available to them. Some of the practices of artisans in their trade have many of the principles taught in standard technical schools and conventional schools that have technical subjects in their curriculum. There is the added advantage of enabling pupils to appreciate what can be done with limited resources and the many opportunities that exist.

7. Indigenous Knowledge Systems and their Economic Potential in South Africa

Otsile Ntsoane
University of the North-West, South Africa

Introduction

'Diet pill: San might sue Pfizer', reads the headline of a story in the 22 June issue of the *Mail and Guardian*, a South African weekly newspaper. 'South Africa may give the world a blockbuster drug, but there are claims that traditional knowledge has been plundered', the subheading continues.

The article details how a small firm based in the UK has made agreements with the giant international drug firm Pfizer to market a 'miracle' slimming drug isolated from a small cactus eaten by the San on their long hunting trips to stave off hunger and thirst. Pfizer believes the 'dieter's dream' may turn out to be as big a money earner in the US $1 billion market for slimming as Viagra has proved to be in the male potency market. Ironically, the small British firm obtained the rights to commercialise the drug from South Africa's Council for Scientific and Industrial Research (CSIR), which has owned the patent since the early 1960s. The San, the *Mail and Guardian* reports, '... are angry, saying their ancient knowledge has been "stolen", and are demanding compensation'. This chapter focuses on the need for countries in the southern region of Africa to introduce and implement ways to protect such knowledge.

Many people in developing countries, including Botswana and South Africa, depend on their environment, the veld, for their survival and to meet basic needs such as fuel, health, food and shelter (Sekhwela and Ntseane, 1994). Sacks (1997) defines veld products as non-grazing products that provide food, craft material, tanning gums and so on. Moruakgomo (1996) shows that veld products such as *Artemissia Afra*, (*Lengana* in Setswana) are supplementary sources of medicines. In the Transkei (South Africa), for example, the plant is used commercially to cure a number of ailments such as swelling and sweating of the feet, and gout.

Van der Vleuten (1998) indicates that indigenous knowledge systems have a crucial role in rural community sustainability in terms of providing employment, enriching nutritional content of foodstuffs and maximising the use of local resources. Few studies have been conducted on a comparative basis in the Southern Africa region on production and utilisation of veld products and their associated knowledge systems. Therefore a study into areas of sustainability and intellectual property rights, and their implications with respect to local knowledge systems, will be a contribution to the need to protect local knowledge systems from capitalist exploitative interest.

Studies by Mushita (1995) show that 75 per cent of 120 active compounds currently isolated from higher plants and widely used in modern medicine, show a positive correlation between their modern therapeutic use and the traditional use of the plants from which they were derived. However, commercialisation of such products often results in rural people losing ownership and control of their natural environment and knowledge systems. This is particularly so when commercialisation of veld products involves local and foreign capitalist companies concerned with profits rather than meeting community needs. Because of their strong dependence on the environment for survival, rural people are vulnerable to such commercialisation and are sensitive to the need to conserve their natural resources base.

Who is Protected?

Respondents interviewed in this study expressed reservations about private companies protecting their veld products and related knowledge systems, because of the companies' interest in profits rather than in the interests of the community, and feared that they would become alienated from the source of their being. Protection of cultural and intellectual components is essential, indivisible and crucial for local survival and development. Linked to this is the right of ownership and control of knowledge and resources.

This observation is supported by studies conducted by Thusano Lefatsheng (1994) in Kang, Botswana, showing that most people preferred the government and local community to provide protection for veld products. Matawanyika, Garibaldi et al. (1994) note that in South Africa the Bakgatla Community Development Organisation (BCDO) uses its tribal structures to mobilise its people's local conservation measures.

Interviews conducted in Magogoe and Dinokana Villages in South Africa showed that the greatest concern was the lack of regulatory measures and capacity to protect veld products and the local knowledge base, and knowing how to deal with agreements intended to benefit local people. Respondents who were members of the Dingaka Association and Traditional Healers

Organisation based in South Africa were concerned about their isolation from government on matters relating to sharing their indigenous knowledge and its benefits, including conservation methods and ecological knowledge.

Interviews conducted in both countries studied revealed a common agreement by respondents on the need to protect their local veld products and indigenous knowledge systems from exploitation and foreign control. They expressed concern about the limitation in South Africa of existing local, national, and international legislation such as the following:

- The Medical, Dental and Pharmacy Act No. 13 of 1928 that served to constrain traditional medicinal practitioners by restricting issuance of licenses to the Minister of Public Health, with the aim of reducing the number of practicing traditional medical practitioners in South Africa;

- The Natal Code of Native Law No. 19 of 1891 requiring that herbalists seek approval to practise from the regional African chief and stating that they must purchase a license to do so;

- A number of laws such as the Witchcraft Suppression Act No. 3 of 1957 which prohibit specific activities;

- The Forest Act No. 22 of 1984 and the KwaZulu Forest Act No 15 of 1980 which theoretically regulate the exploitation of plants;

- Local by-laws such as the Business Act and Tribal Regulations which legislate on trade and influence when and where medicinal products may be sold (Christoffersen *et al.*, 1996).

Legislation affecting the practice of traditional medicine has been in place since 1890, but until recently there was no law that enforced the protection of veld products and their indigenous knowledge systems. However, there are currently a number of Bills waiting to be enacted for the protection of indigenous knowledge systems, including the Bill on Intellectual Property Rights, the Heritage Resources Bill and the Protection of Indigenous Knowledge Bill. South Africa is also a signatory to a number of international laws and treaties that have a bearing on indigenous knowledge systems such as the International Convention on Biological Diversity that recognises indigenous knowledge practitioners and states that they should benefit from any commercial venture that uses their veld products or indigenous knowledge systems. The Convention on International Trade in Endangered Species of wild fauna and flora aims to protect any species that is regarded as endangered, but does not offer protection or benefit to local communities. Such treaties do not recognise the indigenous as defined in the South.

What is Indigenous?

Kaya and Maleka (1996) argue that indigenous does not necessarily mean traditional. They define indigenous as what the local community regards as authentic. Lalonde and Morin-Labatut (1993) support this when they argue that indigenous knowledge systems are not monolithic, because some elements are traditional and passed down from one generation to another with little or no changes while others are subject to innovation and integration of foreign practices. Indigenous knowledge systems are in constant transformation.

However, Lalonde and Morin-Labatut emphasise that indigenous knowledge systems and veld products have value not only for the cultures from which they emanate, but also for the scientific and commercial needs of outsiders. This argument has strong implications for the utilisation of indigenous knowledge systems and veld products in Botswana and South Africa. *Bio-Diversity Campaign News* (1996) states that the key strategy is to ensure that intellectual property rights of local communities are guaranteed, value is added to their knowledge, their entrepreneurial capacities are developed to generate returns to this knowledge and products, and that their cultural and institutional basis for dealing with their natural environment are enriched.

In accordance with Article 8 (j) of the International Convention on Biological Diversity (1992), national legislation on access to genetic resources must ensure the consent not only of the national government but also of the local or indigenous communities from which genetic material is taken or whose traditional knowledge is utilised for commercial purposes. Further to this, the Community Rights (Article 6) states that local communities have the right not to allow the collection of biological resources and access to their traditional technologies, knowledge and innovations, when doing so may threaten the integrity of their natural or cultural heritage.

Sing (1996) emphasises that existing intellectual property rights and regimes give the holder an exclusive monopoly to restrict the use (by copy, adapting and distribution) of the information embodied within the subject matter. It thus becomes a matter of grave concern when intellectual property rights agreements give a monopoly over the use of veld products to big companies which want to control the market (Convention on Biological Diversity, 1992).

A summit held in Ouagadougou in May 1996 was held partly in response to problems encountered when dealing with trade related intellectual property rights and the World Trade Organisation. At the summit, the Organisation of African Unity endorsed a draft Convention on Access to Biological Resources and the Protection of Community Rights. It is on this basis that African countries pass national legislation enabling them to regulate access to their genetic resources and to legally protect the rights of their communities.

The problem that South Africa currently encounters (Sekhwela and Ntseane, 1994) is that strategies adopted usually do not take into account community-related intellectual property rights, traditional knowledge and techniques. Furthermore, whatever experts impose is often not accepted by the communities and thus not utilised because most external strategies contrast with indigenous ones that are authentic to the local community (Tikatikwe, A Supplement in Mmegi, *The Reporter*, 22 August 1997).

Botswana has passed laws, including the Agricultural Conservation Act (1977), that prohibit the extraction and distribution of devils' claws (Harpogophytum Procumbens). Under this Act, members of the public are required to have permits to dig and sell plants that are regarded as endangered. South Africa, on the other hand, has not fully protected indigenous plants from random and unmonitored extraction and distribution.

To ensure that any agreement for development optimises the benefits accruing to the local people is the greatest concern for respondent communities in Dinokana and Magogoe in South Africa. The challenge from the respondents' viewpoint is that Western intellectual property rights do not consider the interests and sustainability of the traditional rights of local communities over their resources and associated knowledge.

In the absence of policy legislation, enforcing agencies and empowered communities, the consequences are that country-related intellectual property rights and genetic resources will be exploited and developed by foreign companies with little gain to either the country or people from whom knowledge is gleaned. A policy structure will commit governments to develop legislation and establish tools to control access to genetic resources including veld products and related indigenous knowledge systems. Such a move will solve a current trend that reveals unfair distribution of costs and benefits in bio-prospecting ventures to the disadvantage of local communities who are the custodians of biodiversity and the related indigenous knowledge.

The scanty availability of information on the ecology and socio-economic impact affects the production of veld products. This was expressed in the fear of the potential hazard of over-exploitation and environmental degradation (Kgathi, 1987). This chapter looks into two examples of existing veld products that are used as medicines or food, and the contribution of veld products to the socio-economic sustainability of the study communities in terms of employment, income generation, health and food security.

The Veld: A Closer Examination

The commercial potential of South Africa's veld-related intellectual property rights and products has been stressed in recent years (Materechera, Hansen and Nyamapfene, 1998), although at present the veld product sector is informal and does not make a specific contribution to GDP. However, for the poor who make up 60–70 per cent of the rural population, veld products are probably more important than livestock. The distribution of veld products has a bearing on settlement patterns since people adapt to their environmental conditions and exploit all available natural resources.

Imbrasis belina

Phane (*Imbrasis belina*) larvae in Southern Africa have attracted the interest of researchers who are investigating this edible species for a number of scientific reasons (Gashe and Mpuchane, 1996). In Botswana, *Imbrasis belina* is the major source of cash income for the harvesters as well as providing other members of the family with employment. The third source of cash income was beer brewing, followed by employment for cash (Ntsoane, 2000a). Dependence of rural communities on such natural resources is linked to their conservation and thus to sustainable development that provides food, generates income and employs rural people in natural resources projects. Most harvesters of veld products, including *Imbrasis belina*, are women who should be empowered to benefit more from their sustaining of *Imbrasis belina* that supplies significant amounts of high-quality protein. *Imbrasis belina* contains amino acids that are easily digested, thus making it suitable as a weaning food. The need for its sustainability is of great concern for the rural poor who depend on it for their livelihood.

Artemesia Afra

Artemesia Afra is another well-known medicinal plant in Southern Africa, known as wormwood in English, Wilde in Afrikaans, Longana in Setswana and Mhlonya in isiXhosa. *Artmesia Afra* belongs to the family of Compositae known as *Artmemisia absinthium*. Economic rural development plans in the Ciskei, South Africa and in some villages in Botswana specifically exploit *Artmesia Afra*. It offers great promise as an alternative crop because of its adaptation to the environment and its high financial return. Consequently, there has been much interest in farming it as a commercial crop (Materechera, Hansen and Nyamapfene, 1998). In North Western Province and other regions of South Africa the plant is used in different preparations for a wide variety of illnesses including lack of appetite; coughs, colds, and chills; dyspepsia; menstrual period pains; stomach ache, colic and other gastric derangements; croup and whooping cough; gout; and as a purgative. The infusion or decantation is used as a lotion to bathe haemorrhoids and as a hot bath to bring out the rash in measles. The vapour from boiled leaves can be inhaled for respiratory afflictions and can relieve neuralgia, mumps, throat inflammations, and sweating and aching feet. It can be used with tea or as a tea substitute.

Artemesia Afra requires lower inputs than conventional crops in terms of planting, tillage, fertiliser and pest control, so that it is relatively easy to establish, manage and maintain (Materechera, Hansen and Nyamapfebe, 1997). The species is rich in essential oils and a small worldwide demand exists for Artemesis-type oils for use as external medicines, perfumery and deodorant soaps. Artemesis also has potential as a substitute for more highly priced oils. A research team in Alice, Ciskei, reported that manufacturing techniques have already been evolved such as standard dry steam distillation procedures for extracting the oil, bulk handling equipment and methods, and for local processing of the crop.

Considering the different purposes and uses of *Artemesia Afra*, its economic potential is huge and its development should not be delayed. The plant should be developed, its economic potential explored and the intellectual property rights retained by the local community who can share the final product jointly with the developers.

Discussion

The term sustainable development stems from the 1980 World Conservation Strategy. The report of the World Commission on Environment and Development, 'Our Common Future' (the Brundtland Report of 1987), gives prominence to sustainable development. The fundamental premise of sustainable development is that there is an obligation to future generations and the notion that we owe them the choice to make their own decisions about the resources we bequeath them. However, there is growing evidence that the planet's natural resources are being steadily degraded and in some cases irreversibly damaged.

The Earth Summit at Rio de Janeiro laid down a challenge to nations to achieve sustainable development. People must change their attitudes to the use of resources, particularly to those from the biophysical environment of the interconnected ecosystem of land, air, water and biological species upon which we depend for our life needs. To help this change in attitude, changes must be made to the laws and institutions that influence our behaviour and relationships with each other, and with the biophysical world. Sustainable development within such a context is a major policy cornerstone of the democratic government of South Africa, as stipulated in the Reconstruction and Development Programme (ANC, 1994).

Indigenous knowledge: some definitions

Definitions related to the topic are brief and to the point, but require deeper meaning that is involving, inclusive and in the interests of people in the southern hemisphere, especially sub-Saharan Africa. In the past, the meaning or the conceptual framework was defined in the interest of Western epistemology with little regard for African or Asiatic definitions of the world. The articulation of the definition, conceptualisation and operationalisation of the term 'Indigenous Knowledge' given here is based on a need to reintroduce an Afro-optimistic approach to knowledge production.

Any search for a definition should not be a short cut such as reverting to the dictionary definition. Neither should it be based on the definition of the coloniser whose language and culture obviously influenced the meaning of the term (Ntsoane, 2000b). North–South tensions have been linked to economic disparities (Mazrui, 1990) where definition was based on Western epistemology with little or no respect for the articulation of aboriginal or indigenous peoples. Such denial of articulation is common and well documented by many authors of Africa origin and scholars from the diaspora.

First, in Africa the issue of knowledge production, generation and use was not academically derived. The process was and is continuous, without words and concepts, or copyright. The process is open, highly participatory and commonly used. The production is not alienating (Ntsoane, 2000b). Ani (1994) puts it clearly when he says that the pragmatic implications of indigenous knowledge systems are that, unlike the European conception of science, they are secular and do not alienate. Rather they liberate, rationalising concepts and knowledge. The African way of explaining the world is not linear or alienating, and it is not written. Such concepts are the basis of the European tradition of science that deals exclusively with the physical world and in which the metaphysical is debunked as irrational, mystical and anti-scientific. Indigenous knowledge production consists of characteristic elements of the traditional heritage developed and maintained by a community of individuals that reflects their traditional expectations. Other definitions include, 'Local knowledge that is unique to a given culture or society. It is the basis for agriculture, health care, food preparation, education, environmental conservation and a host of other activities. Such knowledge is passed down from generation to generation, usually by word of mouth.' Indigenous knowledge is culture-based and practised in ways that are effective, efficient and functional in those communities that hold them. Communities that practise indigenous knowledge also have a technical knowledge component. Apart from such technical knowledge, local communities also have non-technical knowledge or insights, wisdom, ideas, perceptions and innovative capabilities that pertain to ecological, biological, geographical and physical phenomena (Todaro, 1985; Ntsoane, 2000b).

Indigenous practice

This is the application of community skills and experiential knowledge to help people support, develop, and maintain their communities in combination and integrated with the knowledge and skills derived from appropriate professional knowledge systems.

Indigenous community workers

Although employed at the lowest scale, indigenous community workers are often expected to perform specialised functions without training or compensation. Many have years of experience in the service delivery field but receive no recognition of their experience and wisdom.

Conceptualised articulation of indigenous knowledge systems

In the current analysis of the use of veld products and related knowledge systems is the challenge faced when useful indigenous knowledge becomes delegitimised or lost with the growing dominance of imported technologies, Western scientific principles, and conventional development strategies. Most scholars in anthropology and the social sciences use the term indigenous knowledge synonymously with traditional and local knowledge to differentiate the knowledge developed by a given community from knowledge systems generated through universities, government research centres and private industry. Scholars thereby subject endogenous knowledge to knowledge of indigenous people or any other defined community. Unlike the word traditional, which commonly implies that something is static, indigenous knowledge is dynamic.

Indigenous knowledge relates to the ways members of a given community define and classify phenomenon in their physical, natural, and social environments. It provides a basis for local decision-making, frequently occurring through formal and informal community associations and organisations. Communities identify problems and seek solutions in such local forums, capitalising on indigenous creativity and encouraging experimentation and innovation. Indigenous knowledge is tacit knowledge and therefore difficult to codify. It is embedded in community practices, institutions, relationships and rituals.

Larsen (1998), reporting on the outcomes of workshops on indigenous knowledge systems, defined it as concepts, facts, perceptions, beliefs, information and values, as well as particular economic, social and traditional political arrangements. Ntsoane (2000a) defines indigenous knowledge as a fusion of both traditional and local. He adds heritage. He says it is production consisting of characteristic elements of the traditional heritage developed and maintained by a community or individuals reflecting the traditional expectations of such a community. It is local knowledge that is unique to a given culture or society. It is the basis for agriculture, health care, food preparation, education, environmental conservation and a host of other activities. Such knowledge is passed down from generation to generation, usually by word of mouth.

Then comes the word 'endogenous', which means what grows from within. What needs to be conceptualised is the process that takes place during endogenisation on one side and indigenization on the other. Endogenous knowledge, which according to simple meaning is growing and originating from within, is mediated wherein people's common understanding of what is shared, what is found in the group's experience and is strongly linked to their common sources of such knowledge. It is based on ritual about ancestors and speech given from generation to generation by word of mouth. Within the endogenous come the aspects of cognitive experience that are unique to the place and the people who conceal, shape and filter the knowledge utilisation among them. Indigenization and localising, critical thinking and theory correlate easily with the colonial invention of the native, the rural, the uneducated; indeed, the whole list of pejorative and derogatory terms that can be found in the euphemism lexicon.

The skewed insight given to the indigenous by the colonial must be challenged and removed. Hence the endogenization of plural knowledge and practices is needed through mental decolonisation; something that puts the oral history and knowledge that is not written as worth considering. The process of endogenization is that of asserting the notion of thinking with the assistance of the self; the involvement of the liberated self, the involvement of the 'internal brains' and the growing from inside of the paradigm that will be responsible for re-appropriating and partially reinventing local paradigms. The whole process should be seen as a nationalistic reaction against Western domination, against the neocolonial, against the informal globalisation with its neo-capitalist investor notions. The endogenization of African knowledge systems should draw on prestigious cultural traditions of the East. Unless Africa affirms its epistemology, cosmologies, ethical and ecological concerns, the West will set the agenda for her. Plurality of knowledge is what should drive the cultural forces of change in the African renaissance.

Indigenous knowledge systems can be further defined as the combination of knowledge systems encompassing technology, social, economic and philosophical learning, and educational, legal and governance systems. It is knowledge relating to the technological, social, institutional, scientific and broad development of communities. It consists of tangible aspects such as medicine, natural resources, crafts and the like. Intangible aspects, however, consist of the knowledge system behind the technologies, such as indigenous education, philosophy, cosmology, botany, and crop and animal husbandry. In indigenous communities, the tangible and intangibles are closely woven together. This indigenous knowledge is not new knowledge. Senghor (1963) states that we have inherited our own method of knowledge from our ancestors.

Non-South Africans have played an important role in campaigns for environmental justice, bio-watch and sustainable natural resource utilisation, including mobilising South African citizens into forums that have begun to address matters related to the environment and indigenous knowledge systems. It therefore suggests that the role of Africans and other peoples from regions that suffered the effects of colonialism and the appropriation by the West of intellectual property rights can share their experiences in promoting the protection of their indigenous knowledge and natural resources. Except for a few committed Western environmental groupings, most have an agenda and interest in the bio-piracy and biosphere of the natural resources of the South. The South must choose its friends carefully. What is important is to draft laws that will protect the rights of local farmers and of all communities that produce veld products and own the knowledge that is needed for their production.

A strong conveyer belt of indigenous knowledge is needed across the continent. Each country should contribute in sustaining its own cultural niche. Such a niche should be linked to an industrialisation of non-industrialised indigenous technology or natural resources. Through such a network, indigenous knowledge systems will contribute significantly to the renaissance of the continent.

South Africa should use the experiences of eastern countries such as China,

Malaysia and India. Through sharing with this non-South African citizenry, knowledge can be exchanged and thereby increase the awareness and the potential of indigenous knowledge in communities.

The industrialised world can also contribute to the development of indigenous knowledge systems, even if this proves uncomfortable. Just as Europeans and Americans were active in popularising Western knowledge, they should be involved in giving Africa authority over her own indigenous knowledge. The struggle to revitalise Africa's legitimacy over indigenous knowledge systems must be negotiated through a strategic commitment by those who have benefited at the expense of colonies in Africa. There cannot be another colonialism of the mind and resources that are related to indigenous knowledge systems.

Community awareness of the economic potential, as well as the cultural bond that common knowledge brings to nations, will directly result in the popularisation of indigenous knowledge systems as a means of socio-economic sustenance and cultural bonding. Indigenous knowledge should be made popular amongst people of all ages because of its important role in providing problem-solving strategies, especially for the poor. Indigenous knowledge is commonly held by communities rather than individuals, is tacit knowledge and therefore difficult to codify, and is embedded in community practices, institutions, relationships and rituals. Furthermore, indigenous knowledge represents an important contribution to global development knowledge and is an underutilised resource in the development process.

A network between South Africa and other countries will facilitate the development partnership and contribute to learning more about local practices in other countries. It will enable African countries to better adapt global knowledge to local conditions, and thereby help design activities that better serve country needs. The proposed network should facilitate a sharing of indigenous knowledge practices and innovations among local communities in a South-to-South exchange.

Knowledge production and dissemination determine knowledge utilisation. Differences are at the level of interpretation where locally produced knowledge seems to be denied. During the anti-colonial struggle in a number of African countries, knowledge was appropriated whilst knowledge produced in those states that were not colonised remained authentic to local interests. Epistemic communities that share the same source and modes of knowledge disseminate knowledge in modes that retain the meaning and content of such knowledge.

When popularising areas of indigenous knowledge systems and their related science and technology, it is important to consider the nature of the communities involved in the process of development. Knowledge is a universal heritage and a universal resource. The need, therefore, to popularise indigenous knowledge systems amongst schools both inside and outside South Africa is important in post-colonial Africa. Knowledge as a universal heritage has location and models for dissemination. It was in the process of the dissemination of Western knowledge that indigenous knowledge systems were ostracised and disregarded. Indigenous knowledge systems were not included in discipline clusters of scientific knowledge and technology.

Indigenous knowledge systems represent a knowledge heritage that, much as it is universal, is also a unique way of ensuring that it becomes part and parcel of informing policy making, research and teaching modules so that it becomes a pivotal aspect of knowledge development.

Through promoting indigenous knowledge systems in schools, work areas and in our different communities, all Africa will create a platform for articulation, which will demystify the Western domination achieved through the violent and linguistic measures of the former colony. Space allocation by educators for learners to bring their knowledge to classrooms will create a dialogue that will eventually show that the learners' knowledge, which in most instances is based on indigenous knowledge systems, is vital in determining the educators' input. We cannot treat our learners as ignorant of their environmental, social, political, ecological, scientific and technological cultures. It is, therefore, appropriate to adjust the learning areas to the learners' needs and those of the community.

In popularising indigenous knowledge systems around science and technology, special attention should be placed on the paradigm shift from a Western epistemology to an endogenous or indigenous epistemology. Such a shift of mindset demands new areas of articulation. It is at this stage that the knowledge production discourse is engaged. It is for a holistic knowledge framework that seeks to make whole that which was partial, incomplete, in large measure stunted and therefore stunting. The new framework which emerges involves principles that were present all along but were unknown to us. It includes the old as a partial truth and, by its framework, it transforms the traditional positions and the stubborn new observations, reconciling their apparent contradictions (Hountondji, 1997). Indigenous knowledge systems as an operational concept reject the skewed way of analysing the world, the one way of seeing and the only tool through which the masses of humanity can receive accreditation and license to be (Hopper, 1999).

Human rights, democracy and equality as inscribed in our constitution will have no meaning in reality as long as one knowledge system dominates, as long as the 'othering' is promoted. Nothing of social justice can be spoken about until the indigenous knowledge systems of those communities and countries that were colonised and served a resource for the economic development of the coloniser have platforms to influence policy in knowledge generating, validating and dissemination as notions of human rights. In popularising indigenous knowledge systems, we should declare a struggle to emancipate indigenous knowledge systems and thereby contribute to the development of its holistic operationalisation.

8. Promoting Co-operation in Science and Technology in the SADC Region

Professor Michael Kahn
University of Cape Town, South Africa

Progress in science requires various types of co-operation at and between the intergovernmental, governmental and non-governmental levels, such as: multilateral projects; research networks, including South-South networking.

Declaration on Science and the Use of Knowledge, World Conference on
Science, Budapest, 1999

Why Promote Co-operation?

One objective of the South African government is the promotion of regional development. This is a dual goal that is both altruistic and self-seeking. It has the intention of creating and enlarging markets for technological goods and services, and of promoting regional growth and stability. Accordingly, the Department of Arts, Culture, Science and Technology has taken on the responsibility to promote cross-border scientific co-operation. The Department seeks to exercise this mandate in collaboration with other government departments, parastatals and the private sector. The advent of formal apartheid led to schism between South Africa and most African states, and building new trust and relationships necessarily takes some time. It is also important to have a good understanding of what capacity for joint scientific co-operation exists, and to have clarity on the mechanisms and resources that should be put in place to give meaning to intent. Accordingly, this chapter explores scientific capacity, the policy environment and the views of those who might become involved in co-operative activities.

Thus far, the track record of science in national development in most African states has been modest, if not weak. The problems appear to begin at school level, where uptake of science and mathematics is low and performance far from satisfactory. The reasons for this failure are many. One group, arguing from the perspective of dependency theory, sees lack of resources as the problem (Ogbu *et al.*, 1995). Another claims a cultural dissonance between what is termed 'Western science' and the so-called traditional African world view (Ogunniyi, 1996). A third, in what seems to be a modified version of the vocational school fallacy, seeks an explanation in instrumental causes (Dzama and Osborne, 1999).

Whatever the reasons, science and technology at research levels, and science education in schools, technical colleges and higher education institutions, has generally not been important in state funding in post-independence Africa. The more pressing needs of basic education, health, infrastructure and defence have consumed what budget might be grown off the local tax base. An excellent account of these difficulties can be found in a review conducted for the SADC Secretariat (Mshigeni *et al.*, 1994).

How then can South Africa, with its relatively developed scientific infrastructure, engage in scientific co-operation with the rest of the region? It is this aspect of science promotion with which this chapter will engage.

Mere popularisation of the ideas of science cannot alone change the situation. The practice of science must be grounded in the local reality, failing which it is likely to be a rich man's toy. How then to strengthen local capacity? Is it a matter of developing the necessary human resources after which an agenda for research will follow? Who determines the agenda? How is the work to be paid for? To begin finding an answer we now turn to the region.

Science in the Southern African Development Community

The Southern African Development Co-ordinating Conference (SADCC) originated in 1980 as a political and economic response to the damaging effects on the sub-region of the ongoing wars for liberation from South African domination. The nine founding countries were Botswana, Lesotho, Swaziland, Zambia, Zimbabwe, Malawi, Tanzania, Angola and Mozambique. All these countries, except the last two, were formerly subject to British colonial rule and experienced transitions to independence without the widespread loss of life and destruction of infrastructure that characterised the experience of Mozambique and Angola. To a varying extent, institutions such as research stations and standards laboratories existed in these states before independence where they provided a service to the extractive industries and plantations of the colonial era. On the other hand, there were generally few graduates available to the new governments, let alone scientists and technologists to staff these institutions.

The various states have largely remained in the modes of production of colonial times in which a local science capacity was barely necessary. Under those conditions national systems of science and technology did not develop and government spending on science research has thus not emerged.

Taken as a whole, in 1993 Africa had an estimated 72,000 research and development specialists of whom approximately 18,000 were in South Africa. In sub-Saharan Africa, South Africa accounts for nearly 60 per cent of research and development specialists, and in SADC probably for more than 90 per cent. There is a major difficulty in accessing reliable figures since outside South Africa no systematic auditing is carried out. Males are the dominant gender of this knowledge capital stock

The SADCC states, with the assistance of the international community, organised a range of development and rehabilitation programmes that were arranged under the sector responsibilities assigned to the various countries. So Zimbabwe was given responsibility for food security, Angola for energy, Botswana for livestock research, Swaziland for Human Resource Development and so on. However, the cross-cutting nature of S&T, whilst recognised as important, was not given the same sector recognition.

That science and technology is an important driver in socio-economic development was appreciated by SADCC scientists, technologists and administrators and they waged a long but largely unsuccessful campaign to elevate science and technology in their national government policies.

In their efforts to build the modern state, the new governments established institutions of higher education and other science and technology organs. Together, these comprise around 200 entities that support and promote research and development. While there has been some brain drain out of SADC to the West, a significant number of scientists, engineers and technologists remain in SADC. This includes those who have entered state administration, those in research and technology organisations and those in higher education.

If one needs a good example that research spending is driven by economic and social necessity, then the experience of Mauritius, with its 250 years of research into sugar cultivation and processing, is a case in point. A producer-funded research capacity was developed to the extent that through to the present day, government science research spending is dwarfed by the private sector spending on sugar research. This example also serves to illustrate that where the state cannot or will not invest in such research, the private sector, if convinced of its necessity, will do so.

While South Africa's S&T policy development, refracted through its 'total onslaught' mindset, mainly related to Europe and North America, the SADCC states looked toward the OAU and Economic Commission for Africa (ECA) for leadership. CASTAFRICA I in 1974 rekindled the debates begun in Lagos in 1964, urging that the human resource base had to be strengthened to a level of 100–200 scientists per million of population by 1980. This target eluded most SADCC states.

A more forceful move to place S&T on the agenda came through the Council of Ministers Meeting held in 1988. This meeting mandated a SADCC-wide study on S&T that finally got underway in 1991, with the study itself finally published in 1994 as the Mshigeni Report. The report begins with an overview of research capacity, noting that the commercial sector undertakes substantial research through institutes owned by specific agricultural industries often funded through producer levies. The mining sector is dominated by multinationals whose research is pursued offshore and whose local geological exploration activities frequently bypass the existing state geological surveys. Industry, on the other hand, tends to be an importer of technology and generally operates at the lower end of value addition. A complex interaction of the effects of war, hyperinflation, structural adjustment policies, unbalanced terms of trade and devaluation of currencies have eroded industrial capacity.

The report found neglect on the government side of the S&T sector. Of the 10 SADC States in the survey, only four had an official S&T policy in place at the time of the study. In the state sector, agricultural research dominated but had a poor record of impact on communal farming. Research on shelter, water, sanitation and appropriate technology was poorly co-ordinated across countries. Nor had expansion of basic education improved the persistent imbalance of scientists and engineers, technologists and technicians. The situation contrasts with that in the East, where investment in secondary education has begun to show good returns (Lewin, 1993).

In seeking measures to ameliorate the problem the report urged co-operation, gender redress and steps to limit the brain drain out of SADC. The need for investment and reform of school science and mathematics education was highlighted and in particular it was recommended that 'Science education, at all levels, should emphasise the applied aspects, and also involve linkages with entrepreneurships (sic) and joint ventures' (p. 6). While noting that a small pool of highly trained scientists exists, their work was skewed from development toward research. This in part arose since policies did not encourage participation of the private sector but was also caused by 'the lack of properly trained manpower' (p. 8). The Mshigeni Report then argued that a precondition for driving S&T onto the national agenda was that all states should establish a National Research and Development Co-ordinating Body (NRDCB) with access to the highest levels of government. This might be termed a bureaucratic change approach.

A second S&T policy overview is that of Ogbu, Oyeyinka and Mlawa who argue the case that technology drives development. 'African economies require deep technological revolutions to bring about rapid structural shifts … (within) an enabling macroeconomic environment and the ways that environment interacts with an effective technology policy.' For them, technology is central to the development process and long-term structural change is technology driven. Since the growth of systems is an evolutionary process, technological and organisational learning cannot be circumscribed. The authors quote evidence from across African countries to demonstrate those explicit efforts and investments that are essential preconditions for learning and development. In other words, technological capability is not an automatic outcome of capital accumulation and investment. Successful technology transfer involves and requires time, skills of adaptation and continuous learning for which investment must be provided. Technological learning is not automatic and not necessarily expensive. But it must be managed and allowed for.

Accordingly the consequences of a ' … lack of capacity for domestic capital goods and machinery production is a singular characteristic of underdevelopment. … SSA (Sub-Saharan Africa) is extremely weak, lacking the capacity to produce even the most basic tools for manufacturing … [and] maintain the systems.' One of the additional factors that contributes to this weakness is the lack of, or impossibility for interaction among, a network of firms. When there is no domestic capital goods sector, linkages with firms cannot emerge. Technological learning is limited and little technical change will occur. Turnkey projects generate foreign exchange but these do not stimulate local manufacturing, human resource development or R&D. Despite turnkey projects the gap between the G-7 countries and the rest widens since industrial production today rests on a much more complex scientific, information and technological base. Accordingly the state must exercise a stronger interventionist role in the underdeveloped than in the industrialised countries. Implicitly what the authors argue for is management through a set of national systems of innovation with the state actively laying down the regulatory, physical, human and social infrastructure. This is undeniably a systems approach.

With the end of formal colonialism and the liberation of the whole region,

SADCC transformed itself into the Southern African Development Community (SADC). Up to that point no real progress in co-ordinating and developing science and technology policy had been made. However, much had been achieved regarding policy for education and training, with the SADC Protocol on Education and Training (SADC, 1997) coming into force in early 1999. Given the differences in approach across the education systems of the region, the linkage of education with local culture and language difficulties, this was no mean achievement.

The Protocol includes the undertaking that 'Member states agree to urge universities and non-university research institutes to co-operate in the area of research and to forge links with the industry/private sector and other relevant sectors … to lay a basis for developing science and technology.' Here then is a first instrument for forging research co-operation.

Regional Capacity and Co-operation

Written largely from the perspective of higher education, Article 8 of the Protocol lays out guidelines for co-operation in R&D. The Protocol makes provision for higher education and R&D resource sharing, and recommends that within ten years all states should have a national S&T policy in place. This will serve as the basis for formulation of S&T policy for SADC as a whole. Co-operation among the various R&D role players is urged, including the establishment of professional associations through which information might be exchanged and R&D quality enhanced.

Overall there is a call for the promotion of mobility of researchers through relaxation of immigration regulations for the purposes of 'research, consultancy work and related pursuits'. The inclusion of Article 8 in the Protocol reflects the fact that in many SADC states S&T policy and, by implication, R&D often falls within the ambit of a Ministry of Education or Higher Education. The recommendations for R&D promotion and co-operation should be read in the larger context of higher education where co-operation in capacity development is a major thrust. A starting point for an analysis of S&T capacity in SADC begins with some comparisons across the different states.

Among the four most prosperous states, Seychelles has the highest GNP per capita. The other three (Mauritius, Botswana and South Africa) are at the lower end of the upper middle-income range, the unusual case in this group being Botswana whose social composition is unusually homogeneous with a minute expatriate and settler population. Arguably, in terms of GNP/capita, infrastructure and composition of GDP, the three settler 'islands' have most in common with each other.

South Africa and Botswana are members of the Southern African Customs Union (SACU). Both countries in the lower middle-income group (Swaziland and Namibia) are members of SACU and have 'marched together'. The remaining member of SACU, Lesotho, lies in the lower-income group and is the country least endowed with agricultural potential or mineral resources. Until the completion of the Lesotho Highlands Water Scheme its main income derived from migrant labour remissions. As a water and energy exporter one may expect Lesotho's GDP to rise dramatically from 1998 onward.

Two members of the lower-income group are the former Portuguese colonies of Mozambique and Angola, whose economies were largely destroyed during and after independence. The former Belgian colony of the Democratic Republic of Congo has since independence struggled to establish state infrastructure. This leaves the former British possessions of Malawi, Tanzania, Zambia and Zimbabwe. All have a leading university, and in some cases, more than one. While Tanzania and Malawi have predominantly agriculture-led economies, both Zambia and Zimbabwe through their mining industries have an associated manufacturing sector. In the latter case this sector developed strong self-reliance during the period of sanctions from 1965 to 1980.

Among the upper middle-income countries, Mauritius and Botswana are currently making strides in reconfiguring their S&T systems towards national goals. Both have growing economies and well-established universities. Their S&T policies are being operationalised through a small set of institutions that are being developed according to market principles.

The two lower middle-income countries, Namibia and Swaziland, have very small S&T systems and are heavily dependent upon expatriate researchers. Both have niche strengths that provide a basis for external co-operation.

Among the lower-income countries Zimbabwe, given its huge investment in education and the developments around the National University of Science and Technology, may be expected to achieve greater levels of scientific output over the next decade or so.

The institutions that could form the basis for national systems of innovation are in place, but the impact of war, political instability, the imposition of structural adjustment policies and the disastrous falls in commodity prices mean that in many states the systems have all but collapsed. While the institutions are today largely populated with nationals, many units are moribund with demoralised staff and aging equipment. Funds for transport are limited and many scientists perform largely administrative functions.

Promoting Scientific Co-operation with SADC

To seek a mechanism for co-operation, DACST in 1999 commissioned a study that would engage with the main role players in the SADC member states and provide guidelines for a research programme with modest funding to serve as a kick start.

A project team engaged in a series of country visits over a period of some six months and compiled a report that provided an overview of capacity and a set of recommendations. The project took care to navigate the difficult terrain of perceptions regarding South Africa. The skills and resources of the country are desirable, but there are fears that a new dominance could emerge from apparently innocent co-operation.

It is obvious that many of the lower- and lower middle-income countries have become dependent upon donors for the continued functioning of their research systems. This raises the very real concern of who controls the research agenda. Where relationships are so unbalanced, the existence of an official science and technology policy in and of itself is no safeguard against usurpation of the research agenda. A new player on the block adds to the complexity of these relationships.

On the other hand, some country economies have blossomed, institutions have grown and are performing world-class research and development. A network of SADC Centres of Excellence has been established that is actively training a new generation of scientists and carrying out relevant research. The concerns that scientists and administrators raise in regard to international co-operation must, therefore, be understood in the context of three powerful factors – decline, dependence and loss of control.

Broadly speaking the claims, issues and concerns of the major SADC role players may be summarised as:

- Donor-funded projects create well-resourced islands that lead to further fragmentation within institutions.
- The imbalances of power had made some researchers feel as if 'we have moved from being hunter-gatherers to data gatherers' who perform basic

tasks that would accrue to the benefit of academics in the North.

- Donor technical assistance consumed a disproportionate share of funds, which amounted to 'recycling', and was frequently of a nature that could well have been performed by a local researcher.

- The devaluation of local currencies and erosion of income of highly-qualified scientists has led many to turn to consulting as a survival activity. That many donor projects did not recruit local consultants is thus a further source of concern and formation of distrust of motives.

- At the level of country experience there was generally movement of researchers from North to South and students from South to North. This, too, made for a feeling of inequality. This was further exacerbated where projects were made to fit into the northern partner's timetable.

- Co-operation with external partners who had access to greater resources led to 'swamping' within projects, such that the local voice was all but lost.

- It was frequently alleged that external researchers had appropriated data or specimens. This theme was a constant background in discussions and has become an urgent issue in the age of biotechnology and genetic manipulation.

- The absence of ethical regimes for experimentation laid SADC states open to unscrupulous testing of animals and crops by foreign parties within their borders.

- Scientists face the very real prospect of becoming deskilled since they lack the necessary equipment and other resources to work in their fields of specialisation. Put simply, scientific human capital has a finite shelf life.

- There were many forms of brain drain and brain gain in operation, with scientists moving within the region and out of the region.

- Researchers in many states were frustrated that politicians had not grasped the importance of funding research and building S&T systems. They felt that leadership was only interested in activities with a high likelihood of delivering immediate results. There was a problem of managing expectations.

- Fears of dominance frequently arose, directed towards the rich countries of the North, South Africa and even East Africa.

- Some government departments felt a strong need to control research, especially where this intruded on sensitive issues such as threatened minority groups.

- A caution was frequently offered that individual researchers were prone to advocate narrow interests to attract funds toward their own areas or institutions.

- Appropriate technology was to be encouraged; appropriation of technology would be resisted.

These matters cluster around matters such as power relations, preservation of self-esteem, professional mobility and intellectual survival.

What form of co-operation?

At one extreme one might argue that formal nation-to-nation bilateral agreements are needed. However, the time and effort required to establish such agreements would be an obstacle to rapid progress. Where such bilaterals exist they may be used for setting up collaboration, but where they do not exist, other mechanisms must. At the other extreme might be a totally laissez faire approach that relies upon peer-to-peer or institution-to-institution networking. The argument would be that competent scientists know one another, will make contact and will get on with the job. Sadly, where the resources available to the different scientists are highly unequal, the emergent relationship may be flawed. Somewhere between these extremes is where funding is channelled through the appropriate national research and development co-ordinating bodies. Where such bodies do not exist, the national university could assume the position of facilitator.

To the relations between individuals or nations must be added the purpose behind the relations. All countries grapple with the problem of deciding where the self-interest of researchers, both national and foreign, ends and linkage to national interest begins. Where researchers determine the goals, various forms of lack of accountability to local goals may arise. However, this lack of 'goal' accountability does not necessarily preclude funds becoming available from sources external to the state. In an attempt to keep track of such relationships, some SADC governments make use of existing statutes or are drafting legislation that requires the registration of all research projects.

Then there is possible tension between researcher goals and what national parties are prepared to fund. Given multilateral interests, such co-operation frequently involves significant numbers of expatriate researchers being on local ground. This serves to provide additional intellectual capital and project experience for local researchers, but it may feed many of the concerns that were listed above. Another situation that arises from time to time is where researchers are able to access their own funds. Typical cases are where nationals retain links with the foreign universities where they obtained their doctorates or with the donor agency that made this possible. Fruitful work may arise out of such relationships, but they are often felt to threaten the national agenda.

For cash-strapped governments that wish to control the research agenda, there are limits to the extent to which they may be able to persuade multilateral agencies that projects in support of the national goals are what they should fund. Another difficulty lies in getting all parties onto the same timeline.

With the above in mind the following framework for co-operation emerged:

◆ Initially, co-operation should be sought through peer-to-peer interaction, if possible aligned with national goals and effected in co-operation with NRDCBs where they exist.

◆ Activities that are squarely in the public goods domain would be preferred. There are a number of reasons for this position, arising from direct historic relations as well as the general experience of the region. The primary goal must be to establish a relationship of trust with partner organisations. This may best be done through research where the fear of unilateral exploitation is kept to a minimum. By removing commercial gain from the equation along with its concomitant contractual aspects, one goes some way toward this.

◆ As the relationships mature and all parties become secure, more commercial benefit might be sought.

◆ Linkage with the productive sector should be a longer-term goal of the co-operation.

◆ Project identification may be based on goal-directed needs, through an expression of interest or where an existing project is recognised as having mutual benefit.

◆ Where potential projects involve direct social impact it would be expected that stakeholder consultation should be effected as early as possible.

◆ On the South African side a project champion for each project will be identified from among the Science Councils. The project champion will invite 'requests to participate' from SADC S&T institutions that have already identified goal-directed areas as important. An endorsement from the relevant NRDCB that the project is aligned with country S&T goals might be a prerequisite for consideration. The project champion will simultaneously invite participation from South African higher education institutions through open advertisement.

- Given the public goods orientation, charges for goods and services would normally be levied at cost.

- Where feasible, projects should involve postgraduate student development.

- Intellectual property rights arising from the project work will primarily be dealt with through joint publication. A memorandum of understanding (MoU) would normally suffice to protect pre-existing rights. Where a MoU is drawn up to deal with future rights, unless exceptional circumstances prevail, such MoU should be free of long-term disclosure provisions.

- A steering committee should monitor projects in terms of ethical compliance and gender balance, and will be responsible for formative and summative project evaluation. The evaluation criteria should be built into the project design at the outset.

Giving Substance to the Intentions

The DACST study sought ways to promote research across regional borders under circumstances of severe financial constraint. Proposals in the fields of water management, cross-border pollution, food technology, indigenous knowledge protection, soil management, HIV/AIDs and Information and Communication Technology, including GIS and education MIS, were invited. The selection criteria were also made known to bidders. On the South African side, it was stipulated that the cost centres would be located in one or another of the science councils. The choice of partners was left entirely open.

That the research community desired such interchange was more than evident in that when a request for proposals was placed, more than 90 submissions for funding were received. This high response more than justified the effort that was put into canvassing the role players and scoping out the guidelines.

9. Regional Co-operation for Capacity Building in Science and Technology

The African Network of Scientific and Technological Institutions (ANSTI) and the Consultative Group for International Agricultural Research (CGIAR)

Dr J. G. M. Massaquoi
African Network of Scientific and Technological Institutions, Nairobi, Kenya

Mike Savage
African Forum for Children's Literacy in Science and Technology
University of Durban-Westville, South Africa

Introduction

The promotion and popularisation of science and technology can be done through intervention at the local community level, the primary and secondary school level and at the tertiary education level. However, activities at these different levels are not independent of each other, and interventions at one level influence or are influenced by the other levels.

The emphasis at the tertiary level is to train a pool of scientists and technologists, and this is influenced by how science and technology are promoted in both schools and society, since intakes into tertiary institutions depend on students' interest in science and technology at the lower levels of education. In a similar manner, the output of interventions at the tertiary level influences the effectiveness of science and technology learning at the lower levels. Outputs at the tertiary level are trained scientists and technologists who serve as role models as they engage in activities that facilitate the demystification of science and technology. Thus, high-level human resource capacity building in science and technology is an important activity in their promotion. A critical mass of scientists and science-based professionals who can put science into action for community and national development demonstrates the power of science and technology in improving peoples' quality of life. With a large pool of active, high-level, scientific manpower, society will be better able to appreciate the applications of science in such sectors as agriculture, health and industry, thus promoting and popularising science and technology.

To produce this pool of scientists and technologists, the countries of sub-Saharan Africa must provide inputs to demystify science and make science-based professions more popular career choices. Thus, the problem of human resource capacity building can be tackled by addressing resource availability and popularisation of science and technology at the lower educational levels and within society. In this chapter we shall concentrate on strategies to optimise the use of available resources. Other chapters have already demonstrated various strategies for demystifying science.

Capacity building is a process involving the input of resources that include staff, laboratory facilities and libraries. In most African countries there are problems with the availability of these resources, and their inadequacy contributes to secondary problems such as inequity in access to science and technology education, and problems of quality assurance and accreditation. An examination of the status of training and research institutions in the region reveals major problems of staff retention, limited financial resources, weak infrastructures, inequity in access to science and technology education, a shortage of university space for the increasing number of students, weak resource endowment of students, an irrelevance of S&T curricula and a scarcity of learning materials.

Faced with such problems, African countries find it difficult to build human resource capacity in S&T. Fortunately, the problems mentioned are not felt to the same degree by all institutions and countries, and the variations across the continent raises a possibility for regional co-operation as a strategy for human resource capacity building in science and technology. Such co-operation could enable students from any part of the continent to be trained in the best institutions particularly at the post-graduate level. Regional co-operation could also provide opportunities for researchers to have access to equipment and other facilities that may not be available in their own institutions. In theory, therefore, regional co-operation is a useful strategy for human resource development, especially at the higher level in specialised disciplines. In practice, however, this may not readily be achieved because of inherent problems that will be discussed in this chapter.

The same regional strategy can also be useful in the popularisation and demystification of science because it enables countries to share experiences on policies and actions that can be used to overcome cultural and other factors inhibiting the promotion of science.

In this chapter we shall examine two examples of regional co-operation in capacity building, the African Network of Scientific and Technological Institutions (ANSTI) and the Consultancy Group for International Agricultural Research (CGIAR), both centres which are based in Africa, to illustrate the programme strategies involved in institutional networking for human resource capacity building. The chapter gives an account of the origin, the participating countries and institutions, the activities and achievements of ANSTI and CGIAR. It describes how they are structured, managed and administered, and the activities they employ to pursue their objectives. The chapter also analyses problems associated with African networks and discusses their prospects for capacity building. Overall, we hope to show that regional co-operation in capacity building in an environment of resource limitation is a useful strategy in Africa for the promotion of science and technology.

Options for Regional Co-operation

Regional co-operation involves pooling resources for the benefit of the region. Thus, for human resource capacity building there are two main types of regional co-operation – regional centres of excellence for training and research, and regional networks. The former is an example of how financial resources can be pooled to establish regional institutions for research and training in highly specialised fields such as those worked on at the CGIAR centres. The latter is shows how physical and human resources available in existing institutions can be pooled for the purpose of research and training as exemplified by ANSTI. Each type of networking has its advantages and disadvantages.

Major advantages of regional centres include that high-quality facilities and opportunities are offered to a selected few, and that major scientific breakthroughs made by regional centres (in contrast to resource sharing networks) have an immediate and significant impact on national economies and the quality of life of countless numbers of Africans. Disadvantages include issues of control and ownership. Non-host countries tend to feel marginalised and may withhold contributions, and this is particularly true for countries whose medium of education is a language different from that used by the regional training centre, though at the level at which they operate most researchers are multilingual. Another disadvantage is that regional centres only provide training in highly specialised areas such as biotechnology, theoretical physics, agriculture and so on, and are not effective for development of human resources across all fields of basic and applied sciences. Finally, the regional centre approach is expensive, requiring construction of new institutions and facilities, though both types of networking are dependent on external funding.

The greatest advantage of institutional networking is its low cost. It does not require new buildings or facilities, but puts those that already exist in individual countries at the disposal of the region. Through networking, postgraduate students requiring specialist training are moved from institutions with low resource endowment to another with better facilities. Because of the low investment required in establishing networks, the financial contribution by members involved in the co-operation is lower. Furthermore, training can be provided in many scientific disciplines. Among the many universities in the region, it will always be possible to find one with the required resources, and because of the wide range of institutions students will be able to receive training in the language with which they are familiar. Networks also enable members to share experiences on policy implementation and the outcomes of various strategies in training and development of science and technology capacity.

A major disadvantage associated with networking is quality control that arises because training takes place in different institutions with different rules and regulations. Sometimes even the system of education and duration of programmes may differ. Under such circumstances it is a challenge to assure quality of the training.

In short, regional centres are more effective at developing Africa's scientific and technological person-power to the highest possible level, and and at producing scientists whose work has a significant and important social impact. However, despite collaboration with national institutions that effectively develop their research capabilities, compared with capacity building networks, centres of excellence affect fewer people.

Regional Institutional Networking

The preceding paragraphs have shown that as far as regional co-operation for capacity building is concerned, institutional networking offers some advantages over regional training centres in that networking emphasises co-operation in terms of sharing resources rather than joint ownership of facilities. Networking is more stable and less prone to civil conflicts such as the unrest in Liberia that forced the West African Rice Association (WARDA) to relocate in Côte d'Ivoire.

We must distinguish institutional from other networks. There are several organisations that engage in regional networking in science and technology. However, most promote networking among individuals, and build or strengthen the capacity of individuals through collaboration and exchange of information. Networking among individuals is therefore not appropriate for large-scale human capacity development for which institutional networking offers a better alternative. Institutional networks strengthen training institutions not individuals, though the benefits trickle down to individuals. The strengthened institutions are then in a better position to provide training for larger numbers. Institutional networks promote collaboration among member institutions, and facilitate the exchange of staff, students, information and other resources. This enables each member institution to draw on the resources of others in order to enhance its ability to deliver training in certain fields. Furthermore, because institutional networks involve institutions with established facilities for training, they can put a large pool of training facilities at the disposal of the entire region. Networks of individuals on the other hand cannot do so. Institutional networks, by encouraging collective self-reliance in manpower development, promote the full use of the existing institutions.

The African Network of Scientific and Technological Institutions is one of the oldest institutional networks dedicated to human resource capacity building in science and technology in Africa. Indeed, the network is the only regional co-operative activity with a mandate for high-level manpower development in all fields of basic and engineering sciences in Africa. In this chapter we shall use the operation of ANSTI to illustrate the opportunities and problems associated with institutional networks in their drive to foster regional collaboration for human capacity building in Africa. We shall present its history and origins to illustrate how this can affect the success of a network. We shall describe how the programme currently caters for differences in learner abilities and school conditions by fitting learners into different syllabus categories, ranging from the 'hard' or 'pure' sciences to the 'soft' or 'combined' sciences – arrangements that have, to some extent, satisfied the 'science for all' principle. However, current reforms as exemplified by the Swazi project, Linking School Science with Local Industry and Technology (LISSIT), advocate that all learners are exposed to meaningful, applicable and functional school science, at least up to junior secondary school level. Reports on the observation and assessment of classrooms using the contextualised approach indicates that this strategy yields valuable outcomes (Ramsden, 1992; George, 1999) to the extent that it should be regarded as popular school science for all.

The second importance of the context-based teaching strategy emerges as a powerful means to combat Africa's reliance on imported curriculum ideas. A condition for the successful production of context-based material is the necessity for all contributors to be conversant with all vital aspects of the features and culture to be depicted as realities of local S&T in action. If S&T

education should be for everybody, then all requisite resources, physical and human should be aligned to the task of producing the relevant school science. In the LISSIT project, a sample of high-ranking technologists from a variety of local industries collaborated closely with a group of science teachers and educators to develop the contextualised teaching materials.

The History, Structure and Administration of ANSTI

The origin of ANSTI

The African Network of Scientific and Technological Institutions is a regional non-governmental organisation that was established in January 1980 by the United Nations Educational Scientific and Cultural Organisation (UNESCO) with funding from the UNDP and the German government. The network was conceived in response to the resolutions of the Conference of African Ministers of Science and Technology (CASTAFRICA I), held in Dakar, Senegal in January 1974. At that meeting the African ministers present urged UNESCO to help African universities and research organisations engaged in training and research in science and technology to establish linkages to enable them to pool their human and material resources to contribute more effectively to the applications of science and technology.

Although UNESCO initially favoured the idea, the organisation had to be certain there was enough interest in and enthusiasm among African institutions, as well as determining the number and types of institutions that would form the network. Thus, in 1975 they commissioned a consultant to conduct a feasibility study. The consultant visited 19 universities in the region and summarised his reasons for a positive recommendation as follows:

It is difficult to exhaust all the arguments in favour of the creation of the network. The strongest, however, is the fact that practically everybody wants it and everybody is anxious that it should be created, structured, administered, financed and operated in such a manner that it can work to the satisfaction of all.

Thus we can conclude that ANSTI was demand-driven and that the beneficiaries were involved in its development. This is one of the strengths of the Network.

After two expert group meetings on the consultant's report, a project proposal was produced in December 1978 and submitted to the UNDP for funding. The first project document was signed by the UNDP on 4 May 1979 and the Funds-in-Trust Agreement between UNESCO and the Federal Republic of Germany to assist ANSTI was signed on 5 August 1980. ANSTI formally came into existence on 6 January 1980, the day the first Co-ordinator assumed office.

The aim of ANSTI

ANSTI's original aim, which has remained unchanged, was to develop active collaboration among African scientific institutions to promote research and development in the region. The network's specific objective is to develop and implement progamme activities that will facilitate sharing of resources and an exchange of information and staff to implement high-level training in the relevant fields of science and technology.

ANSTI Membership

The network's constitution offers membership to:

i.   University faculties and schools of basic sciences (physical and biological sciences), and engineering and technology.

ii. University and non-university research institutes devoted to any S&T discipline.

Currently there are 99 member institutions from 33 countries. Figure 9.1 shows the distribution of membership in the region. The size and spread of this network makes it unique. The network is probably the biggest regional scientific network in the world in terms of the number of countries involved and the intensity of its activities. The network's size facilitates dissemination of information and scientific ideas throughout the region.

Figure 9.1

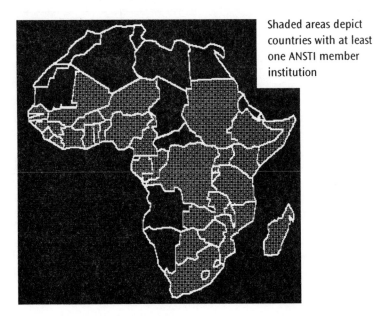

Shaded areas depict countries with at least one ANSTI member institution

---

ANSTI management structure

The structure of the network has gone through many changes. Over the years it has changed twice to adapt to the size of its programme activities and resource constraints. Currently, ANSTI's policy making organs and administration structure consists of a governing council, national focal points and the regional co-ordinating unit (the secretariat). This structure is depicted in Figure 9.2.

Figure 9.2. ANSTI Management Structure

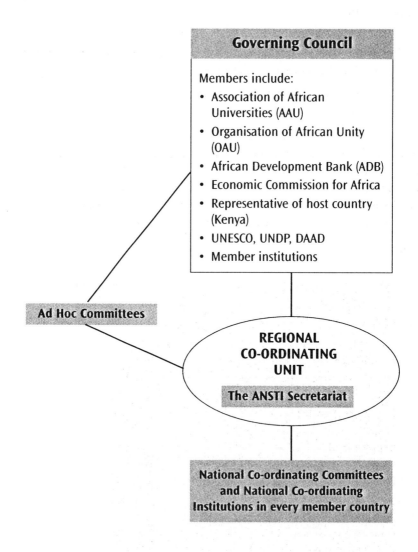

The Governing Council

ANSTI policies are determined by the Governing Council whose membership includes representatives of the Organisation of African Unity (OAU), UNESCO, United National Economic Commission for Africa (UN-ECA), the Association of African Universities (AAU), deans of the member institutions, the German Academic Exchange Service (DAAD) and other financial sponsors of the network. Although the network's policies on building human resource capacity in science and technology are determined by the Governing Council, the policies relating to its administration are those stipulated under the rules and regulations of UNESCO, a decision that has its origin in the history of the development of the network. At the time of the establishment of the network by UNESCO, it was considered appropriate to integrate the financial management of the network into that of UNESCO to minimise overhead costs. This is why the administrative policies of UNESCO are applied to the Network. To facilitate the work of the Governing Council, some activities are delegated to ad hoc Committees such as the Fellowship Committee.

National Committee and National Co-ordinating Institutions

Each country with a member institution of ANSTI is required to set up an ANSTI National Committee to liaise with the regional co-ordinator to co-ordinate national activities designed to popularise and advance the application of science and technology for sustainable national development.

The Regional Co-ordinating Unit (the Secretariat)

The network's regional operations are planned, co-ordinated and implemented by a regional co-ordinating unit based at the UNESCO office in Nairobi, Kenya. To facilitate in-depth collaborative activities in the relevant areas of science and technology, the regional co-ordinating unit supports sub-networks each of which links several departments across many disciplines in all ANSTI member institutions. Current sub-networks are those in biotechnology, material sciences, renewable energy and water resources engineering. Through these sub-networks ANSTI is able to apply the existing scientific capacity to address regional problems.

Programme and Activities
Rationale

ANSTI must develop and implement programmes that ensure that its members 'pool and share' their available resources for post-graduate training. Thus, opportunities must be offered to potential trainees to travel to other institutions where resources such as appropriate staff and equipment are available. The network must also facilitate the movement of staff so that institutions that are not well endowed with scientists in a particular discipline can benefit from visits by professors from other institutions. Similarly, to share knowledge, information or research results and experiences, the network must have programmes that facilitate dissemination of scientific information. Indeed, information sharing is crucial in networking for capacity building.

Based on this rationale, ANSTI has developed and is implementing several activities which can be grouped into six programme areas: Training, Staff Exchange, Seminar/Workshops, Information Dissemination, Research Promotion and Capacity Building in production of learning and training materials.

Training
The network awards fellowships to qualified candidates in the basic and engineering sciences to study at member institutions outside the fellow's home country. This has a dual objective of developing manpower resources as well as the research capacity of the fellow's home and host institutions. The network facilitates training at the highest level, that is, postgraduate studies and research. There are several reasons for this. First, previously-mentioned problems associated with the training of scientists are more acute at this level. Second, the impact of interventions at this level is far greater since it trains future trainers who return to their home institutions to train others. Thus, one candidate who qualifies with a PhD or MSc will, over a period of several years, be involved with the training of hundreds of scientists at the undergraduate level in his or her home country. So, whether one's objective is to produce scientists at the undergraduate level or at the postgraduate level, it is cost-effective for regional organisations to intervene at the highest level in order to train potential trainers who will, in turn, engage in large-scale training in their respective countries. Another reason for intervening at the higher level is that nearly all countries in the region now have training facilities at the undergraduate level, and the major problems associated with these facilities, such as infrastructure and finance, are more appropriately handled at the national level. However, in the case of high-level postgraduate training, institutions are fewer, therefore requiring some regional co-operation for exchange of students and staff.

Other ANSTI training activities include awards of short-term training fellowships and organisation of training workshops. Training technicians to manage laboratories to undertake repair and maintenance of scientific equipment is an important aspect of human resource capacity building since improved skills increase the stock of usable laboratory equipment that in turn facilitates research and teaching.

Scientific seminars and conferences
ANSTI promotes communication among scientists through the organising of workshops, scientific seminars and conferences..

Staff exchange programme
The network awards fellowships that cover travel costs and honorariums to facilitate travel of senior academic staff from one member institution to another to undertake research or teaching. This ensures that the training resources in the region are 'pooled' to train high-level scientists.

Promotion of collaborative research
Research is essential for individual professional development. Through research the individual's knowledge is increased and this may have a trickle down effect if the researcher is a university staff member. When funds are available, the network supports applied research activities in member institutions.

The network also searches for funds to sponsor regional studies using investigators in member institutions. Such projects entail comparative studies with inputs from more than one country. Examples include performance testing or diffusion of new technologies in the region and assessment of a pilot programme on new courses in selected institutions.

Dissemination of scientific information
One of the most important programme activities of ANSTI is dissemination of scientific information. There are two categories of S&T information disseminated by the network. The first is general information of S&T activities and includes:

+ Descriptions of scientific activities, such as research and training, that are carried out in the various institutions;

+ Information on available scientific manpower resources in the region;

+ Announcements of meetings, conferences, workshops and seminars;

+ Reports on important issues affecting science and technology in the region;

+ Information on strategic issues for training in emerging areas of science and technology.

Although such information may appear to be less important than that on scientific research knowledge, the experience at ANSTI indicates that the non-availability of these ancillary types of information gravely affects the success of scientific research and teaching. Access to such information enables the scientists to overcome their isolation and collaborate meaningfully on important research activities. Table 9.1 sets out the different types of information in this group and also shows how the network collects and disseminates them. The main form of dissemination of this class of information is the publication and distribution in print and electronic form of directories, occasional reports and manuals, and circular letters.

Table 9.1: Collection and Dissemination of Ancillary Information to Enhance S&T Activities

Type of Information	Method of Collection	Method of Dissemination
S&T manpower resources for training and research in the region	Questionnaires to ANSTI member institutions (by e-mail)	Publication of directories in print and on the internet
S&T Research and Training Activities in the region	Questionnaires to ANSTI member institutions	Publication of directories (also put on the internet)
Conferences, seminars and other scientific meetings	Direct communication with the organizers	Circular letters to member institutions (by e-mail)
Important issues affecting S&T in the region	Meetings of expert groups	Occasional reports (in print and electronic form)
Strategic issues in emerging technology problems	Commissioning of consultants	Books, training

The second category of scientific information disseminated by the network is that of research results emanating from member institutions. The network publishes the *African Journal of Science and Technology*, used as a medium to disseminate research results.

Capacity building for preparation of teaching materials

The availability of affordable learning materials in S&T is a constraint on human resource capacity building. One way to overcome this is to develop local capabilities for development of suitable teaching and learning materials. ANSTI has a textbook production programme that utilises staff of its member institutions to develop textbooks that use African examples to illustrate theoretical principles. Through a series of workshops, the materials are harmonised, tested and edited. This programme has led to the production of several undergraduate texts in basic and engineering science using over 30 trained authors from member institutions.

Achievements

The cumulative output of the various programme activities is listed in Table 9.2. Activities implemented since 1994 can also be found in the *Directory of*

ANSTI Grantees published by the network. Other outputs, such as those involving dissemination of information, are more difficult to quantify.

Table 9.2: Output

Description	Quantity (Nos)
Training and capacity building	
Post-graduate Fellowships	27
Visiting Staff Fellowships	79
Short-term International Fellowships	8
Travel Fellowship	5
Fellowships for Technician Training courses	6
Sponsorship for Training courses	16
Seminars and Workshops	
Sub-network (Scientific) Seminars	76
Training Workshops on Maintenance	8
Other Training Workshops	4
Dean's/Director's Conferences	8
Research Promotion	
Grants for Research	20
Publications	
African Journal of Science and Technology (Series A, B and C)	38
Directory of ANSTI Institution	2
Engineering Textbook	8
Science Textbooks	4

The network's achievements should be presented from the viewpoint of the original objective, which is to foster collaboration among African scientific institutions to develop high-level scientific manpower. Thus we shall look at achievements in terms of the number of trainees, the number of ANSTI member staff whose research or teaching ability was strengthened and the level of collaboration among institutions.

Training

In any particular year, some 11 network-supported students graduate with MSc or PhD degrees in basic and engineering science. Over the years, the young graduates trained by ANSTI have joined staff at their own or other universities. Nearly 50 per cent of ANSTI institutions now have at least one member of staff trained by the network. In addition, ANSTI institutions can boast of technicians who have attended one of the training workshops at which 30–50 are trained each year.

Strengthening individual staff

ANSTI has enabled over 80 senior African academics to visit other institutions where they have carried out research that enriched their experience. The beneficiaries of the visiting staff programme have usually returned to their home institutions with increased knowledge and new perspectives. Furthermore, through the network's conference grants, ANSTI institutions' staff have attended meetings that have strengthened their research capacity. Members also use the network's *African Journal of Science and Technology* to disseminate their research results and promote discussion.

Enhancing post-graduate training and research capacity

Programmes such as staff exchange, post-graduate training fellowships and research promotion have effectively contributed to capacity building of African institutions. An outstanding example is that of the water resources engineering programme at the University of Dar es Salaam. Unfortunately, other institutions where similar efforts were made could not sustain the capacity after withdrawal of ANSTI support.

Enhancing inter-university co-operation

Through ANSTI, several faculties and schools of science and engineering in African universities have established contacts where there were none before that have yielded savings in costs of student training, staff recruitment and assessment by external examiners. For instance, more institutions now use external examiners from neighbouring African institutions rather than from traditional sources in Europe and North America. More African professors spend their sabbatical leave in the region, and the network will strengthen this co-operation further when the revised edition of directories and databases is distributed to member institutions, enabling staff to learn about the scientific activities of their colleagues in other countries.

The network disseminates information on S&T activities to 99 faculties of science and engineering in 33 countries. That a significant number of member institutions pay their annual membership fees is a sign of growing confidence in the network's ability to produce results.

Contributing to the identification of science and technology issues

An important part of any capacity building exercise is the identification of strategic issues involved in science and technology education. ANSTI, through meetings of deans and other experts, has in the past identified several issues that affect S&T education in Africa. Some of these findings are published in occasional reports, which are circulated to the deans of member institutions. The most recent include *Strategic Issues in Engineering Education in Africa* (1996), *Quality Assurance and Relevance of Engineering Education in*

Africa (1998) and *Innovative Strategies in the Financing and Management of Engineering Education* (2000).

Building capacity for the production of learning materials

Human resource capacity building in S&T in Africa is constrained by many factors. One is the non-availability of relevant teaching materials. ANSTI has contributed to its alleviation by developing the capacity for preparation of learning materials. The network has provided training and experience to staff of ANSTI member institutions for the preparation of learning materials in basic and engineering sciences. Through this experience several textbooks have been published and distributed to member institutions at very low prices. The books cover mathematics, physics, biology and all first year courses in the three common disciplines of engineering, namely civil, electrical and mechanical engineering. The most significant attribute of the textbook writing programme is that it facilitates the production of textbooks that rely on African examples to illustrate principles.

What has not been Achieved

The network's greatest weakness has been its inability to build women's resource capacity in science and technology. Although participation of women in ANSTI has been in the same proportion to that of their general representation in science and technology, the network should make additional efforts to increase female networking in the sciences because the problem of professional isolation is even more acute for women scientists and engineers. In accordance with the ANSTI programme of thematic sub-networks to address important regional problems such as food production and water supply, a sub-network dedicated to female resource development in science and technology in Africa should be set up. Such sub-networks would be different from existing female networks since it would have access to the training facilities of ANSTI member institutions and the network's other resources such as publication, and fellowships.

Another area of weakness is ANSTI's inability to have a significant impact at the macro-level. Most of the network's achievements have been at the micro-level, that is at the level of the individual and some minor achievements at the institutional level. For the network to have any achievement at the macro-level, the S&T human resources it develops must be used directly in the national development process. At the moment most ANSTI capacity development interventions are in the university environment and contribute to national development through teaching and research. It would also be useful if the sponsored research was oriented towards the solution of national problems and if their results were used in problem solving to enable ANSTI to have a bigger impact at the macro-level. In addition, capacity utilisation always enhances the capacity building process because it motivates graduates and potential students. Networks should, therefore, engage in programmes such as university–industry partnerships that facilitate the use of the science and technology capacity of member institutions. Such partnerships could be used in many ways, including development of curricula that are relevant to national development so that students can better understand the role science plays in society, and this would further promote the subjects. Such demonstrable applications of S&T know-how to the solution of the societal problems would help to popularise science.

Lessons learned

The experience of the last few years has taught ANSTI several lessons that could be useful for other efforts in capacity building through regional institutional networking.

At its inception, the network was designed and presented as a single project comprised of several activities. Funds for the entire project were provided by three main donors who were also members of the Governing Council. The network was given a lump sum and it was left to the Governing Council to formulate activities for its use. This provided some independence, but experience has shown that to mobilise funds from various sources the network needs to adopt the role of an executing medium for, or work in partnership with, agencies involved with human resource development in science and technology. There are donors that may provide support for specific activities but are unwilling to give grants for the running of a network and all its overheads. Donors may use regional networks just like they do with any project grantee. Under such an arrangement, the network would advertise its nodes as centres for training, research and consultancy, and would present staff of its member institutions as the resource base for different types of activities. The difference between this approach and that of the original ANSTI design is that donors would not be faced with large grants to support major programmes. Rather they would see networks as partners assisting in the implementation of the donor's programmes.

The original structure of the network also posed some problems. It was made up of several committees, including an editorial committee, a programme committee and sub-network committees that met at least once every two years. The unwieldy nature of the management structure made administrative costs high and there was an obvious need for the streamlining that was subsequently carried out.

In connection with the network's programme activities, experiences showed that implementation of programme activities in research promotion in science is difficult unless the research grant has components for basic equipment, since most ANSTI member institutions are poorly equipped.

In the post-graduate training programme, the biggest problems are variations of admission requirements and a lack of information on the true status of the post-graduate programmes in the member institutions. Basic admission requirements for post-graduate training also vary from one institution to another, and there is an additional problem in establishing the equivalence between French and English qualifications. Some post-graduate training programmes also lack staff and equipment. On one or two occasions this led to the frustration of ANSTI postgraduate fellows and the costly transfer to other institutions.

Finally, one useful lessons is that regional institutional networks are most effective in sharing resources and exchange of experiences in the development and applications of S&T.

Prospects for ANSTI and networking
The prospects for networking as a strategy for capacity building in science and technology remain good for the following reasons:

◆ The perception of the development problems that led to the founding of ANSTI is still valid. Mechanisms for bringing about regional co-operation and the integration of science and technology into development in Africa are still relevant, especially in a time of deteriorating economies.

◆ An alternative to networking is the establishment of centres of excellence, such as the CGIAR centres, where specialised research and training are conducted in science and technology. However, though such centres make vital breakthroughs that impact on national economies and the quality of life of countless citizens, the human resource development component is limited to a few top-level researchers. In addition, the autonomous nature of such centres raises problems relating to ownership and control.

◆ Networks also serve as umbrellas and media for communicating information on training activities supported and organised by other agencies. This is a role which ANSTI has played very well in the past and, through the internet, will do so even better in future. Availability of information is very important for training.

◆ Institutional networks provide opportunities for sharing experiences on the implementation of policies and strategies relating to science and engineering education that is vital in any effort to promote a science and technology culture in the region.

The CGIAR Centres

The Consultancy Group for International Agricultural Research (CGIAR) provides another example of the power of networking. The 16 centres are distributed worldwide and four are located in Africa, with some others represented by small regional offices. The major CGIAR centres on the continent are the West African Rice Association whose headquarters are in Côte d'Ivoire; the International Institute of Tropical Agriculture (IITA) in Nigeria; the International Centre for Research in Afroforestry (ICRAF) headquartered in Kenya; and the International Livestock Research Institute (ILRI), also located in Kenya. All the centres have representative offices in other countries in the region and elsewhere. With generous budgets – the CGIAR budget for 2000 was US$331 million – all the centres are equipped with the most up-to-date equipment and facilities and can attract an international staff of leading researchers. However, since strengthening national research is a major component of the CGIAR mission, a significant percentage of centre staff are African. Indeed, the CGIAR has done much to keep the best African scientists working in the continent addressing key development problems rather than working elsewhere on issues that have little or no application to Africa.

Established in 1971, CGIAR is an informal association of 58 public and private sector members that supports a network of 16 international agricultural research centres. The World Bank, the Food and Agricultural Organisation of the United Nations (FAO), and the UNDP are co-sponsors of CGIAR, and national governments and many donor agencies and foundations contribute funds.

CGIAR has outlined its aims as follows:

The mission of the CGIAR's centres is to contribute to food security and poverty eradication in developing countries through research, partnership, capacity building, and policy support. The CGIAR promotes sustainable agricultural development based on the environmentally sound management of natural resources.

Challenges posed by the interrelated global issues of poverty, hunger, population growth, and environmental degradation confront the world ... Sustainable agriculture has to be part of the response to these challenges, because agriculture is the cornerstone of development in poor countries, where over 70 per cent of the people depend on the land for their livelihood. Experience shows that agriculture, including forestry and fisheries, is a powerful engine for development, helping to:

♦ *increase food security and lower food prices*

- *create employment and generate income for the rural poor*

- *alleviate rural and urban poverty*

- *protect and conserve the environment*

- *stimulate development in the rest of the economy, and*

- *ensure overall prosperity through the stimulation of global trade and greater global political stability.*

Agricultural growth has to be achieved with methods that preserve the productivity of natural resources, without further damage to the Earth's precious life support systems – land, water, flora, and fauna – that are already under stress. Research is the means by which the world's knowledge of agriculture is increased and improved. Agricultural research, conducted to help the world's poorest people make lasting improvements in their lives, and in the lives of their children, is, therefore, critical to human progress.

CGIAR centres conduct research programmes in collaboration with a full range of partners in an emerging global agricultural research system. Food productivity in developing countries has increased through the application of research-based technologies. Other results include reduced prices of food, better nutrition, more rational policies, and stronger institutions.

The CGIAR focuses on five major research thrusts:

- Increasing productivity by building into plants greater resistance to insects and diseases that adversely affect productivity and the stability of production in the tropics. While protecting farmers from losses, these improved plants protect the environment because they require little, if any, chemical inputs.

- Protecting the environment by developing farming techniques and systems that reduce the impact of agriculture on the surrounding environment, new research methods to identify long-term trends in major agricultural environments and solutions to pressing environmental problems.

- Saving biodiversity through holding one of the world's largest collections of plant genetic resources that contains over 500,000 accessions of more than 3000 crop, forage and agroforestry species, including farmers' varieties and improved varieties and, in substantial measure, the wild species from which those varieties were created. The germplasm within the in-trust collection is made available to researchers around the world, on the understanding that no intellectual property protection is to be applied to the material.

- Improving policies since producers are heavily influenced by public policy.

The CGIAR's policy research aims to help streamline and improve policies that strongly influence the spread of new technologies and the management and use of natural resources.

◆ Strengthening national agricultural research by working with colleagues in national programmes, strengthening skills in research administration and management, and formal training programmes for research staff.

The West African Rice Development Association

Founded in 1971 and located in Côte d'Ivoire, WARDA has regional sites in Senegal and Ibadan. Its mission is to

... strengthen sub-Saharan Africa's capability for technology transfer and policy formulation, in order to increase the sustainable productivity of rice-based cropping systems while conserving the natural resource base and contributing to the food security of poor rural and urban households.

(http://www.warda cgiar.org/, p. 2)

WARDA's 17 member states include Benin, Burkina Faso, Cameroon, Chad, Côte d'Ivoire, Liberia, Mali, Mauritania, Niger, Nigeria, Senegal, Sierra Leone and Togo.

Rice is the staple of more than 240 million people in West Africa and demand is growing, resulting in imports valued at an estimated US$1billion. To meet this crisis, research at WARDA is poised to bring a rice-based green revolution to West and Central Africa through the development of interspecific rices. Cellular biology techniques in interspecific hybridisation can overcome hybrid sterility barriers, leading to their rapid adoption in recent years by over 20,000 farmers in Guinea alone. Such an impact depends not only on 'edge' level scientific research, but also on WARDA's close co-operation with farmers, national research institutions, other centres and advanced level research institutions throughout the world.

WARDA, like other CGIAR centres located in sub-Saharan Africa, provides a dynamic model for pooling Africa's scarce research capacity and limiting the brain-drain of Africa's best scientists and technologists from the continent through provision of good terms of service, high-quality research facilities and professional contacts with science as practised at the highest level throughout the world. WARDA's links with national universities and other research institutions provides national researchers with limited financial support, and a professional challenge and dialogue. As important, through these links WARDA itself benefits from the experience and wisdom of grassroots level farmers.

The International Institute of Tropical Agriculture

The International Institute of Tropical Agriculture was founded in 1967 with a mandate for improving food production in the humid tropics and to develop sustainable production systems. IITA is staffed by approximately 80 scientists and other professionals from over 30 countries, and approximately 1300 support staff. Staff are located at the Ibadan campus, and also at stations in other parts of Nigeria, and in Benin, Cameroon, Côte d'Ivoire and Uganda. Others are located at work sites in several other countries throughout sub-Saharan Africa.

IITA's mission is to enhance the food security, income and well-being of resource-poor people primarily in the humid and sub-humid zones of sub-Saharan Africa by conducting research and related activities to increase agricultural production, improve food systems and sustainably manage natural resources, in partnership with national and international stakeholders.

IITA conducts research, germplasm conservation, training and information exchange activities in partnership with regional bodies and national programmes, including universities, NGOs and the private sector. The research agenda addresses crop improvement, plant health, and resource and crop management within a food systems framework and is targeted at the identified needs of four major agroecological zones – dry savanna, moist savanna, humid forests and mid-altitude savanna. Research focuses on smallholder cropping and postharvest systems and on the following food crops – cassava, cowpea, maize, plantain and banana, soybean and yam.

The International Livestock Research Institute

The International Livestock Research Institute works to improve the well-being of people in developing countries by enhancing the diverse and essential contributions livestock make to smallholder farming. Two-thirds of the world's domestic animals are kept in developing countries, where over 90 per cent are owned by rural smallholders. Ruminant animals provide poor farmers with the resources they need most – high-quality food, animal traction and transport, manure to fertilise croplands, a daily income through dairying and insurance against disaster. ILRI research products are helping to solve the severe problems that hold back animal agriculture, sustainable food production and economic development in the tropics.

ILRI, whose headquarters are in Nairobi, Kenya, is a non-profit institution governed by an international Board of Trustees. The institute belongs to the CGIAR. ILRI began operations in 1995 with consolidation of staff and facilities of two former CGIAR livestock centres: the International Laboratory for

Research on Animal Diseases (ILRAD), based in Nairobi, Kenya and the International Livestock Centre for Africa (ILCA), based in Addis Ababa, Ethiopia.

Feeding an extra 90 million people a year, most of them in developing countries, while preserving the earth's land, water and biodiversity, will challenge the world well into the first century of the new millennium. To help meet that challenge, ILRI supports Future Harvest, a CGIAR public awareness campaign that builds understanding of the critical role international agricultural research plays in forestalling a food and environmental crisis of the first order in the twenty-first century.

ILRI addresses these problems in seven programmes. Six programmes conduct research primarily to develop technologies that enhance tropical livestock enterprises. Three of the programmes focus on improving livestock nutrition, health and genetics – the traditional pillars of enhanced livestock productivity. (ILRI's animal health research is also applied in human health research with collaborating institutions.) Two programmes analyse policy instruments and interactions among people, livestock and the environment to isolate enabling agents for sustainable and equitable development of livestock agro-ecosystems. The sixth research programme integrates information from the other five programmes in systems models that help ILRI set priorities and assess the impacts of its research.

Work in a seventh programme helps to strengthen capacity for livestock research in developing countries. ILRI staff co-ordinate research networks, train technical staff in laboratory and field techniques, supervise and mentor graduate students, and provide information products and services to research, development and government workers. The programme helps organisations deliver the products of livestock research to farmers who need them most. ILRI also leads multi-partner research projects conducted largely in the field. These production-to-consumption projects target four systems: dairy production (Africa, Asia, Latin America), meat and milk enterprises that transect regions and economies (West Africa), mixed crop-and-livestock farming in the highlands (South America, Central Asia, East Africa), and rainfed crop-and-livestock farming (Southeast Asia).

ILRI also conducts research within a Systemwide Livestock Programme. This programme awards competitive grants to research projects submitted by ILRI and other Future Harvest centres of CGIAR, most of which work to improve production of staple food crops. The Systemwide Livestock Programme is co-ordinated by ILRI and representatives from 10 participating CGIAR centres. The projects funded by the programme aim to improve food and natural resource management through research products that refine the integration of crop and livestock processes on small farms. ILRI supports livestock-related research in more than a dozen other initiatives and consortia of CGIAR and its partners.

The impacts of ILRI's work benefit the developing world. The main benefits are more income, food and natural resources for poor people. The end-users of ILRI's research-based technologies are predominately smallholder crop-and-livestock farmers in humid, sub-humid and semi-arid regions of the tropics and subtropics. The first users of ILRI's products, information and expertise generally are development agencies and the national agricultural research systems of developing countries.

Regardless of discipline or research topic, ILRI staff and their partners attend to issues spanning livestock agro-ecosystems as a whole – from environment to farm to market to consumption. They think through issues across the research continuum – from discovery to delivery to impact. Without worldwide partnerships with organisations that possess complementary expertise and resources, ILRI could fulfill none of its development objectives. ILRI offers opportunities for outsiders to collaborate not only in ILRI's research work but also in multi-institutional projects funded by the CGIAR Systemwide Livestock Programme. ILRI scientists leverage the institute's resources to form partnerships with other CGIAR centres and advanced research institutes around the world, with national and regional agricultural research centres in developing countries, with international research and development organisations, with non-governmental organisations and with the private sector. ILRI's collaborators thus gain entry into a global mega-network of livestock research for the poor.

The International Centre for Research in Agroforestry

Established in Nairobi in 1977, the International Centre for Research in Agro-forestry is an autonomous, non-profit research body supported by CGIAR. ICRAF aims to improve human welfare by alleviating poverty, improving food security and enhancing environmental resilience in the tropics. ICRAF conducts strategic and applied research, in partnership with national agricultural research systems, for more sustainable and productive land use. It has five research and development themes: diversification and intensification of land use through domestication of agroforestry trees; soil fertility replenishment in nutrient-depleted lands with agroforestry and other nutrient inputs; socio-economic and policy research to allow policies that will benefit smallholders; acceleration of impact on farms by ensuring that research results are used; and capacity and institutional strengthening through training and the dissemination of information.

ICRAF works mainly in six ecologically distinct regions: the sub-humid highlands of Eastern and Central Africa; the sub-humid plateau of Southern Africa; the semi-arid lowlands of West Africa; the humid tropics of Latin America; the humid tropics of Southeast Asia; and the humid tropics of West Africa. These regions were chosen because they allow ICRAF to simultaneously tackle major poverty and environmental problems that can be addressed by agroforestry, with benefits in both areas. The first three eco-regions tackle the issue of overcoming exacerbated land degradation in areas of Africa with decreasing per capita food production. In the humid tropics, ICRAF is looking for alternatives to slash-and-burn agriculture at the margins of the world's tropical moist forests, where major global environmental damage is being done in the midst of rural poverty.

Conclusions

Ideally, capacity building should be a national effort. However, because of the high costs of training and the non-availability of staff and other training resources in some scientific disciplines in some countries, regional co-operation and centres of excellence for high-level manpower development remain viable alternatives. Both forms of networking make important contributions. Institutional networking as a concept for regional co-operation, as described in the Lagos Plan of Action, stressed that co-operation and collective self-reliance can only be effective when African states pool their resources to strengthen and make full use of the existing institutions. This, indeed, is the basis of networking.

The ANSTI model is an example of an institutional network for capacity building in science and technology that has produced results in the face of resource limitations. It has contributed to staff development in ANSTI institutions through training, research promotion, dissemination of science and technology information, and production of learning materials.

The CGIAR model as an example of networking has produced different, but equally important, results. Major breakthroughs have made, and are making, significant differences to national economies and peoples' quality of life. The centres retain Africa's best scientists to work on critical development problems, and through partnerships inspire many scientists working in national institutions. Unlike the ANSTI model, however, fewer personnel are involved and costs are much higher.

PART III

The first two chapters of Part III provide overviews of critical issues in science and technology education throughout the continent of Africa. Chapter 10 highlights effective ways to promote problem-solving science and technology education, particularly those aimed at girls. Chapter 11 reviews how media has been used to promote public understanding of science and technology. Subsequent chapters present country-specific case studies. Chapter 12 describes in detail what problem-solving science and technology education can look like, first in a primary school in Malawi whose work reaches into family lives in the community, then in a village level environmental centre in Zanzibar. Chapters 13–18 are case studies of promoting understanding of science and technology in Malawi, Swaziland, Ghana, South Africa, Sierra Leone and, again, Ghana. Chapter 13 describes how environmental education is used as a subject to prime change in science and technology education in Malawi. Chapter 14 describes a secondary school project in Swaziland that effectively popularises science and technology by linking school science with that practised in the manufacturing sector of the economy and Chapter 15 describes similar efforts in Ghana. Chapter 16 discusses policy changes to reorientate the type of science conducted in South Africa as well as summarising the supporting programme thrusts, while Chapter 17 shows the power of basing educational programmes of indigenous knowledge systems in Sierra Leone. Finally, Chapter 18 presents a vivid personal account of the use of television to widely promote science, technology and mathematics.

10. Improving Girls' Participation and Performance in Science, Mathematics and Technology-based Education

Dr Jane Mulemwa
Education Service Commission, Kampala, Uganda

Introduction

This chapter discusses some efforts specifically aimed at improving girls' participation in science education in the sub-Saharan countries of Africa. While mathematics is an independent subject and cannot be subsumed into science, in most sub-Saharan African countries it is a major tool of science and is usually a requirement for the pursuance of science-based subjects at post-primary levels. Mathematics is generally considered to be difficult, as are science and technology. In most of the countries of the region, technology has not yet been developed as a subject at the primary or secondary school levels, but much that is included in science at these levels involves technology. Most countries have technical education at the post-primary levels as a separate strand of education parallel to mainstream secondary school education. Given this scenario, and knowing the close interrelationship between science, mathematics and technology (SMT), particularly at lower levels, the efforts that have addressed any of these three areas of education will be referred to as SMT-based education. The chapter will not be exhaustive because of the paucity of literature and information on the theme under discussion as well as on the many developments in sub-Saharan Africa. This needs urgent remedy and is something which this publication is trying to address.

Girls' Participation and Performance in SMT

The poorer access, participation and performance in SMT education of girls and women relative to boys and men, is a worldwide issue that was recognised long ago in developed countries who have been addressing it for some time. As a result, in developed countries the gender gap in SMT-based education has been greatly narrowed, while that in access to education in general has been almost closed. Unfortunately for Africa and other developing countries, the gender gap, with girls and women being greatly disadvantaged, is still a major problem that contributes to the lack of rapid development being experienced in these regions. Hence it needs urgent attention.

For a long time, the study of SMT subjects was considered the preserve of boys and men and a 'forbidden' area for girls and women. In Africa, this fallacy was exacerbated by the cultures, traditions and practices that deem women less intelligent, and even less hardworking, than men! Consequently, on the African continent, girls and women still lag very far behind boys and men in SMT-based education, jobs and careers. This presents a major problem for the continent, particularly in this era where knowledge and application of SMT is vital for survival and development.

That girls' access, participation and performance in education in general and SMT-based education in particular is much lower than that of boys has been well-known in Africa for some time. However, this was not seen as a problem because it fitted in with African cultures that generally perceive a woman's major roles as being only those related to reproduction, making a home for the family and social care. With such attitudes and beliefs, girls' education, particularly in the 'hard' SMT-based subjects, has been seen as a luxury rather than the necessity it has turned out to be. In the recent past, the problem of gender inequality in education has been clearly recognised in Africa and in other regions as a major issue that needs urgent attention. For example, the Forum for African Women Educationalists (FAWE) was founded in 1992, with the overall goal of closing the gender gap in education in Africa, where women continue to lag behind men in access and participation. The 4th UN Conference on Women, held in Beijing in September 1995, further highlighted the problem of lack of education of the girl child as a critical area. Since then, countries have endeavoured to double their efforts to close this gender gap in education, with increased assistance and support from funding agencies and world bodies that have long recognised the problem, such as UNICEF, UNESCO and the World Bank.

Background

This chapter is a series of overviews of what is happening in Africa in gender and SMT-based education. Some initiatives that address gender issues in SMT-based education in the different countries of the region are discussed. A more elaborate treatment has been given to those interventions that are major and involve many countries in the region, as well as to those that are innovative since if Africa is to develop, particularly in the SMT field, there is a need for multi-pronged, innovative cost-effective approaches to alleviate the problems, given the lack of financial resources. The different initiatives are divided into the following categories:

- Major regional programmes and projects;

- Other innovative projects;

- SMT education research and networks in Africa.

Each initiative is briefly described, its achievement outlined, its significance highlighted and its prospects indicated.

Major Regional Programmes

Female Education in Mathematics and Science in Africa (FEMSA)
In 1996, the Association for the Development of Education in Africa (ADEA), through its Working Group on Female Participation (WGFP), funded the first phase of FEMSA. This is an African regional project whose overall goal is to strengthen girls' participation and achievement in science, mathematics and technology through improvement in the quality of teaching and learning at primary and secondary school levels.

Information on girls' access, participation and performance in SMT subjects in Africa was already available. However, not much was taking place to address the problems. The FEMSA project therefore decided to probe more deeply to seek solutions among those most intimately affected by the problem, namely the girls themselves, their male peers, their teachers and their parents. Consequently, during the pilot phase of 2 years, the FEMSA studies concentrated on an in-depth study of a sample of between 12 and 16 primary schools and between 10 and 14 secondary schools in each of the four pilot countries, Cameroon, Ghana, Tanzania and Uganda. In each country a local team of researchers, led by a national co-ordinator, carded out the work. The studies verified the current status of girls' access to education, and their participation and performance in SMT subjects and national examinations. The problems the girls experience in their study of SMT, as well as possible solutions, were also identified. The main outcome of this phase was a Country Profile of the status of girls' participation and performance in SMT in each of the four countries, the problems they experience and suggestions for possible solutions to address the identified problems. The detailed country reports are available from the FEMSA secretariat, FAWE offices, in Nairobi, Kenya.

The data collection approaches
Empirical data from schools, the 'School Studies', were complemented with data from 'Desk Reviews' on issues of policy, curricula, access and performance; examinations; and research, interventions, innovations and donor support with reference to gender and SMT.

Several research methodologies were employed in the school studies to obtain triangulated data, and hence more reliable information. The instruments were originally designed by a central project committee, including the national co-ordinators, but each country team had the liberty to, and did, modify them to suit their own situation. However, care was taken to ensure that the key questions to be answered remained the same for the four countries. The instruments included questionnaires, classroom observation schedules and guidelines for group discussions and interviews.

The participatory learning approach (PLA), using group discussions with students, teachers and, where possible, parents and community leaders, was an effective and interesting strategy. PLA was pioneered by the Uganda team and used extensively by them in their school studies (O'Connor, 1997). It involved intensive brainstorming, first with female and male only groups, and then in mixed groups of participants to discover the reasons for the poor participation and performance of girls in mathematics and science, and then to come up with solutions that might alleviate these problems. The PLA methodology ensures a systematic and deep analysis of issues. The method was extremely effective in creating awareness and sensitising the participants about the seriousness of the problem. Participants were assisted to realise that they themselves and their traditional and often chauvinistic attitudes were the principal cause of the situation and that the solution, therefore, lay largely in their own hands (Mulemwa, 1997).

The two-year phase culminated into the organisation of National Dissemination Workshops and Seminars, held between August and December 1997.

Major findings of phase 1

While there were results peculiar to each country, there were some major findings which generally applied in all four countries (O'Connor, 1997; FEMSA Country Reports, 1997). These are briefly discussed below.

Some general issues

1. Access, participation and performance of girls in SMT is poorer than that of boys, and the gap widens at the secondary school level.

2. There is a paucity of both research and interventions in the area of gender and SMT.

Reasons for girls' poor access to education

Two major reasons identified for girls' poor access to education relative to that of boys are the negative attitude of parents and society towards girls' education and poverty at the household level. Thirdly, girls' dropout rates from school are higher, particularly at the upper primary and lower secondary school levels, due to early marriage, pregnancies and poor academic performance caused by factors beyond the girls' control.

Major reasons for girls' poor participation and performance in SMT

1. Negative attitudes

There is a strong, deep-seated, traditional and conservative belief among parents, teachers and students, including the girls themselves, that the study of mathematics and science subjects is only for boys and men. Despite much lip-service to the equality of girls and boys, there is a strong belief among all these categories of people that most girls have neither the ability nor the determination to study and succeed in SMT subjects because these are very difficult subjects. Therefore, many people, including teachers, advise and actively discourage girls from studying SMT subjects. Moreover, the girls believe that even if they succeed in SMT, there are very few opportunities for them and they are not likely to attain their full potential in what they perceive to be male-dominated professions and careers.

2. Lack of awareness of gender issues in education

Many teachers are not aware of gender issues in education and the difficulties that girls face in learning SMT. They are insensitive to the different out-of-school experiences that girls bring to the study of SMT. They do not take account of the anxiety many girls experience when they start menstruating, when topics such as reproduction are discussed in the classroom, or when girls are asked to use unfamiliar equipment and apparatus or cope with live specimens. They do not understand when girls, especially from traditional and conservative backgrounds, seem unwilling to enter into discussions or ask questions, especially in mixed classrooms. Girls therefore appear less bright and capable than boys, and are relegated as less enthusiastic and intelligent.

3. The instructional methods employed

The classroom approach to the learning of SMT at the primary level was found to be almost entirely didactic. It consisted mainly of a lecture, followed by note taking and question and answer sessions. Then long exercises were often given as homework, particularly in mathematics, whose objective seemed to be to drill pupils into recognising, rather than understanding, the principles and concepts involved. Although there was often a shortage of equipment and consumables, very little practical work was done even when these materials were easily found in the environment. Hardly any group work was observed and pupils were discouraged from 'talking in class' thus prohibiting any useful peer discussions, sharing of ideas and learning from each other. In general, the development of a scientific way of thinking and of inquiry was abandoned in favour of learning nomenclature, definitions and standard procedures.

4. Inappropriate and irrelevant syllabuses

O'Connor (1997) summarised this problem, stating 'Most mathematics and science syllabuses do not take account of the needs of girls in their lives after school, both at the primary or secondary level. An exception is the Uganda Primary Science syllabus, which is the only one examined that addressed girls' needs. Most secondary school syllabuses put far too much emphasis on definitions, laws, formulae and abstract procedures and little on mathematics and science as a way of thinking and looking at the world around us.'

5. Lack of role models and information on SMT-based careers

In all four countries, the majority of girls in the education system come from rural homes or from the urban poor. They rarely see a female scientist, mathematician or technician. Consequently, the world of SMT hardly ever enters their dreams. This lack of role models is exacerbated by the girls' almost total lack of information on jobs or careers where a mathematical and scientific way of thinking would be an advantage.

Main solutions proposed

1. Sensitisation

The major strategy that emerged as a solution was the sensitisation of the different categories of society to the vital need for girls' education, particularly in SMT. People need to be aware that girls have just as much ability to study all subjects, including SMT, if they are provided with an appropriate environment. Such people include policy-makers and implementers, parents, teachers and students, both the girls themselves and the boys.

2. Training of teachers

Modules on gender issues in SMT and in education in general must be developed and included in all teacher-training pre-service and in-service courses. Teachers must also be equipped with effective teaching strategies and methodologies which address girls' needs.

3. Revision of syllabuses and examinations

SMT syllabuses need to be revised so that emphasis is put more on the processes than the products. They must help the development of scientific and mathematical ways of thinking which reflect the needs of girls, as well as of boys, in life outside school. Similarly, the examinations should test more of the students' ability to apply their knowledge rather than simple recall and rote-learning.

4. Role models and information on careers open to girls

More serious efforts must be made to use effectively the existing successful women scientists, mathematicians and technologists to encourage more girls to enter these fields of study. Information must be provided to girls regarding the SMT-based careers that are open to them at each of the different levels of education. This strategy is equally important in helping to change the attitudes of parents and society towards girls' education in SMT education. It would further help in raising the aspirations of parents for their daughters and thus motivate them to encourage and support the education of girls.

5. Further research

There is need for research that determines the kind of SMT content which is relevant to girls' lives outside school, so that it can be included in the school syllabuses. There is also need for research into the instructional methods and other strategies that facilitate girls' active participation and improved performance in SMT.

Lessons from FEMSA Phase 1

1. A comprehensive partnership between key players must be developed to address the problem effectively. These include Ministries of Education and departments dealing with curriculum design, examinations and teacher training; the school communities, namely students, teachers and parents; interventionist organisations and NGOs; funding agencies; and society at large.

2. There is a great deal of good will towards funding pragmatic solutions to the problems.

3. People are not unwilling to take action, but the problem has never been recognised as serious, particularly at the grassroots level, and hence it has never been given serious thought. Having been sensitised to it, people seemed ready to take some action, with assistance and guidance.

4. There is need for some umbrella body to co-ordinate the activities required to address the problems, which will inform overall policy decisions and liaise with other bodies, NGOs and funding agencies active in the field.

5. The literature review indicated that girls' access, participation and

performance in SMT in other African countries was generally similar to the situation found by FEMSA. Therefore, other countries should be encouraged to begin with the prioritisation of the identified problems and/or solutions, using PLA discussions, so that they can design their own appropriate national plans of action and quickly move into the phase of implementing interventions.

The significance of FEMSA Phase 1

1. In addition to quantitative information, FEMSA provided current solid qualitative data by probing deeply into the views, feelings and attitudes of the key players. Such information is most appropriate in terms of what can be done to alleviate the problems.

2. The research deeply involved those categories of people who are often not consulted and yet are directly concerned and affected, namely the girls themselves, the male students, their teachers and parents, and the political and opinion-leaders in the communities. The research documented their views and started to build a partnership between them.

3. Through the National Dissemination Workshop, the key policy and decision-makers and implementers, and other concerned people, were sensitised to the issues. FEMSA highlighted a problem that is most pertinent to the developing countries of Africa, at a most opportune time when many countries are planning future approaches to faster development through education, particularly the learning and application of SMT.

4. Since the problems and the solutions were identified by those most affected, any interventions based on the finding are likely to be more effective at alleviating the problems if they are properly implemented.

5. Some audio and video materials were gathered. These materials can be edited and made into modules appropriate for enriching both pre-service and in-service teacher-training programmes that aim at building awareness of the complexity of girls' problems in SMT education and sensitising teachers.

Otherwise, the findings of Phase 1 were published in small, 'user friendly' booklets, under 16 different themes, and disseminated widely particularly in Africa and to other organisations interested in SMT education both within the region and internationally.

The activities of Phase 2 of FEMSA

The second three-year phase of FEMSA started in June 1998, with eight additional countries joining the project, namely Burkina Faso, Kenya, Mali, Malawi, Mozambique, Senegal, Swaziland and Zambia. The major focus of this phase, particularly in the four pilot countries is the implementation of interventions to address the problems identified in Phase 1. The action plans, consisting of global and wide-ranging proposals devised at the national workshops and seminars, are being translated into pragmatic and feasible activities on the ground. The new countries are studying Phase 1 findings and working out how they can use them to move fast into the FEMSA Phase 1 focus of implementing interventions.

Each country has set up a national FEMSA centre to implement and co-ordinate FEMSA activities. They are located in institutions of national repute, but have reasonable autonomy to engage in FEMSA activities and try to incorporate FEMSA concerns into mainstream educational activities. Interventions are being developed at both the national and school and community levels.

The bulk of the activities so far implemented in the four pilot countries can be categorised into four broad areas. First, there are the sensitisation and awareness-building activities for male and female students, the parents, policy-makers and implementers, and the general public. These have included the use of mass media, short talks, seminars and workshops. Sensitisation materials such as video and music tapes, calendars, posters and T-shirts have been produced and distributed. The communities continue to be sensitised and mobilised to support the FEMSA schools' activities through songs, dance, drama and plays. The second category of motivational activities includes FEMSA clubs, visits to female SMT-based practitioners in the field, FEMSA awards for good academic performance, as well as career guidance and counselling programmes for girls and parents. The instructional materials development intervention involves the identification of gender biases in the existing scholastic materials and the preparation of gender-sensitive and gender-inclusive supplementary materials for the school curricula. The fourth category of activities is teacher capacity building, where teachers are given in-service training workshops to discuss teaching of difficult SMT content as well as gender-inclusive classroom instructional methods and practices. Other activities being carried out are remedial classes in SMT for girls, social guidance and counselling on AIDS and sexual harassment.

It is expected that by the end of this three-year phase in June 2001, the 12 countries will have developed a rich repertoire of methods and interventions to address different problems that girls experience in access and learning of SMT at both school and national levels. These will be shared with other countries in Africa and elsewhere.

The UNESCO special project on Science, Technical and Vocational Education of Girls in Africa

The special project in Science, Technical and Vocational Education (STVE) of Girls in Africa is a six-year project (1996–2001) executed by the UNESCO Section for Science and Technology Education, and Technical and Vocational Education Division for the Renovation of Secondary and Vocational Education. The project is taking place in collaboration with local, national and international NGOs, notably Gender And Science And Technology GASAT. It is in line with UNESCO's International Project on Technical and Vocational Education (UNEVOC), which was launched in 1992 (Dyankov, 1996). The organisations have identified two target areas of action (UNESCO Project Document):

* Enhancing scientific and technological literacy for all through non-formal education;

* Ameliorating the quality, relevance and appropriateness of STVE through curricula programmes, education materials, teacher training, career guidance and counselling, social environment and linkage with the world of work.

Activities

The project started with an assessment and planning phase prior to development of project activities. In this phase, 31 countries were requested to participate in a survey to determine:

1. The status of girls and women in social life (recent trends at home, in school, in the community and in the workplace) and a generalised evaluative statement of the effectiveness of gender-related policies and measures;

2. Factors (both positive and negative) determining the orientation of girls towards science education and technical and vocational education;

3. Existing measures to promote equal access of girls to science education and technical and vocational education;

4. Specific information concerning science education such as data on girls' attainment in science, technology, environment and health education, and on whether science is compulsory or not, and integrated;

5. A brief description of future strategies and plans.

The findings of Phase 1

The results of the above survey were presented at UNESCO sub-regional meetings on STVE for girls in Africa. For example, during the September 1997 workshop in Harare, Malpede (1997) summarised the results of the surveys in Ethiopia, Ghana, Kenya, Malawi, Namibia, Nigeria, South Africa, Swaziland, Tanzania, Uganda, Zambia and Zimbabwe. Similarly, Simelane (1997) presented her findings from the Southern African countries of Botswana, Lesotho, Malawi, Mozambique, Swaziland, Zimbabwe and Zambia. On the whole, the findings of the surveys reflected what has been described in some detail in the discussion of the FEMSA project above. Girls' access and participation in STVE, particularly at the secondary school level, was poor in most countries relative to that of boys. There were even fewer girls in the area of technical education, and few women in STVE fields of employment.

The workshop was attended by participants from at least 13 different African countries, and discussed and developed skeletal frameworks for interventions in key areas such as 'Teaching Methodologies and Learning Materials', 'Teacher Education' and 'Preparing Girls for the Workplace'.

In its second phase the project is collaborating with bodies that have similar interests, such as FEMSA and GASAT, to implement the identified solutions. It will, therefore, be another source of relevant strategies for improving girls' participation in STVE. For example, the project commissioned a booklet concerning the promotion of girls' participation and performance in STVE (Mulemwa, 1999). It is primarily written for developing regions, particularly Africa, where the gender gap in STVE is still wide. It is intended specifically for teachers and for developers of curriculum and material who are involved with STVE at the upper primary and lower secondary school levels. The booklet is titled *Scientific, Technical and Vocational Education of Girls in Africa: Guidelines for Programme Planning* and addresses curriculum and educational materials, teacher training, guidance and counselling and motivating girls in STVE.

The African Forum for Children's Literacy in Science and Technology

AFCLIST is an informal association of African educators, scientists, technologists, media specialists and international resource persons, who promote children's literacy in science and technology. The AFCLIST mission is to develop the base for a strong science and technology culture among the young people in Africa. It aims to generate understanding by young people in Africa of practical applications of S&T, an understanding based on an active interaction between learners and their environment, peers, teachers, other adults in the community and the accepted views of science. Only then,

AFCLIST believes, can young people develop the confidence and ability to adopt and use the ever-increasing science based technologies that impinge on their lives. AFCLIST further believes that any attempt to popularise science must be sensitive to local educational and cultural practices.

Activities

AFCLIST supports small innovative projects by groups, or even individuals, that aim at improving children's interest, understanding and effective participation in S&T subjects and activities. All projects must address gender issues and work closely with FEMSA and FAWE. AFCLIST also supports projects that link school and community science and action research that develops models for how schools can change at the system level or within an individual school. It have supported media-related projects that sensitise and increase awareness of science issues. AFCLIST has supported projects in more than 12 countries, including Ghana, Kenya, Lesotho, Malawi, Namibia, Nigeria, Sierra Leone, South Africa, Swaziland, Uganda, Tanzania and Zimbabwe. Some of the projects so far supported by AFCLIST, which specifically target girls, include:

♦ **Girls Learning Science from Toys.** This is an interactive exhibition of African toys, developed by FAWE, to show how toys can be used to encourage girls' learning in science.

♦ **Girls' Performance in Science Subjects.** This Nigerian study looked at factors that contribute to secondary school girls' choice of, and performance in, science subjects.

♦ **Girls into Science.** This project in Zanzibar was a community-based participatory project aimed at increasing girls' interest, participation and performance in science subjects.

In a publication edited by Savage and Naidoo (1997), *Improving Girls' Participation and Performance in Science Education in Africa,* five AFCLIST-supported projects are described. These are:

♦ **Enhancing Girls' Participation in Science and Mathematics,** carried out in Zanzibar;

♦ **Gender Issues in Science and Technology: Lessons from Nigeria;**

♦ **Improving Scientific Reasoning Skills of Students in Secondary Schools in Malawi;**

♦ **Biographies of Black Women Scientists: Case Studies from South Africa; Science and Technology Education Through Home Science,** carried out in Sierra Leone.

The significance of AFCLIST

AFCLIST has supported at least 100 small-scale projects. Its major contribution and significance is in its support of innovative projects that demonstrate alternative strategies for improving children's literacy in science and technology. AFCLIST-supported projects must be gender aware. They encourage group work to ensure continuity and proliferation of good projects, a strategy that can also promote the participation and training of young researchers, particularly women. This is of vital importance because the African region is still in dire need of a critical mass of researchers, including women, in all SMT-based areas.

Future prospects

AFCLIST is now working to implement its plan of setting up and developing Centres of Excellence in different parts of the continent, known as 'AFCLIST Nodes' (Fabiano et al., 1997). This is an effort towards capacity building in different parts of Africa, while addressing some of the most pressing problems of the region in science education. The nodes include:

- **Gender and Action Research**, to be developed in conjunction with FEMSA;

- **Large classes**, to develop strategies and methodologies of teaching large classes;

- **Industrial and Indigenous Technology**, to explore the relationship that should be developed between industry, indigenous technology and school science curricula;

- **Assessment and Evaluation**, to develop appropriate methodologies;

- **The Fellowship Programme**, to assist members to travel and reflect, and analyse and document their work in supportive but challenging intellectual environments.

Each node will be hosted by countries that show interest and have done some work in the area. For example, the Industry and Indigenous Technology node is now being developed in Ghana and Swaziland, while Environmental Education nodes are becoming established in Malawi and Zanzibar. AFCLIST also offers consultancy services through its unique network of science education scholars, practitioners and media specialists throughout the English-speaking world and greatly encourages the participation of women in this service.

The planned activities of AFCLIST, many of which are being implemented, promise to be beneficial to the continent, as they will address some of its main problems in SMT- based education. They will develop expertise and eventually a critical mass of gender-aware science educators who will work to improve existing systems. AFCLIST has started institutionalising its planned regional nature by having its programme secretariat hosted in two different countries, South Africa and Malawi. In addition, it has appointed professional associates who act as its representatives in West Africa, East Africa, Central Africa and Southern Africa. Professional associates assist AFCLIST to identify, develop and monitor fundable, gender-aware proposals and projects; assist with the establishment of nodes; and act as AFCLIST advocates in their sub-regions and elsewhere.

The Teacher Management and Support Programme

The central role of the teacher in the education system has long been recognised, particularly in Africa where the learning process still heavily depends on teachers. The Teacher Management and Support (TMS) Programme is a programme of the ADEA Working Group being implemented by the Commonwealth Secretariat. It is organised so that different countries and regions of Africa work in collaboration.

The July–September 1995 Newsletter of the then Development of African Education (DAE), now ADEA, reported on the meeting of the Francophone TMS group held in June 1995. The group, comprising delegations from Burkina Faso, Chad, Côte d'Ivoire, Gabon, Guinea, Madagascar, Mali, Mauritania, Niger and Senegal, deliberated on action plans on issues such as 'The rationalisation of personnel management so as to enhance the quality and efficiency of education'. *TMS News*, January 1998, reported on work being done in the East African countries of Kenya, Tanzania (mainland), Uganda and Zanzibar (EAC-TMS) and the SADC countries – Botswana, Lesotho, Malawi, Mozambique, Namibia, Zambia and Zimbabwe (SADC-TMS). Each region has a secretariat which co-ordinates activities. TMS also operates in the West African Anglophone countries of Ghana and Gambia.

In Uganda, for example, the programme is known as the 'Teacher Development and Management Systems' (TDMS) programme. It targets the primary school level and is complemented by another programme, the 'Support for the Uganda Primary Education Reform' (SUPER) project. While SUPER originally provided textbooks, it now works closely with the TDMS programme and the Curriculum Review Task, and together they have produced a number of materials for this level, including:

◆ National integrated syllabuses for the primary leaving examinations for Integrated Science, Mathematics, English and Social Studies. The new curricula emphasise 'Integrated Skills Production' and an 'Integrated Approach' to all disciplines. The curricula are gender inclusive.

♦ Self-study modules as an alternative way to train teachers since the formal two-year teacher education pre-service programme, presented problems. The plan is to develop this form of distance education, through a 'National Primary Teacher Education Self-Study Series' into a nationally recognised certificate course. This strategy is likely to benefit women, not only because of its flexibility, but also because female teachers are in a majority at the primary school level.

♦ A community mobilisation called 'Community Mobilisation Training Manual: Training Parents and Community Leaders in Improving Quality Education' developed in response to the need to sensitise parents and the community about the important role they play in education, particularly at the primary level.

♦ TMS News, 1998, reported that the SADC-TMS group had developed training modules for school inspectors to induct them and assist them do their work more efficiently. Botswana had plans to start a three-year project in support of management development training at the basic education level. This would have a teacher upgrading component through distance education; school-focused interventions to develop training and teaching materials; teacher-focused interventions that would organise short school-based and residential upgrading programmes in mathematics, science, English and social studies; and an information technology support-for-schools project that would train teachers to pilot a computer awareness syllabus for junior secondary schools.

The 'Improving the Education Quality' Project

The 'Improving the Education Quality' project (IEQ) is a project of the Institute for International Research, in collaboration with different countries in the developing world. It has three major purposes: to learn about the school and classroom experiences of educators and pupils; to work in partnership with host country colleagues; and to gather and share information that reflects the educational priorities of each country. African countries so far involved are Ghana, Mali, South Africa and Uganda. The data gathered through IEQ has resulted in the re-examination of some national initiatives. It '... becomes a catalyst for dialogue, seminars and workshops, and a basis for proposing changes such as instructional strategies at classroom level, and re-examining national initiatives to support girls' education' (Schubert, 1996).

In Uganda, IEQ was implemented as a research arm of the national reform effort at the primary school level. It identified five factors that seemed to be central in determining the effectiveness of primary schools in Uganda. These were the state of the basic facilities, community involvement, support from the education system, leadership of the head-teachers and quality of teachers. The data analysis indicated that the teacher factor was the most important variable. The second phase concentrated, therefore, on the context in which primary school teachers operate, their perceived and actual experience of this context, and how these impinge on learning outcomes. The major finding was that the working environment of teachers was generally bleak, and that in such a situation most teachers become apathetic and are either unable or unwilling to update their teaching notes (Munene et al., 1997). Such a situation affects a practical subject such as science more than other subjects. It further affects girls' participation more adversely that that of boys, as the FEMSA findings indicated. The overall recommendation was, therefore, that emphasis in the reforms should be placed on the teacher. This is a conclusion that underscored what was already known and the challenge is how it can be implemented effectively, given the huge numbers involved and the limited financial resources.

Improvements in curricula and test design

Currently in Africa, there is an ever-growing realisation of the need to make SMT curricula more gender-sensitive and relevant to national and community needs (Mulemwa, 1999). Many countries have therefore undertaken curricula reviews in content, methodology and examinations, as exemplified below.

Some curricula reviews

The ZIM-SCI and BOTSCI curricula

Zimbabwe reappraised its national science curriculum to provide science for all. The new Zimbabwe science curriculum, known as ZIM-SCI, produced science kits that make use of materials that are available in the local environment. These were more affordable and hence enabled the provision and popularisation of science education in many schools, particularly in remote rural areas. The ZIM-SCI curriculum received recognition in some other African countries that studied it for adaptation and adoption. One such country was Botswana which produced a curriculum known as BOTSCI. ZIM-SCI won the Comenius Medal, awarded in recognition of curricula innovations, at the 45th International Conference on Education held in Geneva in 1996 (Takundwa, 1997).

Curricula reforms in Uganda

Uganda is undergoing substantial SMT curricula changes in the education sector, starting at primary school level. There is a new science curriculum for the formal school which is being improved through development of appropriate supplementary materials, including teachers' guides, to support its more effective implementation.

Another curriculum effort is the 'Complementary Opportunities for Primary Education' (COPE), a project for out-of-school youth that specifically targets girls. It employs and trains community-based school-leavers as instructors. COPE condensed five years' work of the primary school curriculum into a three-year curriculum that is flexible, child-centred and practical. It also developed a corresponding set of instructors' guides and pupils' books. It has been piloted for three years in four districts of Uganda and has gained growing community recognition as a significant alternative way to impart basic education. The plan is that graduates of COPE should be able to join the upper primary school at primary six level. The challenges for COPE include forging linkages with the formal school system and developing modalities to involve communities in sustaining such a programme. If COPE proves to be successful it will address one of the major problems in many countries of the region, namely that of educating out-of-school young people, who include many girls. Review efforts to improve the SMT curricula at the secondary school level are also in progress (Mulemwa, 1998).

Curricula review efforts in South Africa

South Africa is in the unique situation of having to develop new policies and strategies in all areas of development in order to redress the huge imbalances created by apartheid. Its S&T curricula reforms in started with a White Paper. It carried out a baseline survey of macro indicators in preparation for 'Education 2000+' (Bot, 1997). The development of curricula content and materials which aim to achieve the stated general policies is the major educational challenge with which South Africa is now grappling. The Science Curriculum Initiative in South Africa (SCISA), a network of individuals and organisations concerned with change in science education, has provided a model for teacher education that seeks to bridge the gap between pre-service and in-service functions (Savage, 1995). All these efforts have gender components.

Improving test design

Many African countries have examination-driven curricula and hence any improvements in the quality of learning greatly depends on what is examined and how. Most examination systems in the region use norm-referenced types of final examinations that do not provide information about the success of an education system in imparting the knowledge and skills as stated in the curricula. In recognition of this, many countries are making efforts to improve their assessment instruments. In two volumes, entitled *Improving Test Design*, Bude and Lewin (1997) discussed the efforts of more than 12 Southern and East African countries to improve their examination instruments for science and agriculture, in terms of their validity, reliability and technical efficiency. Similar efforts in West Africa include those in Ghana where the role critically examining the role of assessment in the current education reforms (Harris, 1996).

Recently, Bude and Wippich (1999) edited another volume of primary leaving examination papers for science and agriculture from 12 African countries. The papers of each country were reviewed by a group of colleagues from the region who discuss the papers in terms of their cognitive demand, relevance, reliability, practical activity and gender balance. They '... contain a wealth of constructive criticism and helpful proposals that might assist countries to further improve future item design in their examination papers', says Bude.

Project 2000+

The UNESCO Project 2000+ is a worldwide project aimed at improving the relevance, and the teaching and learning of science (UNESCO, 1993). In Africa, the project concentrated on fundamental key areas of concern, namely the need to popularise science in such a way that it becomes a culture and way of life rather than subjects to be learned at school. It was therefore code-named 'POPSTAFRIC', standing for Popularising of Science and Technology in Africa and is organised on a regional basis. The themes focused on include:

- The development of supplementary materials for school-based S&T and S&T Clinics for Girls;

- S&T audiovisual materials for the out-of-school populations.

Some sub-regional workshops have taken place as part of Project 2000+, such as one for the Southern African region in Harare in 1994. Since then, however, few activities have been undertaken, basically because of lack of funds, though many countries are carrying out projects that address the objectives of Project 2000+. The project has produced materials such as the UNESCO book, *Practical Guide For the Development of Instructional Materials For EPD in Africa South of the Sahara*, 1996.

Some Other Innovative Projects

In this section some country-specific projects are discussed.

The In-Service Secondary Teachers' Education Project

The In-Service Secondary Teachers' Education Project (INSSTEP) is a four-year programme of support to secondary education in Uganda. It aims at '... increasing the efficiency and effectiveness of secondary education through establishing a national network of Teacher Resource Centres (TRCs) and developing a systematic programme of in-service teacher education in the core subjects of English, mathematics and science'. The project has created a TRC in each district in Uganda and equipped them with resources and facilities for teachers including basic reprographic equipment, mathematics and science teaching resource boxes for loan to schools, materials for in-service teacher-training courses and reference materials for teaching. The TRCs act as information and meeting centres. In each district, centre co-ordinators and two subject teachers have been trained, workshops held for head-teachers, school management committees briefed and resources made available for loans to schools.

The in-service training and support to teachers through the TRCs is provided by a variety of personnel including tutors from nearby national teacher training colleges, part-time teacher-trainers and district inspectors who have received training through the project. INSSTEP places special emphasis on gender equality and tries to ensure that the project benefits male and female teachers equally. INSSTEP has therefore developed training materials including worksheets for units such as the following:

- Science Activities: Objectives. Approaches and Outcomes; Improvising Materials

- Preparing Worksheets; Laboratory Management

- A module on 'Gender Issues in Science Education'.

The INSSTEP approach to teacher-training may offer a viable, less expensive and more effective alternative for training teachers on the job, both at the pre-service and in-service levels, and improve the resources available to teachers. The TRCs also have considerable potential for the in-service training of teachers at the primary school level.

The Children's Science (CHISCI) Publications in Africa

The Foundation for the Promotion of Children's Science Publications in Africa is premised on the conviction that the development future of Africa lies in its children, and on how deeply and intimately science and technology is reintegrated into African culture (Odhiambo, 1997). Its mission is three-pronged:

+ To stimulate and promote a reading and creative science and technology culture in Africa – at home, in the villages, at school, out-of-school, at play and at the workplace – from a very early age;

+ To stimulate and promote the design, development, production and distribution of relevant quality children's books and creative toys with innovative, culturally-sensitive science and technology content;

+ To promote ownership of reading materials and a lifelong book-buying propensity by children and their families (siblings, parents, grandparents and guardians).

In fulfilment of these objectives, CHISCI has:

+ Organised more than 55 seminars and workshops focused on the development of skills for writing, editing, illustrating, publishing and marketing children's books in Africa, including science books;

+ Organised a Pan-African Children's Book Fair (PACBF) for one week in Nairobi in 1992;

+ Established a children's library for daily reading, story telling and other activities in 1996. Since then, a creative science workshop and children's toy library (with its own production workshop) have been added. CHISCI reports that on average 80 children use the campus daily and the number greatly increases during school holidays;

+ Piloted the concept of the 'Children's Mobile Reading Tent' and exhibited the tent in Kampala, Uganda in 1998;

+ In 1992 CHISCI established the Children's Science Press on a small scale and now publishes its own occasional newspaper, *Challenger*.

CHISCI has a strategic plan of action for the medium term, starting in 1998, to strengthen and expand the above activities that aim to develop a reading and scientific culture in Africa. It is particularly interesting and exciting because it targets children at an appropriate age. CHISCI promises to become a creative way to improve scientific and technological literacy in local populations.

Science camps for girls

School science curricula tend to build more on the out-of-school experiences of boys than those of girls. Consequently, efforts have been made to give girls extra assistance in learning science such as special camps, like those held for over 10 years in Ghana known as the Science, Mathematics and Technology Education (SMTE) Clinics for girls. In these two week residential 'clinics', girls are given intensive tuition and engage in hands-on-work in SMTE to give them experience, facilitate understanding and help them to develop confidence in handling SMTE subjects and materials. The facilitators of such clinics, who include role models, are carefully selected to create interest in SMTE among the students, and when funds permit, students and role models are invited from other African countries.

In 1995, Zimbabwe tried the Ghana experiment in a two-week 'Science Camp for Girls' (Takundwa, 1997). The camp was organised as a 'booster' in physics, chemistry, biology and mathematics. Participants came from Botswana, Ethiopia, Gambia, Lesotho, Kenya, Malawi, Mozambique, Namibia, Uganda, Swaziland, Zambia and Zimbabwe.

In Zanzibar, annual science camps are held for junior secondary and primary school students and teachers. Gender equity is an important selection criterion. Savage (1995) stated 'The Zanzibar Science Camp and its participants from all levels of education, from the Minister of Education to pupils from schools, actively promote the improvement of science education at the primary, secondary and teacher education levels. This is the most innovative project in participatory curriculum development in science education, at a national level, that I have seen in operation'.

The Zanzibar experience has been a model for at least one other initiative. In South Africa, the Institute for Partnerships between Education and Business (IPEB) hosted two successful camps in association with the national electricity producer (SAARMSE, 1998).

This girls' clinic or camp approach has been evaluated and seems to work, at least in the short run. However, there have been reservations. First, clinics are extremely expensive considering that only a tiny proportion of girls attend, and that for an insignificant percentage of their education. More importantly, it is doubtful whether such a one-off, two-week activity can have any long-term effect on the participation and performance of most girls, particularly when nothing is done to change the school environment to which the girls must return. It may, therefore, be more cost-effective and sustainable to train teachers and provide them with a supportive environment in their schools so that they can endeavour to implement the concept of science camps in their schools. In response to these and other reservations, the Ghana SMTE camps have been decentralised to the regions to reach more girls while reducing costs.

Science and technology road shows

In 1991 an S&T Travelling Exhibition was organised in Botswana and taken to the two major cities. The exhibition included hands-on experiments and succeeded in arousing participants' interest. However, like the science camps and clinics, it is expensive and not cost-effective in relation to its long-term effect on participants. South Africa organised a S&T road show as part of its 'Year of Science and Technology' in 1998 to serve as a re-awakening tool to all South Africans about what is going on in the world in S&T, and the need for the country to get more involved in these vital areas of human endeavour.

The Girls' Attainment in Basic Literacy and Education project

The Girls' Attainment in Basic Literacy and Education (GABLE) project is one of Malawi's key initiatives in primary education. It aims at increasing enrolment, achievement and persistence of girls in primary school. It supports a Gender-Appropriate Curriculum Unit that develops curricula materials such as pupils' textbooks, teachers' guides and teacher-training support materials which contain positive messages about girls' and women's roles in society and school. GABLE supported the University of Malawi in launching a nationwide social mobilisation campaign for pupils, parents and local communities to reinforce the value of girls' education. In this campaign, the project works with a theatre group from the University of Malawi to present gender-sensitive morality plays. There is considerable evidence that the GABLE project has helped to improve girls' enrolment, retention and self-image in Malawi, and that it has made parents, teachers and government more gender-sensitive (Dorsey, 1996). Malawi produces comic books in SMTE. Other gender-sensitive materials produced include:

- *JOIN IN*, a mathematics and science magazine for secondary school pupils, produced by the Science Teachers' Association of Malawi (STAM) and the Mathematics Association of Malawi (MAM);

- *Linking Community Science and Technology with School Science Projects*, newsletter of the Malawi Institute of Education.

The incentive grants scheme

Uganda currently has a grants scheme that specifically targets primary school girls. Under this scheme, funds are awarded to primary schools that excel in maintaining the enrolment of girls from one class to the next up to P7 as well as excel in the primary leaving examination. The grants range from the equivalent of US$500–1,000. This scheme targets only those districts that have low enrolment rates, high drop-out rates, low achievement and low transition rates for girls. It is hoped that this incentive will enable school communities to devise effective ways of keeping girls in school for the whole primary cycle so more will be exposed to basic SMT education.

SMT Education Research and Networks in Africa

The African region is developing internal networks and associations to combat issues of lack of SMTE and development. All emphasise participation of girls and women, which is now recognised as a key issue, and encourage research. However, there is a general paucity of research that focuses on issues of gender and science, and particularly on measures to address the problems of girls' access, participation and performance in SMTE. Some of the known African networks in SMTE and a few known research projects that cover several countries are briefly outlined in this section.

The AFCLIST network

AFCLIST has sponsored a number of networking activities including:

♦ An intensive two-week print production, science education workshop in Nairobi, Kenya in August 1994, involving professionals from nine African countries. In December 1995 AFCLIST convened a meeting with the University of Durban-Westville of over 100 participants from four continents, but mainly from Africa. This meeting of science educators prioritised issues that are now being used to guide the development of AFCLIST, such as formation of a consultancy service and development of centres of excellence on key SMTE issues in Africa.

♦ In January 1991, 120 science educators from 15 countries met in Harare, Zimbabwe, to share and generate new ideas for science teaching and teacher education – hence the title of the conference, the 'Harare Generator'. A report was produced documenting the process and outcomes of the conference. It was supplemented by a set of coloured slides and a three-hour videotape of some of the conference activities. Units were developed on themes such as Encouraging Pupils' Involvement, Developing Creativity and Thinking, Exploring Low-Cost Materials, Using Real-World Resources, Introducing Technology and Regenerating Science Education. While gender sensitivity was not an focus area, the materials were developed with the involvement of actual pupils and are therefore most appropriate for science education and a valuable resource for teachers at all levels of education.

- A 'WHO'S WHO' of science education professionals and their research interests was produced (Enjiku, 1997) to improve communication and promote an exchange of ideas and networking among interested people. It will be updated from time to time so as to include upcoming professionals.

- The Zomba workshop was held in June 1997 to disseminate the materials that were developed in the Harare Generator and AFCLIST-sponsored projects. Participants also had opportunities to further develop their project-writing skills.

AFCLIST Publications

AFCLIST has taken on the important and needed role of publishing and disseminating research and information in SMTE. They have, for example, published the following books or manuscripts:

- *Improving Girls' Participation and Performance in Science Education in Africa*, edited by P. Naidoo and M. Savage, 1997;

- *African Science and Technology Education into the New Millennium: Practice, Policy and Priorities*, edited by P. Naidoo and M. Savage, 1998;

'◆ *Using the Local Resource Base to Teach Science and Technology: Lessons from Africa*, edited by P. Naidoo and M. Savage (1999).

Gender And Science And Technology – Africa

Gender And Science And Technology (GASAT) is an international association of people concerned with issues arising from gender and S&T. GASAT holds international conferences every two to three years and has established strong and influential networks of individuals and organisations engaged in research and grassroots level activities that promote gender equity in S&T. The major activity at these meetings is sharing results of research and interventions. A case in point is the international research on 'Science and Scientists' (SAS), which started as a small contribution to the GASAT 8 meeting in India in 1996.

GASAT aims at finding out the images that young people aged about 13 years, from different parts of the world, have of science and scientists, with particular emphasis on gender aspects (Sjoberg *et al.*, 1996). The premise is that it may be important for science educators to address the perception of pupils so as to increase interest in, and facilitate understanding of, S&T. This cross-cultural study was initiated by three researcher from different parts of the world, India, Norway and Uganda. Over 20 different countries are participating in the research, including eight from Africa. Although all the results have not been thoroughly analysed, there are indications that generally pupils of the developing world, including African countries, believe that science is very useful and reflect hardly any negative effects of science, in contrast to pupils from the countries of the developed world, such as Norway (Sjoberg, 1997) who find science more harmful than useful, and have issues such as environmental pollution and degradation uppermost in their minds.

In October 1997, the Africa region held its first sub-regional meeting, GASAT-Africa, in Lilongwe, Malawi. A major aim was the preparation for the International GASAT 9 that was to be held on the African continent for the first time, in July 1999 in Ghana. The main theme of the GASAT-Africa conference was, 'Towards Sustainable Development Through Gender Equity in Science and Technology'. Research papers were presented on sub-themes such as:

- Efforts in Reducing the Gender Gap in S&T;

- The Role of Gender in Natural Resource Management for Sustainable Development: The Effects of Policies on Gender Participation in S&T;

- The Role of Women in the Development and Utilisation of Indigenous S&T;

- The Establishment of Information Technology Networks and Gender Issues;

- The Impact of Cultural Practices on the Participation of Girls and Boys in S&T.

Participants from over 15 African countries attended the meeting, a beginning that the region should endeavour to build on so that it becomes a forum for creating a critical mass of researchers with a focus on gender and SMTE.

The theme for the GASAT 9 conference in Ghana was 'From Policy to Action in Gender, Science and Technology for Sustainable Development in the 21st Century'. The conference had sub-themes and presentations that addressed some of the problems that are most pertinent to the Africa region. These included education and training; gender issues in employment and work; gender issues in information and new technologies; and valuing women's knowledge and skills. About 15 African countries participated, and the conference was a beginning of collaborative and networking activities.

The International Organisation for Science and Technology Education
The International Organisation for Science and Technology Education (IOSTE) was established to advance the cause of education in S&T as a vital part of general education and to provide scholarly exchange and discussion in field of science and technology education. It holds international meetings

every two years and has achieved recognition by UNESCO as an official NGO. A number of African countries have participated in IOSTE activities. The most recent meeting of IOSTE took place 26 June–2 July 1999 in Durban, South Africa. The theme was 'Science and Technology Education for Sustainable Development in Changing and Diverse Societies and Environments'. One sub-theme was 'The participation of women and girls in science and technology education for sustainable development'. Small interest groups have developed from these meetings, such as groups on environmental education, and gender and science education.

The Southern African Association for Research in Mathematics and Science Education

The Southern African Association for Research in Mathematics and Science Education(SAARMSE) aims at promoting mathematics and science education research, regionally, nationally and internationally, by means of fostering a sense of community among researchers (Levy, 1994). It has several specific objectives among which are:

◆ Promoting research to improve and develop mathematics and science education programmes in Southern Africa in response to current and future needs;

◆ Organising conferences at which results of research undertaken by members can be presented;

◆ Encouraging research and discussion around key issues in mathematics and science education;

◆ Providing avenues for local publication of findings in mathematics and science education research.

Apart from its role in networking and sharing ideas, SAARMSE is another important organisation for the creation of a critical mass of researchers in Africa. It produced the first volume of its journal in January 1998.

The Forum for African Women Educationalists

The Forum for African Women Educationalists (FAWE) is an African regional association of women Ministers of Education, Vice-Chancellors, prominent women educationalists and male Ministers of Education. Its goal is to improve girls' education in Africa by trying to ensure that good, gender-sensitive education policies are not only enacted, but also translated into action. FAWE therefore engages in advocacy and strategic resource planning programmes, and sponsors innovative projects in advocacy, demonstration, policy, research and tertiary education. As such the education of girls in SMTE is part of its mandate. For example, FAWE co-sponsored the GASAT-Africa conference and administers the FEMSA project.

FAWE has national chapters in 20 countries: Benin, Burkina Faso, Cameroon, Ethiopia, Gabon, Ghana, Guinea, Kenya, Malawi, Mali, Mozambique, Namibia, Senegal, Seychelles, Sierra Leone, South Africa, Tanzania, Uganda, Zambia and Zimbabwe. It has sponsored projects in countries such as Chad, Seychelles, Ethiopia, Kenya, South Africa Uganda and Zimbabwe.

FAWE is a programme of ADEA through its working group on female participation. ADEA is an umbrella association of African ministers of education donors with an interest in the field. It aims at developing institutional capacities within Africa through technical skills development and networks for the exchange and sharing of successful strategies and innovations.

FEMSA
As pointed out earlier, the activities of the second phase of FEMSA focus on implementing interventions that address some of the problems that girls experience learning SMT. The findings of good practices, strategies and interventions are shared first amongst the 12 FEMSA countries during the biannual regional project committee meetings. The findings are then refined and printed in small booklets for dissemination throughout Africa and beyond the continent.

The African Academy of Sciences
The African Academy of Sciences (AAS) focuses on science, including science education. It has produced materials such as guidelines for gender analysis of textbooks and teaching materials in an African context, as well as profiles of African women scientists, which not only give their addresses but also their areas of research interests, and works to facilitate networking. AAS works closely with the Third World Organisation for Women Scientists (TWOWS), and both organisations carry out gender-focused research in all fields, including SMTE, and disseminate their findings widely, especially in Africa.

The Way Forward

The efforts discussed above clearly indicate that Africa has now seriously woken up to the need to address the problem of gender inequality in education, and particularly in SMTE. As a way forward, the African region and individual countries need to intensify their efforts to ensure a drastic and fast improvement in the access, participation and performance of girls in

SMT-based education and hence in jobs and careers. To maximise their effect, these efforts must, as far as is possible, occur simultaneously at the regional, national and local levels.

At the regional level, another initiative of the Gender Advisory Board (GAB) of the UN Commission on Science and Technology for Development is to set up an African Secretariat to co-ordinate the implementation of its recommendations to the 4th World Conference on Women held in Beijing in 1995. These recommendations are contained in a report of the Gender Working Group of the Commission (UN Report, May 1995). This is in addition to the regional bodies and projects identified earlier, such as FAWE, FEMSA, AAS, TWOWS, AFCLIST, GASAT-Africa and the Africa Regional Office of UNESCO (BREDA-UNESCO) in Dakar, Senegal, that should continue to carry out work in the areas of SMTE.

At a national level, many countries of the region need to re-examine their education systems and programmes to ensure gender equality in access, participation and performance. Many countries are already implementing strategic planning exercises in education, and particularly SMTE, that are at different stages, as the examples given below illustrate.

In Mozambique, the government has plans for '... the promotion of equal access of girls to education' and has defined what should be done. However, none of the actions have been implemented for financial and political reasons (Januario and Mariano da Jasso, 1997). In Botswana, the government has made detailed 'Strategies for Mainstreaming and Institutionalising Gender Equity in Science Education and Vocational Training' and has started implementing some of them (Mannathoko, 1997).

In Uganda, the government is seriously implementing the 'Education Strategic Investment Plan' (ESIP) for its education sector; girls' education in SMTE is included. The six-month periodic review of the implementation of ESIP as it moves into the second year was completed between 3–14 April 2000.

ESIP, which is a six-year, sector-wide plan, developed a series of detailed investment programmes for specific sub-sectors of education, such as primary, and teacher education. Within ESIP, there are major cross-cutting issues that are given due emphasis, such as quality, access, gender and poverty. For example, the 'ESIP and GENDEW' strategy aims at a target of 100 per cent enrolment and universal primary education, and a significant increase in the participation of females at the secondary school level. There is a consultative group on the 'National Strategy for Accelerating Girls' Education', and within this SMTE is given emphasis. As ESIP, which focuses on the primary level, was being developed, another committee was charged with the development of a strategy specific to 'Science, Technology and Management in Secondary Schools' (STEMSS). It prepared a feasible work plan to develop STEMSS that ensures maximum effectiveness and benefits from the available limited resources in the ministry. It has so far produced a concept paper outlining what should be done and how. It then has to do a feasibility study before producing a report on the implementation of STEMSS.

Conclusion

This chapter has highlighted some current efforts in the African region in girls' access, participation and performance in SMT-based education. The focus of these interventions is and should deliberately be at the primary and secondary school levels because this is where efforts must be maximised to involve more girls if there is to be a substantial increase in women's participation in SMT-based jobs and careers. It is vital that the individual countries and the region as a whole should work towards the development and inculcation of an SMT culture among youth, and hence a scientific and technological way of life. This is because the 'SMT culture' is fast becoming important for personal survival as well as national and regional viability. The efforts discussed in this chapter provide positive experiences for possible ways forward. The FEMSA project, for example, has been discussed in some detail because its findings and broad suggestions for ameliorating the situation, as well as its general approach, are feasible and would be beneficial to many countries of the region.

It is hoped that the sketch of activities presented here will stimulate concerned people and organisations to double their efforts in improving girls' participation and performance in SMTE. This should ensure that the new millennium starts with a promise of having significantly more women in Africa participating actively in science, mathematics and technology.

11. Using the Mass Media to Promote Science and Technology

Mike Savage
African Forum for Children's Literacy in Science and Technology
University of Durban-Westville, South Africa

Introduction

In much of sub-Saharan Africa there is no mass media in the sense that messages reach the bulk of the people. Only elites have access to television. Radio, which was once the furthest reaching of the mass media, is becoming less used as economies deteriorate and the price of dry-cells goes up. Newspapers reach only cities and the larger villages, and are often days late. Magazines are treasured, wrapped in brown paper and read over and over again. For the most part, recurrent budgets restrict publication to only the occasional leaflet by ministries such as those of agriculture and health. The most widely available reading material is the bible, or the Koran in Islamic areas, followed by ancient, out-of-date, school textbooks. Mass media in sub-Saharan Africa remain basically traditional and oral, and unlike in industrialised countries, schools are the most frequently found and visible source of input to these traditional networks. No discussion of how to use the mass media to disseminate science and technology can ignore targeting young people with school-based programmes and activities such as science clubs, or interpersonal media such as local science centres and museums. Furthermore, a dearth of modern mass-media infrastructures in sub-Saharan Africa, together with a continuing power of traditional media that are oral and interpersonal, implies that to maximise the effectiveness of what modern mass media exists, it must impact on and be culturally sympathetic to traditional media.

A school-based museum

One of my favourite museums used to be located in an old wooden classroom block in a village primary school in Kenya that was organised and run by the school science club. Along the back wall was a row of rabbit cages, each with its notebook of records on feed, breeding, diseases and so on. Pupils claimed that if the rabbits were fed a certain local plant they stopped breeding, but as soon as the plant was removed from their diet they had much bigger litters than usual. Their records certainly seemed to support their hypothesis. There was a table with cardboard boxes from which two wires emerged. Question cards on the table challenged one to use the dry cells, wires, bulbs and other materials to try to find out what electrical circuit was inside each box. The bones table had an elegant display of femurs, from that of a giraffe to that of a minute shrew. A rabbit's skeleton invited one to try to assemble it; there were saw blades and various chemicals to explore the properties of bones. Questions and a variety of named liquids motivated one to try to identify 'mystery' powders on another table. The variety of displays was stunning and constantly changed. During my first visit I noticed cardboard boxes under each table and asked what they were. 'Well, you know what teachers are like, Mr. Mike', one boy responded. 'They always just lecture so these are kits of materials they can borrow so they can do some practicals.'

Self-help associations

Sierra Leone
Until recently, far across the continent in war-torn Sierra Leone, groups of displaced young people could be seen throughout the country gathering together in the evening. Sometimes they go to a disco, sometimes they just hang out, sometimes they plan community activities. With help from the Home Economics Association of Sierra Leone, these young people were rebuilding their shattered lives.

Members of the Association were perceptive enough to realise that the primary need of these youngsters was a low-stress social life, hence the initial assistance with organising discos. Predictably this grew into something much more. Whilst hanging out, local problems could be discussed and action campaigns planned. Sanitation, preventive health and littering nearly always arose, and of course HIV/AIDS. However, a universal concern was how to earn a living, however modest. The Home Economics Association provided contacts, funds and appropriate back-up training to enable selected individuals to become apprenticed as dyers, weavers, carpenters, hairdressers, roadside mechanics and so on. When necessary it supplied loans to help them start up in business. A surprisingly high percentage of these young people did become successful within their own terms, and soon they in their turn became the master-craftspeople who could train other youngsters from throughout the country.

Malawi
Recently, the Wildlife Society of Malawi supported a campaign in one of the poorest regions that used youth to raise village communities' awareness of the need to use local resources in a rational and sustainable way. The campaign used wall art and street or path theatre to stimulate debate. The finals of the

drama competition were held in the regional capital and were attended by over 10,000 people.

The impact of another project, PAMET (the Paper-Making Educational Trust), can be seen in many schools and training institutions throughout Malawi. Using scrap paper scavenged from printers, embassies and donor offices, children in many primary schools make their own notebooks and classroom notice boards. Women's groups make more sophisticated products such as art stationary, cards, school globes, envelopes and diaries. Through clever marketing, regionally as well as nationally, PAMET is a financially viable institution that continues to help school children and local community groups to see the potential of science and technology to improve their lives.

Educators in Malawi are fully aware of the role of schools in community education and development. Indeed, the most recent wave of primary curriculum reform was called Community Orientated Primary Education (COPE). Multimedia teacher development materials advocate basing children's science and technology learning on community practices and understanding. School environmental clubs monitor community water supplies and institutional resources, and become engaged in activities such as tree planting together with the local community. *Join In*, the magazine of the science and mathematics teachers associations, regularly runs competitions for the best entries on community activities such as local technologies, indigenous medicines and teeth hygiene habits. The science teachers' association created a special category for school science fairs for out-of-school youth.

Zanzibar

Zanzibar has a thriving network of teachers' centres that it uses for community science and technology education. One project works in these centres by the coast with teachers, students and community leaders to implement action campaigns on the rational and sustainable use of coral reefs. I became aware of another campaign when I talked with a group of Standard Four pupils about whether they knew of the activities of the centres. 'They are the best thing that has ever happened to this village', a traditionally dressed Islamic girl exclaimed. 'They have taught the people here about women's rights and now us girls are given time off household chores to do our homework just like the boys.'

Modern Mass Media

There are examples of the use of modern mass media to educate the public, especially young people, about issues involving science and technology. Most are targeted at schools, and have come to realise that for maximum impact they must include face-to-face, interpersonal elements.

Print media

Action magazine, published in Zimbabwe, is an outstanding environmental magazine for young people. With a plentiful use of graphics, *Action* uses cartoons, puzzles, competitions, stories, interviews and so on to motivate young people to discuss a full range of environmental and health issues. Often, the magazine is the only print material to be found in schools. Distributed free of charge, 10 copies of *Action* are sent to every primary school, secondary school and training institution in Botswana, Zambia and Zimbabwe. On occasion special editions, for example that on HIV/AIDs, are translated into local languages and also distributed in other countries such as Angola, Namibia and Mozambique. Whenever possible *Action* organises visual literacy workshops for teachers, education officers and community leaders. Since the magazine is intended for the poorest in very poor countries, its publication is in no way sustainable despite attempts to market it to elites and tourists, so *Action* sells its considerable design and publishing skills to many other local organisations.

Join In, the magazine published in Malawi for students jointly by the mathematics and science teachers' associations, has already been mentioned. Other professional associations throughout sub-Saharan Africa, such as those in Ghana and Lesotho, publish similar magazines intended to involve students in using the local community and resources to learn scientific and technological skills, building bridges between school learning and community knowledge and thus enriching both. A similar approach has been effectively used by Mazingira, a Kenya-based NGO, that has published cartoon booklets on, for example, animal husbandry, that reach community members through schools. The Kagera Writers and Publishers Society on Lake Victoria far from the Tanzanian capital published a monthly newspaper with a youth section, as well as supplementary materials for schools. The society cleverly solved distribution and marketing problems by 'piggy backing' on farmers' co-operatives that had appropriate infrastructures. For years Jacaranda Designs in Kenya ran a section for youth in the largest-selling newspaper that included sections relating to science and technology, as did newspapers in Uganda, Ghana and other countries. Alas, the experience has been that as soon as the newspapers feel they could do the job themselves, quality as well as sales falls.

Television and videotape

Though many programmes in sub-Saharan Africa, such as STAG and the teacher development programme in Malawi, use videotape and slide-tape, few use broadcast television. Television is costly both to produce and to receive. Perhaps not surprisingly one of the most effective uses of this media is *Spider's Place*, a South African science and technology programme for upper primary and lower secondary school children. Spider, an adventurous girl, is the leader of a multiracial gang of puppet characters that in every episode get themselves into some scary scrape from which they escape thanks to their scientific and technological skills. The programme is broadcast on radio for schools without access to television as well as through comics for places that have neither. Sophisticated though *Spider's Place* is, Handspring Puppets, the production company, went into partnership with another NGO with a large teacher development programme.

Museums

Many museums in Africa use their permanent displays, good or bad, for special educational school tours. Few have exhibits especially designed for young people, indeed for anybody other than those who attended museums anywhere in the mid-twentieth century. The National Museum of Kenya is an exception, with an exhibit that travels to regional museums illustrating the potential for learning science, technology and mathematics using local toys and games. The exhibit is, however, static and non-interactive. The Cape Technikon, in Cape Town, South Africa, does have an interactive display mounted in a large truck that tours schools and provokes much excitement when it visits.

Discussion

To most people the term 'mass media' connotes film, television, radio, newspapers, magazines and information technology – all terms drawn from industrialised countries. I contend that even within that context such means of communication may not be the most effective. I am sure that most people have shared my experience of having been shown round a display – for me it was the optics exhibits in the Exploratorium in San Francisco – by the designer or some other knowledgeable enthusiastic person. I became completely absorbed by pinholes and their images, positive and negative. To this day, the hairs stand up on the back of my neck when I point to any spot in the air around me and think of the mass of information there that I could read if I had the appropriate instruments. Museums in industrialised countries have headphones that can be hired for the tour, but despite my attempts they always ignore my questions and anyway I do not believe I could ever make friends with that voice. Perhaps media in industrial countries have come to rely on technology because labour costs are too high. Maybe we are fortunate in Africa that we can maintain a strong element of the personal in our media.

The contrast between the experience of being a visitor in the village museum I described in Kenya with that of touring the national museum was striking. Not only was the personal milieu more sympathetic – so too was the cultural.

Traditionally, modern mass media is designed on the assumption that the audience is solitary and has little time. Neither is the case in Africa. In many parts of the continent the arrival of strangers is welcomed as the entire village congregates to hear the news they bring. Story-telling, drama, poetry, song and dance are some of the mass media in Africa; all have their own conventions, a deep knowledge of local culture, establishment of a personal relationship and time.

I have argued that those concerned with mass communication in the countries of sub-Saharan Africa, whatever the message, must be sensitive to these conventions of traditional media. They must target modern mass media in ways that can be absorbed rapidly and deeply by traditional media networks. One of the most effective mass media campaigns I have participated in took place in Mogadishu, Somalia in the mid-1980s. A group of health education curriculum staff were developing materials in schools, and it happened that they tested a series of games, puzzles and stories during Ramadan. The very night they had introduced these to a handful of schools, adults were playing the games in tea-bars. Parents with children in other schools clamoured for the materials to be given to them. School attendance figures shot up. Curriculum staff were pestered in the streets by adults and children for the next instalment of the stories that were printed as broadsheets. In the long evenings of breaking the fast, whole extended families entertained themselves with the materials. Poets composed appropriate songs about the major characters in the stories. What else had they to do? There were few television sets, movie theatres, books or DV drives, yet Somalis are well-known story tellers who value the poet and the musician much more highly than the warrior. The curriculum staff had stumbled on an effective way to feed messages into the traditional culture.

A final point: this chapter has largely focused on the use of schools as the entry point for mass media educational programmes, contrary to recent research in industrialised countries that shows the limited impact that schools have on young people's learning compared with what they learn from the modern media. I justify this focus since very few of the people of the countries of sub-Saharan Africa have access to television or film, though the advent of the VCR is leading to an outburst of rural and urban 'cinemas'. In any case, most governments lack the financial resources to programme for these media. Newspapers reach urban areas and major rural villages and some efforts are made in Africa to use these to carry scientific and technological messages. However, most communities in Africa have moderately easy access to schools which, apart from the small store, are the most widely distributed manifestation of modernisation. Communicators, I argue, would do well to target schools directly and use them as entry points to the rural and urban poor of Africa.

12. Malawi and Zanzibar: Exemplars of Inquiry Science in School and the Community

Mike Savage

African Forum for Children's Literacy in Science and Technology
University of Durban-Westville, South Africa

Science Kasungu Demonstration School

An old metal trunk stands on its end in the corner of a mud-brick hut in a village in Malawi, one of the poorest countries of the world. A 12-year old boy, let's call him John, proudly asks me to open it. Even before I do, I can feel that it's cold. Inside is a big clay pot filled with cool water and a bottle of soda that John insists that I drink to prove his 'cooler' really works. It is refreshing on this very hot day. The 'cooler' is lined with charcoal held in place with sacking that dips into a tray of water that is replenished periodically. John lectures me about water and the latent heat of evaporation as he takes me to the science club in a nearby primary school. As we walk, John explains how energy is needed to turn liquid into vapour and that is why we feel cooler when we sweat. When we reach the science club it's obvious why John brought me. A group has two similar old book boxes also made from metal set up with the same sack and charcoal arrangement. However, one has a rewired electric motor fixed in its top with a fan attached. They claim that the fan will increase the rate of evaporation, and that the box will become cooler more quickly. The data in their well-thumbed notebook fails to convince me.

I comment on the strange looking stoves I saw outside some huts in the village. One had clay packed round the outside of the usual metal charcoal version. Others were filled with sand or appeared to use ground up old maize cobs as fuel. Mary is the science club's expert on stoves and reports the results of her research. This time the meticulous experimental design and records convince me that insulating the metal stoves and using fuels such as kerosene poured on sand indeed leads to savings.

In a very different house, the mathematics tutor at the training college proudly shows me various electrical gadgets such as the radio that his son has repaired. He tells me that this son has become much sought after by his colleagues since he is a better repair man than any of those in the nearby town. He also shows me with equal pride a poster presentation with models of the history of calculating machines made by his daughter. The tutor expressed his astonishment, saying that he had no idea that his daughter had any interest in mathematics at all until he had seen her display at the annual schools science fair. And she got her ideas from an old journal that I'd left lying about the house, he exclaimed.

Diary entries, 1998–2000, Mike Savage

These diary extracts serve to illustrate the impact that the activities of the school science club have on the lives of the communities served by Kasungu Demonstration Primary School. The school is a modern, pleasant building that is part of the complex attached to the training college that was built recently. By the standards of most primary schools in Malawi, the school is extraordinarily fortunate though it lacks a room where work of the science club can be permanently on display. The science club itself is astonishing. There is always a rich variety of children's work, especially things electrical.

On one visit boats were the craze. About a foot long, made of wire covered with plastic from discarded bags, the boats were attractive, well-made models that sped down the artificial river children had made. One was a mono hull, another a catamaran with a searchlight mounted on its bows. Driven by small electric motors, the engines were mounted so that they could be raised from the water by pulling a lever. These boats, children said, were like the ones they saw on the lake. Their 'fire' boat was not! Children had bent a thin metal tube over a candle's flame, the two open ends bent under the water on either side of the boat. Expanded hot air bubbled from the tube propelling the boat forward. But not for long, and not with much force. During discussion the children had lots of ideas about what they could try next: coiling the tube or attaching a tin instead of the tube above the flame; squeezing the outlets of the tube to make them smaller – all ideas showing children had grasped the problem, though on my subsequent visits children reported that these ideas never did work.

On one occasion, a couple of girls had made a series of microscopes. I forgot to ask where they'd found the lenses. The optics weren't grand, but the microscopes did magnify. The real problem the girls had identified was how to ratchet the scope to bring objects into focus. Each microscope design was an improvement on previous models but the girls weren't satisfied. The same girls were also exploring pinhole cameras and making light-sensitive paper.

A striking display was a flood monitoring station. This was an elaborate, beautifully made model village. A bucket was the river. Children told me they had found out that flood water is more acidic or basic (I've forgotten). A piece of cloth dipped into the river. The other end was in contact with a piece of paper soaked in some plant juice. Pour acid into the children's river and the paper changed colour giving advance warning of floods. Pouring water into the bucket to simulate a flood caused a float to rise inside a tube. Bells rang in the village flood monitoring station. After a while, they stopped. As water continued to rise, the bells rang again and this time bulbs festooning the outside of the monitoring station light up. Then silence and darkness reigned again. The final warning was a light flashing atop a big tower in the middle of the village with continuous ringing of the bell.

A couple of very young girls were busy developing what they called a classroom museum. A long, thin cardboard box contained a series of envelopes arranged alphabetically and labelled food, health, leaves and so on. Open an envelope and it might contain big cards labelled protein, vitamins, or energy foods. Smaller cards had individual food items such as avocados, roast chicken or rice drawn on them. One was challenged to stack smaller cards on the appropriate large cards. Rubber bands held a series of matchboxes together to make something similar to a craftsperson's toolbox. The girls conceded there was a problem since taking out an individual box caused others to fly all over the place. They were working on that, they claimed. Each box was labelled. Seeds, beans, elastic bands, paper clips, pins, small stones – the girls had collected all sorts of small things they thought others might find interesting or useful. A current display on the desktop that girls said they changed every now and then, was of fruits, some cut into sections. They had written questions about the items, challenging visitors to observe more closely and think about what they saw.   Diary entries, 1998–2000, Mike Savage

By now I am a well-known visitor to Kasungu, but I can never anticipate what I will see the next time I visit. On one occasion it was a complex working model of a bakery, on another a weather station and a fishpond. But my visit in late 2000 was the most striking of all.

AFCLIST had given Andrew Nchesi, the teacher who inspired such work, a small grant for him and his students to write supplementary curriculum materials and to see what they could do to inspire similar work in six nearby schools. Over 30 schools, both primary and secondary, had signed up. Many had built similar weather stations. The research on placing fans in 'coolers' was taking place in one of these other schools. Students in another were involved in finding out local knowledge of the night sky. Teachers met to engage in tasks such as planning schemes of work and lesson plans, and designing ways to assess and test students work. They had organised science fairs that aroused great local interest and community support. Inspired by the work of children in Kasungu Demonstration School, student teachers had set up their own science club.

The important lesson to be learned from Kasungu is that with minimal encouragement and support, inspired teachers can transform attitudes to science and technology not only in their classrooms, but in their school, neighbouring educational institutions and, most important, the entire local community. Indeed, Nchesi has influenced more than his immediate community. Through his students' exhibits at national science fairs, the school science club has been visited by the Head of State; they have won international awards offered by organisations such as the Forum for African Women Educators and the British Council; they receive regular media coverage and all Ministry of Education officials are aware of the level of work pupils can achieve when they are motivated. No mass media campaign could have such a deep and lasting impact.

Out-of-School Programmes

ZALA: The Zanzibar Land Animals Park

You see the first signpost to ZALA, the Zanzibar Land Animals Park, after driving for about half an hour southwest of Stonetown, Zanzibar. Fifteen minutes more and you're there. ZALA is in Muungoni, a typical, Zanzibari village. The only building with electricity is a petrol station that opened in November 1998. ZALA is modest. It blends with its surroundings; the buildings are built with the coral blocks and lime that is so characteristic of these islands. Yet some 350 visitors come to this quiet village each month and ZALA is the attraction.

Muungoni is not the sort of place where you would expect to find the only land animal park in Zanzibar, but there it is. For the most part the animals are snakes, lizards and amphibians. Such animals are not usually the most popular, but at ZALA they look so healthy and at home that they are a joy.

Diary Entries, 1998–2000, Mike Savage

Mohammed Ayoub started ZALA, it was not called that then, from very small beginnings. In 1988 he began to collect snakes, identifying them using *The Field Guide of Snakes of East Africa*. Mohammed reports that people thought he was crazy, calling him 'Mchawi' or witch doctor. To begin with he kept them in big plastic bottles but Mohammed could see that the snakes were not happy. In 1994, he built an enclosure outside his house from local materials that cost about Tsh. 25,000, quite a lot of money for a teacher only earning Tsh. 28,000 per month.

Mohammed's neighbours and people from nearby villages began to visit to see the snakes. Questions he could not answer motivated Mohammed to find out more and more about snakes. Periodically he brought classes from his school, and as staff from the Ministry of Education found out more about Mohammed and his snakes, they brought visitors. That was how Professor Bob Lange of

Brandeis University, Massachusetts, USA became a strong advocate of ZALA.

With support from Bob, Mohammed built a library, furnished five more enclosures for various reptiles and named the park. As important, his contacts with Bob made Mohammed reflect about the purpose of ZALA. He is clear that ZALA's objectives are to educate, promote conservation and to engage in research. In late 1994, ZALA was first officially open to visitors.

Like many activists, Mohammed Ayoub can be impatient. To regularise ZALA, in 1997 he registered it as a business organisation, an action he now regrets since it is difficult for the Ministry of Education or donors to support a business. However, he plans to re-register ZALA as an NGO. To become independent and self-sustaining, ZALA must make money (though not a profit). Tourists already visit ZALA, but with tourism rapidly growing in Zanzibar, it plans to promote itself better. It has already developed plans to put together a package with the nearby Jozani Forest Protected Area that is home for families of the rare red colobus monkey, as well as having an untouched mangrove forest.

The educational programme

Visitors can see reptiles, amphibians and other small animals in ZALA. A favourite with some, and regarded with suspicion by others, are the chameleons. This is not surprising – the chameleon is a strange animal until one becomes used to it as many visitors do. Handling them perhaps does something to allay the many superstitions surrounding chameleons such as the bad luck they are supposed to bring if you see one crossing from left to right, the idea that you will die if one drops on you and that its touch causes a skin disease. Another belief involves the plated lizard. Though harmless, it is threatened because a local belief has it that if one bites you, the only cure is to sleep with your sister! Even ZALA finds it difficult to keep the lizard. A large one was recently stolen, since a massage with its fat is said to cure arthritis and rheumatism. People believe the python carries away babies, hatches monsters and that smoke from its burning skin cures headaches. Some believe that backward babies will crawl if they see a snake and that seeing snakes fighting leads to divorce or a break with a best friend. The people of Zanzibar have many superstitions. ZALA believes that only by changing such beliefs can the people of Zanzibar conserve one of their most important resources.

To convince villagers that science and technology is relevant to their lives, Mohammed is in the process of building a typical village household – but one with a difference. Bamboo guttering will collect rain-water to be stored in a huge clay pot. The household will have examples of fuel-conserving stoves and evaporation driven 'coolers'. Inside, the mud from which the walls are made will be moulded to make sitting and sleeping bays. The outside pit latrine will be deep with the walls made of mud and arranged to provide privacy, as well as being well-ventilated with a chimney. Mohammed's current enthusiasm, shared by everyone in the local community, is devising improvements that can be made to local dwellings using local resources.

ZALA does not charge Zanzibaris an entrance fee. It charges tourists about US$1.5, using this and other funds to subsidise school visits. Table 12.1 shows the number of visits between 1995 and November 1998.

Table 12.1. Visits by Tourists to Schools in Zanzibar

Year	No. of tourists	No. of Zanzibaris	Schools
1995	433	564	3 plus 1 college
1996	688	1024	5 plus 2 private
1997	1345	1242	8 plus 1 college
1998	2644	1354	12

Visitors' comments give some indication of the response to ZALA.

Very Interesting! Very well kept reptiles. Good luck! Really enjoyable.
Jane Portman, Northampton, England

Needs encouragement. Good to find another enthusiast. Good luck and keep in contact.
Bill Thomas, Kalimba Farm, Lusaka, Zambia

A man dedicated to snakes. Very interesting.
Dave and Peta Corrall, Curators, The Zoo, RSA

Heart stopping. Breathtaking.
Judie Ratar, Editor, Kenya

Very good and beautiful.
Broccati Guzio, Italy

Astonishing and very interesting.
Jurgord Sashia Ashraf, Holland

Exciting and beautiful animals.
Perinelli, Dagmar, Germany

The conservation programme
ZALA is active in the local community where it has helped establish branches of the Zanzibar Wildlife Club and the Mangrove Rehabilitation Club with a membership of some 30 women. The village school now has a thriving

Environmental Club with Mohammed Ayoub as its adviser. Since 1997, ZALA has conducted a breeding and release programme called 'Young-to Young'. The park breeds selected protected species such as chameleons, the plated lizard and the suni – a charming, rabbit-sized antelope. When the animals are mature, local children take them to the nearby Jozani Forest Protected Area and release them in their natural habitat, thus re-stocking the environment.

The Park is a member of several international conservation organisations such as the British Herpetological Society, Fauna and Flora International, the Association for the Study of Reptiles and Amphibians, the Africa Bird Club, the Environment and Development Group and the World Society for Protection of Animals, for whom Ayoub organises school visits to Changu Island where the Zanzibar giant tortoise is protected. Mohammed regularly attends the monthly meetings of the Wildlife Conservation Society of Tanzania, occasionally addressing it. Mohammed's membership of such organisations puts him in touch with the current literature and brings him professional contacts throughout the world. One such contact with the Jersey Wildlife Preservation Trust (UK) led to an invitation to attend a course at the zoo in Jersey; British Airways paid transportation costs.

The research programme

The Commission for Natural Resources has commissioned ZALA to help with several projects such as the Rat Eradication Project on Chumbe Island; the Blue Duiker Translocation Programme on Chumbe Island; and the Rat Eradication, Reptiles and Amphibians, and Conservation Programmes on Misali Island. ZALA periodically communicates with Professor Kim Howell, a herpetologist at the University of Dar es Salaam. As a result, in February and March 1996, two research students from Ireland spent a month updating the reptiles and amphibians of Zanzibar. To facilitate such contacts with researchers, in 1997 ZALA completed a small, fully-equipped guest cottage that also houses the ZALA office and library.

Discussion

This chapter has shown what is possible. An inquiring approach to science and technology education can make a significant impact on the lives of students and, through them, on the communities within which they live. Some may argue that Africa lacks the resources to implement such an approach. My response is that Africa lacks the resources for the traditional science and technology education whose failure to impact on lives throughout the continent is amply demonstrated everywhere. I wonder what are the resources that Africa lacks since inquiry science demands little other than an environment rich in phenomena. Others may argue that such questioning is not part of our traditional culture. My response is twofold. First, I suggest that if this is true, how did Africa make any progress at all? Second, perhaps our traditional ways of schooling so rarely provide children with an appropriate learning environment that this explains why such intellectual vitality is so rarely seen. An argument that I frequently hear is that we have so few dedicated and resourceful teachers to which I respond again with the question: how often do we encourage our teachers to teach this way? I suggest that the biggest obstacle is inertia. With the vision, political will and an appropriate theory of change, education in Africa could be transformed. A subsequent chapter suggests such a theory.

13. Non-Formal and Formal Approaches to Science and Technology Education in Malawi

Dr Matthew Chilambo

Chancellor College, University of Malawi, Zomba, Malawi
Umgeni Valley Environmental Centre

The Umgeni Valley Environmental Centre near Howick in KwaZulu-Natal provides training in environmental education and produces curriculum materials for environmental education. AFCLIST sponsored a Malawi and Zanzibar delegation to a week's workshop at the Centre. During the week (6–13 December 1999) participants visited various environmental education facilities at Umgeni Valley and attended lectures as well as field trips to Treasure Beach Environmental Education Centre, Midmar Dam Environmental Education Centre and the Sea World Aquarium and Dolphinarium. During the week the proposal for developing environmental education nodes of excellence was completed. Malawi had just completed a project funded by the Rockefeller Foundation through AFCLIST. The following is a brief preview of the findings.

Malawi Environmental Education Project

Malawi's population was expected to be 12 million by the year 2000. With a population growth rate of 3.2 per cent, there is severe pressure on cultivatable land. As a result, environmental degradation is worsening every year. Conservation of natural resources requires strong measures and government efforts to curb degradation are hampered by a high level of environmental illiteracy. The Environmental Action Plan launched in June 1994, the Environmental Management Act of 1996 and the Forestry Act of 1996 are proof of government's concern for the environment. Within the Environmental Management Act environmental education features as one tool for combating illiteracy. NGOs such as the Geography Teachers Association run projects aimed at enhancing environmental education and natural resource conservation. This paper describes a project sponsored by the Rockefeller Foundation through AFCLIST, that demonstrates the effectiveness of environmental conservation by students in 25 secondary schools spread throughout the country.

Project objectives

The project's two main objectives were:

♦ To introduce interactive teaching-learning activities aimed at reducing environmental degradation by motivating students to work with the local community to analyse and deal with causes of specific environmental problems;

♦ To develop students' understanding of the importance of science and technology in environmental protection and instill positive attitudes towards the environment.

The problem

In spite of earlier efforts to integrate environmental education in the geography curriculum in Malawi, its teaching was handicapped because fieldwork topics and course work projects were too broad and did not focus on specific environmental issues. The project hoped to develop approaches that would be easier for teachers and students to implement using resources within their local environment.

Methodology
School sample

The project team consisted of members from Chancellor College, the Malawi Institute of Education, the National Commission for UNESCO, the Department of Environmental Affairs and selected secondary school teachers. The study drew on a representative sample of 25 schools with a varied geographical location in all three regions. Five were girls' schools, one was a boy's school and nineteen were co-educational. This ensured an adequate representation of girls in the study.

School orientation

The project team briefed geography teachers and their school heads at a workshop on the approaches they would use. For the project to be able to develop effective localised curriculum approaches and materials, it considered orientation necessary to:

♦ involve teachers as curriculum developers;

♦ expose teachers to a style of teaching through which they in turn would involve students and members of local communities as curriculum developers;

♦ deepen teachers' understanding and commitment to using local resources to demonstrate that geography can lead to an improvement of the quality of life of local communities.

During the workshop the project team particularly stressed a need for community participation, interaction between students, and the role of teachers in sensitising students and other teachers on the chosen environmental problems. The workshop assisted participants with activities such as:

- planning field surveys;
- guiding students' fieldwork and their relationship with the community;
- developing appropriate research tools, for example when analysing water;
- helping students to conduct environmental audits;
- ways students could raise community environmental awareness using methods such as drama and dance.

The project provided each school with a small grant (approximately US$40) for basic equipment and negotiated with head teachers for their support in explaining the project to other students and teachers, monitoring progress, establishing relationships with the community and minimising transfer of project teachers. Schools agreed to conduct project activities during time allocated to geography, and if this proved inadequate, to conduct activities in out-of-school time such as weekends. Only 39 per cent of teachers reported that most project work was done during weekends.

The orientation workshop helped school heads and teachers to identify their school's environmental project. Thirteen chose to tackle deforestation. Three schools chose water for their case studies. Of these one decided to monitor water quality by collecting and testing samples from local sources. A second was concerned with water conservation and planned to construct a collecting tank to harvest rainwater. The third school studied the sources of water in their area. One school wished to establish fish farming, while six wanted to study human habitat degradation. Another school planned to rehabilitate a nearby mining area, and a further school chose to study the local threat to biodiversity.

Evaluation of the orientation workshop indicated that 97 per cent of participants expressed confidence in carrying out their project, 83 per cent considered that the orientation was very good and 59 per cent thought the guidelines were very good. Participants' main concern was that the project grant to schools would be inadequate.

Implementation of school case studies
Case studies involved students in identified local problems that required action. Students' action required a deeper understanding of the environmental

issues, required an understanding of how science and technology could contribute to their solution and that they develop ways to mobilise community resources. During implementation of the case studies, members of the project visited schools to monitor and assess their impact on their selected environmental issues. Students and teachers were given written questionnaires towards the end of the projects two-year cycle. In addition, the team graded students' written project reports. The media was involved to raise public awareness about the issues under study. As described below, this media coverage led to the project director's co-option to the national task force of the Cabinet Committee on Health and Environment.

Community involvement

One school, Providence Industrial Mission (PIM), involved six neighbouring villages in environmental activities. The project team observed healthy seedlings in villages and in school. Interestingly, village chiefs refused to consult the District Forestry Officer since they believed that trees along the river that they wanted to rehabilitate had been cut down with his authorisation, and that he received bribes from the timber sawyers that cut them down. As a result of the students' project, the community became so aware of the importance of reforestation that they donated sections of their farms on the banks of the river for tree planting. However, other schools such as St. Michael's Girls, Mlanda Girls and Ekwendeni Girls reported vandalism by the community in which seedlings were uprooted and goats and cattle grazed on the nurseries and areas where seedlings had been transplanted. In response, students from these schools negotiated with chiefs to let them conduct awareness campaigns where they used poems, songs and drama to highlight the issues.

Students from St. Mary's Girls Secondary School worked with villagers in Namalaka to survey water pollution and clean the surroundings of boreholes. Villagers and students collected bricks and sand to build an apron to drain excess water, and effectively sought assistance from Zomba Central Hospital in testing water samples and donating equipment. The Bottom Hospital in Lilongwe Old Town gave similar assistance to students at Bwaila Secondary School involved in a human habitat degradation project. Hospital staff gave the school masks and gloves to use when cleaning hospital drains during clean-up campaigns. The community in Masasa Township in Mzuzu worked with students at Mzuzu Secondary School to clear and rebuild drains, replanting grass on bare areas.

School projects on fish farming were disappointing. At Liwaladzi private secondary school, authorities had given students an old dam to clear and stock with fish. On their visit the project team saw no fish. The proprietors had suspended the teacher involved in the project and had given the team erroneous information. Students at Ludzi Girls School had to change their project from fish farming to human habitat degradation after digging two dams since pumps promised by the school proprietors did not materialise. Mulunguzi Secondary School built an effective rainwater tank that enables savings to be made on the school's water bill.

Most seedlings in schools involved in tree planting wilted and died during the long vacation since no arrangements had been made for watering them when students were away. Students at Bandawe Secondary School actually cut down indigenous trees to clear an area for tree planting on the advice of the agriculture teacher and district forestry officer!

Written reports

Twenty-two of the 25 schools submitted written reports though teachers rather than students. Most reports had maps and photographs illustrating their activities. Students' maps showed that students can learn map-making skills as well as environmental concepts, skills and attitudes. Many schools used scientific skills to record and analyse data. For example, Ekwendeni Girls Secondary used tables and graphs to record the growth rate of trees. Those that did so reported the slow growth rate of many indigenous trees, stressed the importance of their conservation and reported on awareness campaigns that they conducted based on their observations. Some schools used various scientific tests to analyse water sources such as rivers, streams, springs, boreholes and taps. St. Mary's School identified and traced bacterial agents such as escheria coli and salmonella to water sources in Zomba, conducted surveys and interviewed inhabitants to map associated diseases, and communicated their findings to health authorities. Most schools designed and used technology tools, for example to construct water collection and storage tanks of make aprons round boreholes.

As schools implemented their projects, they learned much about topics such as the conditions necessary for growth, growth rates, ecology and interdependence, and the etiology and symptoms of disease.

Rewarding best school case studies

The project team administered questionnaires to students and teachers in the project schools. They used an observation schedule to check progress on school visits and to record evidence of community involvement. The team observers rated project activities from 0–15, evidence of community involvement from 0–15, student interaction with the environment from 0–5, initiatives by teachers and school principals from 0–5 and completion of tasks from 0–10. The project administered a 20-item objective test to 5222 students in 23 of the 25 project schools. The items covered environmental concepts that students should have learned as a result of participating in the project. One question asked pupils to identify difficulties they had experienced in implementing their projects. Each member of the project team read all the school reports and marked them out of 50. Marks awarded were the average of the scores awarded by the five team members.

The project team used the teachers' questionnaire to determine their level of competence to teach environmental education through geography.

To motivate schools, the project announced that the best 10 schools would be awarded cash prizes. An additional motivation was that the best case studies would be edited and published in an environmental education teaching manual by the Geography Teachers' Association and distributed to participating schools free of charge.

Findings
Student performance
Scores on the objective test, together with those of the school reports, ranged from 45–75 per cent with a mean of 58 per cent and a standard deviation of 8. Overall 56.5 per cent of project schools were above and 53.5 per cent were below the mean.

On-site assessment
Scores on relevant project activity together with those for evidence of community involvement, student interaction, and teacher and principal initiative ranged from 3–77 per cent with a mean of 37 per cent and a standard deviation of 19. Forty-four per cent of schools were above average, 17 per cent were average and 39 per cent were below average. Three schools failed to implement their project because of teacher transfer.

Teacher competence
Twenty-eight teachers completed the questionnaire. Seventy-one per cent had learned about the project during the first year and 29 per cent during its second year. Forty-four per cent had attended the orientation workshop. Teacher drop out rates were substantial due to transfers.

All project school principals were aware of the project, though 25 per cent of teachers reported limited co-operation from them. All respondents reported that staff meetings had been held in schools to launch the project and that other teachers knew about it. Seventy-five per cent reported working with lower classes to ensure continuity.

Thirty-nine per cent of teachers reported using only timetabled lessons, with 61 per cent stating that students also worked on their projects on weekends. However, 61 per cent thought that environmental education could be taught as any other topic in the geography syllabus.

Ninety-three per cent of teachers reported that they formed a project student committee to plan and manage the project, and 71 per cent held student briefing sessions shortly after the orientation workshop. Eighty-six per cent of teachers defined environmental education satisfactorily, and 90 per cent could articulate the objectives of their school projects. Though 96 per cent indicated that they could teach environmental education through geography, 64 per cent suggested that it was not easy to do so and 36 per cent claimed that they had difficulty doing so. Fifty per cent of project teachers recommended that environmental education should be taught through geography, 14 per cent recommended that it be taught through biology, while 36 per cent thought it was best taught as a separate subject.

Sixty-three per cent of project teachers thought environmental education complemented the school curriculum, and 89 per cent stated that it had raised student awareness on environmental issues considerably. Eighty-six per cent of teachers thought that students had shown a sense of ownership of their projects, 75 per cent said the project had contributed considerably to development of students' interpersonal skills and 85 per cent thought that to a great extent the project had helped students to feel a sense of control over environmental events. Eighty-three per cent were confident that the project had impacted positively on students and members of the community.

Classroom and school trials
The project team observed that implementation of the school case studies varied from poor to good. Three schools failed to implement their project due to transfer of their teachers. The best school, Ekwendeni Girls Secondary School, worked on afforestation of the school surroundings. They planted and monitored the growth rates of the indigenous trees and conducted awareness campaigns in the community. With assistance from the Central Hospital's laboratory, the second best school, St. Mary's Girls Secondary School, studied water quality at the Likangala, Bwaila and Namichimba rivers and boreholes in the municipality of Zomba. The third best school, Mlanda Girls Secondary School, also grew indigenous trees to rehabilitate the slopes of Mlanda Hill near the school. They cared for the trees and took measurements of the rate of

growth. The most poorly implemented case study demonstrated ignorance of environmental conservation. Students had cut down existing indigenous trees in order to plant new ones. When asked why, they admitted they were advised to do so by their agriculture teacher and the district forestry officer!

Lessons learned

Students in some pilot schools demonstrated that with minimum supervision they could interact with the environment, use the intellectual and analytical skills of science in their interaction and mobilise community members to conserve natural resources. The media was represented when the Minister of Education, Hon. Brown Mpinganjira and the Hon. Mayinga Mkandawire, Minister of Forestry, Fisheries and Environmental Affairs, gave prizes. *The Weekly News*, 1–3 September 1998, commented that the winners, the girls of Ekwendeni Secondary School, were proud of their trees. They had learned to care for them and appreciate their rate of growth. The editor further observed that the findings in Zomba by St. Mary's Girls that salmonella was present in the water drunk by some communities was an important and disturbing finding.

The project had less impact on teachers, some of whom were reluctant to implement the project since they saw it as additional to their normal classroom geography lessons. Teachers need orientation when environmental education activities are introduced to the curriculum. As important, enabling structures such as appropriate policy and examinations must be in place before most teachers are willing to adopt a case study approach to environmental education.

However, the project considered that the experience gained from its implementation demonstrated that with little input, secondary school students can engage in local environmental issues, becoming aware that school geography, science and technology can contribute to solving local problems, and that implementing effective solutions requires that they develop the interpersonal and political skills of community mobilisation.

The Way Forward

The project team, together with the editor of the *Malawi Geography Magazine*, edited the reports from the 10 best schools. These reports and the feedback from project schools formed a basis for developing and printing a teachers' resource manual for teaching environmental education through geography. It is the hope of the project team that the manual will help teachers and students learn how to conserve delicate and finite natural resources. The young people of Malawi should learn to reduce, recycle and re-use – the 3Rs of environmental education. Teachers should be encouraged to use interactive teaching strategies.

As a result of media publicity for the project, the co-ordinator was co-opted as a member of the task force of the Cabinet Committee on Health and Environment. One of the committee's functions is to develop appropriate project proposals. The committee charged the project director with the task of drafting these proposals. They include a suggestion that funds should be allocated for printing more copies of the manual produced by the project. An unexpected outcome of the project, this illustrates that environmental education can empower not only individual students, and through them communities, but with appropriate strategies such as an appropriate and propitious use of the media, it can empower the nation through influencing policy.

14. Popularising Science and Technology: The Case of Swaziland

Dr Bongile Putsoa
University of Swaziland

Introduction

This chapter illustrates the evolution of a country's attempt to establish a science and technology culture that is publicly perceived as a local challenge rather than an imported idea. This is illustrated by school science curriculum reform that promotes strong links with the scientific and technological applications practised in local workplaces. It is hoped that the meaningful and useful school science derived from learning through these concrete local contexts will cultivate scientifically oriented values and abilities among society's youth. Such attributes are regarded as important sources of power which will enable local people to take charge of their country's socio-economic development.

Historical Background

The phrase 'popularising Science and Technology' gained currency in Swaziland as far back as the mid-1970s. It was understood to be about a set of verbal and practical activities aiming to disseminate information that was considered vital for society's socio-economic development. It was expected that such activities would raise the awareness, understanding and interest of the majority of ordinary people about S&T explanations, practices and devices that were increasingly dominating the world. The concern then, as now, was the alarming gap in S&T knowledge and skills between the developed and underdeveloped countries. Hence, there was a need to raise the level of 'scientific understanding' among the peoples of the developing countries. It was expected that this action would accelerate the industrialisation of these countries and so improve the living and working conditions of all their people. This was a global issue initiated by UNESCO. African enthusiasm for the idea of linking national development to popular S&T education for all age groups and social classes was secured during the late 1960s and early 1970s through the declarations of forums such as the Conference of Ministers of African Member States Responsible for the

Application of Science and Technology to Development (UNESCO, 1983).

Swaziland was a relative late-comer to these developments. It became involved after the reports of an African sub-regional conference held in Zambia on 'promoting the public understanding of science and technology' (UNESCO, 1972). At this conference, countries had the opportunity to reflect on what they had done and could do to achieve 'scientific literacy' for their populations. Encouraged by UNESCO, various schemes that had the potential of drawing public attention to S&T practices were proposed in Swaziland by science-oriented non-governmental groups and attempts were made to put some into action. Examples of these activities were the radio talk series on various forms of scientific knowledge that were organised and presented through the voluntary collaboration of the science and science education staff of the local university. Unfortunately these talks fizzled out within a couple of years before their impact on society was assessed or reliable public reaction had been elicited. There was little support from government, either financially or in the form of alternative ideas or future plans for developing a popular S&T culture which could possibly contribute towards the nation's future socio-economic prosperity and avert the danger of being left behind.

Other potentially interesting plans for mass S&T education included the establishment of a Science and Technology Park or a Science Museum in the same way as had occurred in some developed countries. However, the envisaged donor funds for these commercially driven schemes never materialised and the plans fell through. These two examples of short-lived ideas underpin a recurring undesirable theme: that ideas for S&T development often occur as imports into Swaziland to be used mainly for execution, rather than for generating local meanings and strategies for action among the general population. If imported ideas were used for the latter purpose, the implementation stages would possibly be executed with greater facility and on a wider scale because of the perceived relevance of the ideas to local circumstances.

Nonetheless, the importance and benefits of S&T are recognised by individuals and the state. Tangible S&T products, mostly imported into the country, are ubiquitous and constantly sought after or acquired by the majority among all age groups; thus, everyday human needs are served. Unfortunately, the easy access of ready-to-use S&T products brings to the fore some problems typical of many African countries, such as encouraging the following undesirable tendencies:

- a greater reliance on using or trading in available S&T products, and less on creating or producing the desired S&T commodities;

- holding on to static traditional modes of thought and action, such as authoritative instruction, as against scientific or rational modes (Horton, 1967; Tsuma, 1998).

The outcome of such characteristics is related to what Clark and Juma (1991) referred to as 'the vicious circle of technological dependence'; they are inimical to the expressed desire of developing countries to achieve modern industrialisation. Strategies to counteract these forms of mental stagnation, such as those suggested by Wright (1999) and others before him (Hountondji, 1997) on the need for a determined search and documentation of practical indigenous ideas, as well as exogenous ones currently practised in African communities and workplaces are useful starting points. Such invaluable information would then be linked appropriately with the well-documented modern S&T systems of the developed countries in order to evolve powerful sets of endogenous knowledge in a given country. The availability, wide dissemination and effective use of such contextualised S&T knowledge through formal and non-formal education channels could be the right strategy for inculcating a techno-scientific culture among a large mass of the population (Tsuma, 1998). Moreover, the popularisation of local S&T models is likely to increase the chances of improving their effectiveness, quality and status, thereby contributing towards human welfare on a comparable scale with other global S&T creations. In this way, the chances of improving the continent's constantly poor performance in economic, scientific and technical growth and, instead, raising its self-esteem are enormous. These are prime issues and cogent reasons for promoting massive S&T popularisation campaigns in African countries, for these could advance the global goal of the 1960s and 1970s of 'bringing about a scientific temper ... as well as the promotion of creativity and innovation among the population' (Irvine, 1985). This would not only apply to the general population but, most importantly, it would improve regular school science programmes.

The Current Image of School Science

Government policy
Since Swaziland gained its independence in 1968, the government has taken some commendable steps towards popularising science in schools by enacting policies on the curriculum which are in line with development-oriented global trends. Thus, for instance, when the call for 'science for all' was strong in the 1980s, curriculum reform was activated in the country, with international assistance, to ensure that science as a subject was included from the first to the

last year of schooling. The goal during that period was to accomplish 'scientific literacy' for individuals and societies; this was a departure from the tenets of the 1960s when the curriculum emphasised the expertise of learners in the content of subject matter. In recent times, the incessant impact of modern technology on Swazi society has generated a clearer recognition of the need to implement school curriculum policies that take account of technology.

Three main strands of action indicating the country's practical concern for the development of scientific and technological literacy can be identified. The first relates to the output of ongoing research and development activities for curriculum renewal during the 1990s. Sets of secondary school science curriculum materials that illustrate a teaching and learning approach based on local technological contexts were developed through two consecutive non-governmental projects. The first, referred to as the Matsapha Lessons, operated during the 1992–95 period (Lubben *et al.*, 1995) and this was followed by the project on Linking School Science with Local Industry and Technology (LISSIT), 1996–99 (Putsoa, 1999). As the positive outcomes of these projects emerged, the Ministry of Education (MOE) issued a science policy document in 1998 which clearly advocated the use of the contextualised teaching and learning approach throughout the 12 years of schooling. A government policy statement relating to a single school subject was unprecedented and was highly regarded by local science educators as a progressive step. However, other areas of the school curriculum have not, as yet, emulated such valuable official guidance.

A second strand illustrating the government's capacity for occasional bold moves relates to the unemployment problem, in so far as it relates to S&T education. Since the 1980s, policy-makers have perennially expressed regret over the worsening low levels of employment among school leavers. As a practical solution, a National Education Review Commission recommended in 1985 that the most viable solution to the unemployment problem entailed the introduction of vocation-related secondary school subjects. This, it was expected, would cultivate a positive mentality towards locally available types of work and develop entrepreneurial skills among youth. However, the implementation of this idea was delayed for more than a decade mainly because of the fear of replicating the negative experiences of other African countries. Notwithstanding, a pre-vocational curriculum that emphasises the use of modern technological skills has been piloted by the MOE since 1998 in a number of secondary schools that are progressively being equipped with the requisite technological gadgets, through donor funds, for the chosen practical skills areas.

A third area of current change pertains to the sharing of responsibilities with government, not only for activating, but also for funding, S&T curriculum renewal activities. A measure of willingness to contribute towards S&T education has recently been indicated by some of the country's major businesses which have committed themselves to providing equipment for pupils' competencies in the area of Information and Communication Technology (ICT). Thus, since early 1999 preparations have been underway between the MOE and the private sector to purchase and install computers in a specified number of secondary schools per annum. This input is additional to the LISSIT curriculum research and development project referred to earlier which greatly benefited from the voluntary participation of industry throughout its activities during the 1996–99 period. Such enterprise could help cushion some of the familiar financial difficulties experienced in developing countries of failure to continue with curriculum activities that initially relied on short- or long-term donor grants or loans.

The three experiences of the 1990s described above signify a salutary shift from the country's near-total dependence on imported curriculum ideas, and the government's sole responsibility for propagating them, to the creation of a new sense of common ownership and joint responsibility between government and non-governmental groups for the country's educational affairs. The wide dissemination of such accomplishments within the country is important for generating some national self-esteem and thereby stimulating further ideas and activities that are likely to build up and sustain a desirable S&T culture among the youth and society. Hence, these examples provide evidence that locally-driven S&T education is progressing well, in that ideas for relevant action which subsequently become government policy are derived not only from within its own corridors, but also include the initiatives of various national groups. There will perhaps be a stage in future when tangible socio-economic benefits can be realised as a result of current co-operative efforts in advancing a scientific and technological culture among the school-going Swazi population. These positive outcomes are anticipated despite the numerous and powerful hurdles confronting school science.

Problems of S&T Education and Amelioration Possibilities

The phrase 'scientific literacy' appears frequently in the literature as a desirable school science goal for individuals and society. Recently, the American National Academy of Sciences (NAS) issued a set of 'national standards' for attaining a scientifically literate society. To this end, the academy stated that school science should enable individual learners to:

- Experience the excitement of knowing and understanding something of the natural world;

- Apply appropriate scientific concepts and skills in making personal decisions;

- Discuss public matters on science and technology intelligently;

- Increase their economic productivity by using their acquired scientific knowledge and skills in the workplace.

It is noteworthy that the four NAS statements are a recapitulation of goals stated since the advent of the Science, Technology and Society (STS) movement in the 1980s (Yager, 1990; Solomon and Aikenhead, 1994). Nonetheless, this repetition is valuable in that it reflects the difficulty of achieving these life-skills goals and is essential in the continuing search for strategies likely to help teachers steer clear of pedagogies that emphasise conceptual knowledge as the main aim of school science. An ancillary NAS document on the above standards is titled 'Project 2061'. This title is intended to convey the idea that scientific literacy goals are a long way from being realised; but that the effort towards their attainment should remain a continual process until entrenched expository methods are eliminated from the school programmes of future generations.

Some of the persistent and seemingly intractable constraints militating against the above goals in African countries such as Swaziland are worth recounting, for they justify current attempts at curriculum reform that advocate a contextualised teaching-learning approach.

First, all science curriculum reform in Africa has always endorsed the principle of practical work as the basis for learning, because this approach nurtures the development of virtually all of Bloom's (1956) educational objectives for cognition, as well as capacities for imagining and creating ideas. Regrettably, practical work is known to be a rare occurrence in many African science classes. Some of the reasons proffered for this paucity, such as the overcrowded classrooms that can be a severe problem for teachers, are legitimate. However, other defences are related to teachers' difficulty in shedding expository teaching methods and/or finding ideas for procuring or improvising resources. Notwithstanding, the quest for science classes based on practical work must continue because it is expected that the product of such a curriculum will not only know science, but will have continuously learnt to do or create something with their acquired knowledge. Regrettably, such practical capacities are never reported to have occurred as outcomes of Swaziland's school science system through public examination results.

The science curricula of developing countries must be potentially able to cultivate enduring higher order thinking abilities that are critically needed and are often facilitated by practical work. Such practical activities are not just about the repetition of standard experiments, but should be those that enhance pupils' ability to face challenges or create something, such as constructing a plan of action or modifying the structure of an existing local product. Black *et al.* (1985) refer to such practical work that appropriately links S&T ideas as a 'Task-Action-Capability' approach to school science.

A second noteworthy constraint closely related to the above limitations on practical work concerns a disturbing popular interpretation of success and achievement in schools, as reflected through end-of-year assessments. For the individual learner, success is about being promoted to the next class, through whatever yardstick is used by the school, and this adequately provides for the individual's satisfaction. For society, the focus of attention shifts to the number and quality of passes obtained by schools in public examinations. The public media spend much effort analysing which schools have performed better than others, thus fuelling and perpetuating the public understanding of success or high-quality education to mean the performance of schools in attaining the highest score from the group examined. This yardstick of evaluating successful learning is far removed from any of the goals for achieving the scientific literacy of individual learners. Nonetheless, a few Anglophone countries have expended some effort, through curriculum reform, in gradually removing this misunderstanding. To this end, goals for criterion-referenced assessments of the abilities of individual learners have been set up, starting with Britain's 'Attainment Targets' for different school levels during the late 1980s to South Africa's 'Outcomes Based Education' (OBE). It is to be hoped that many more African countries will want to change their perceptions of learning and will effectively borrow and lend one another various strategies for change.

A third persistent problem is the attitude which consistently portrays school science as an abstract and difficult subject. It is common knowledge that this image of science foments apathy towards science or engenders low self-esteem among learners. The problem emanates from an excessive or even exclusive emphasis on the content of the discipline to the extent that learners fail to see how the concepts and skills of science relate to their real world. As a result, the subject matter is rendered irrelevant and worthless in that learners cannot readily relate their lives to it or use it for dealing with everyday encounters. It is also common knowledge that science has become the prerogative of a few capable learners beyond the compulsory junior secondary school level because the majority could not cope with such an agenda. This exclusiveness was unsuitable not only for the egalitarian sensibilities of modern societies, but runs counter to the agenda of popularising S&T as the basis for the everyday thought and action of all individuals and the essential constituent of the nation's economic advancement.

A possible remedy for this long-standing malady requires the reconstruction of curricula that are meaningful to the learner in so far as the content overtly relates to relevant local contexts and applications. In addition, the curriculum must promote the learning of useful scientific knowledge and skills that have a practical bearing on the socio-economic welfare of individuals and their societies. In this regard, there is a clear implication for weaving a close relationship between school science and local technologies to reflect the fact that everyday encounters and problems often have both a scientific and technological aspect. Hence, the search for local technological contexts and applications, in order to link them appropriately with school science, is important for promoting a sense of useful learning that emphasises productivity, thus raising the chances for learners to develop capacities in problem solving and creativity. Science-related abilities such as being able to suggest the cause of an event, what might be done in a problematic situation, an awareness of how science affects the lives of people living in their community and how, in turn, people affect their environment, are of high priority in many African societies. In this sense, science education goals have become oriented towards the socio-economic development of individuals and their societies. This is the science educator's challenge for promoting popular science at the school level.

Similar goals are relevant for the general population, but different activities for various age groups can be set up to run alongside those focusing on the school situation. This perspective of school science has been reiterated in African forums during the 1980s and 1990s as part of the preparation for Africa's ability to take responsibility for its own development in the next millennium. The LISSIT project aimed at promoting this perspective within those forums that were engaged in curriculum reform for Swaziland.

This background of problems and aspirations takes us to the rationale and strategies used in the construction of the LISSIT curriculum material.

Teaching and Learning Relevant Science for All

Major school science curriculum reform during the latter half of the twentieth century in the English-speaking countries of the West has been consistently emulated by most African countries (Ajeyalemi, 1990). Studies of these reform movements by Roberts (1982) and Solomon and Aikenhead (1994) reveal that change has repeatedly been inspired by the need to achieve what was perceived at a particular time as relevant school science. Although some controversy exists about the notion of relevance, Wellington (1989), for instance, was of the view that it 'is of little value in planning the science curriculum', but that it cannot be easily discarded, for it does provide some measure of the value attached to a phenomenon at a given time and place. Hence, the science that is taught and learned is relevant in so far as it reflects what is regarded by a community as beneficial.

As one of the most recently stated goals for achieving scientific literacy (NAS, 1996) shows, the understanding of science by learners and consequently society as a whole has always been a prime aim of school science. However, relevance takes it cue from the interpretation of what this understanding entails or what its valued outcomes should be. Makhurane and Kahn (1998) identified two operational levels, 'high science' and 'low science', that have to do with worthwhile outcomes of school science in society. At one extreme, this continuum refers to science or technology research activities that contribute to the discovery of new knowledge; at the other, it relates to the various human activities that apply scientific and technological knowledge and skills to everyday encounters. Both these levels of S&T activity are vital for the advancement of African societies; hence, decision-makers and implementers of the science curriculum must ensure that both these expected outcomes are accorded equal importance. The main difference between the adult practitioners of these levels lies in the number of participants who will emerge as school science products for each of these activity types. In the present era of attempts to raise the consciousness of African populations of the value of S&T knowledge and applications for the development of their communities, the majority of citizens should expect to be empowered to engage in practical 'low science'. Such an outcome is of greater benefit than that of learners loaded with much school science knowledge that leaves the majority unaltered in their static non-scientific modes of thought and action. Science educators are therefore challenged to improve the quality of education by ensuring the availability and use of teaching and learning modes that are particularly amenable to raising capacities of the majority to, at least, the 'low science' category.

The LISSIT group responded to this challenge by constructing an illustrative set of curriculum materials that would project the method of teaching and learning scientific ideas through local contexts as highly relevant and feasible. The main lessons emerging from the LISSIT experience begin by responding to some of the current school science problems.

Relevance as meaningful and useful science

It was stated earlier that developing countries have stressed the need for meaningful curricula as a means to combat the negative image of a subject that appears abstract and difficult to understand. Science as useful knowledge should be added to the quality of meaningfulness when identifying and constructing contexts to facilitate the learning of scientific ideas. The first action taken was to decide on a theme to guide the construction of contexts. The LISSIT group agreed to focus on the country's production of commodities, ranging from formal large-scale industries to informal small-scale or everyday activities. The meaningfulness of subject matter would be expedited by the learners' possible familiarity with the depicted occurrence and its usefulness in that the issues would often relate to circumstances in local workplaces. In this way, the meaning of a science concept or skill was made real, understandable to the majority, applicable to local situations, achievable and therefore interesting, rather than abstract, irrelevant and therefore difficult. Learners could also visit the simple S&T sites portrayed in their learning material to improve the understanding of ideas and their usefulness. This link between subject content and the learners' environment should drastically reduce the elitist character of science and makes 'science for all' feasible.

It is, therefore, imperative that every effort is made by the science education community to identify and document local occurrences that learners can identify with. These findings, both indigenous and exogenous, must be analysed in relation to their links with S&T precepts. In this way, scientific and technological concepts are not learnt and understood merely for their own sake, but can be perceived mostly in terms of their fruitful purpose in the daily life of individuals and their communities.

Science for all

The shift towards a more utilitarian 'science for all' necessitates the development of intellectual and physical capacities that are within the learner's scope. The school science curriculum in Swaziland, as in other African countries, currently caters for differences in learner abilities and school conditions by fitting learners into different syllabus categories, ranging from the 'hard' or 'pure' sciences to the 'soft' or 'combined' sciences. Such arrangements have, to some extent, satisfied the 'science for all' principle. However current reform, as exemplified by the LISSIT's viewpoint, advocates that all learners should be exposed to meaningful, applicable and functional school science, at least up to junior secondary school level. Reports on the observation and assessment of classrooms using the contextualised approach indicate that this strategy yields valuable outcomes (Ramsden, 1992; George,

1999) to the extent that it should be regarded as popular school science for all.

Local co-operation effort
The second important feature of the context-based teaching/learning strategy emerges as a powerful means to combat Africa's reliance on imported curriculum ideas. A condition for the successful production of context-based material is the necessity for all contributors to be conversant with all vital aspects of the features and culture to be depicted as realities of local S&T in action.

If S&T education is to be for all, then all requisite resources, physical and human, should be aligned to the task of producing the relevant school science. In the LISSIT project, a sample of high-ranking technologists from a variety of local industries collaborated closely with a group of science teachers and educators to develop the contextualised teaching and learning materials. In fact, industry's contribution went beyond the provision of expert practical S&T knowledge to financing the participation of their technologists in the joint curriculum development venture. Research into the industrialists' reactions to their unprecedented participation in curriculum development yielded positive perspectives among most of them (Lubben et al., 1998). This finding is an indication that continued partnerships with industry in S&T education are worth pursuing.

It is worth noting that varied reasons are proffered by different organisations for establishing links between school science and technology with industry. For instance, a cogent set of goals for Ghana's progress twoards becoming an industrialised country is described by Anamuah-Mensah (1999) as the rationale for school science links with industry. The LISSIT link with Swaziland's industry, through the development of materials for a syllabus that did not require the learner's familiarity with local productive processes, was regarded as a relevant step towards nurturing an interest in the country's productive sector. The possibility of preparing learners to be future workers, or pre-empting the requirements of industry, hardly featured as an aim. It was expected that this link between school science and the country's economic activities could promote in the young generation what a UNESCO-based effort of an earlier era referred to as the development of an 'S&T temper' (Irvine, 1985) among the peoples of developing countries.

Strategies for achieving the applied science approach
A government policy document calling for extensive school curriculum reform was issued in 1985, but little had been implemented to accomplish this goal a decade later. This lack of action challenged the country's science educators to

provide some direction on how the desired curriculum renewal could be executed. Research findings in the country had shown low levels of cognitive ability among learners to apply their scientific knowledge in rational ways to various local situations (Putsoa, 1992). This weakness has been corroborated recently (Campbell et al., 2000). The finding provided some guidance on the direction to follow in reforming the curriculum. Thus the project created a set of inquiry-based, interactive learning materials that modified the current junior secondary school science curriculum. The materials illustrated a strategy which maximised the meaningfulness and usefulness of science to learners and thereby minimised some of the serious problems of S&T education.

LISSIT was a University of Swaziland project. However, the project directors were convinced of the necessity for an all-inclusive reform activity characterised by the participation of a wide spectrum of stakeholders in the country's S&T sector. Thus, the project team consisted of participatory representation from the Science Inspectorate Division of the Ministry of Education, practising teachers from each of the country's four regions, industrialists representing a reasonable variety of technologies and science educators at the University of Swaziland.

Frequent reference has been made in this Chapter to contextualisation and in the literature (Lubben et al., 1995, 1998; Putsoa, 1999) to three central components, contexts, applications and investigations that characterise the teaching and learning approach adopted in developing the materials. These elements are briefly explained below.

Contextualisation
Contextualisation refers to a teaching style based on linking local experiences that learners have, or are likely to encounter in their environment, with the relevant scientific ideas to be learnt. Experience has shown that these contexts, which serve as starting points to lessons, tend to diminish the abstractness of scientific ideas, promote their relevance to the learner's circumstances and raise the learner's interest in tackling the conceptual problem embedded in the story line created for each context. The identification of contexts related to the country's productive activities was the main research activity carried out by the project team of teachers who combed the rural and urban countryside while industrialists focused on events at their workplaces. The collaboration that occurred between the science teachers, educators, government inspectorate and industry representatives in working out appropriate contexts for each of the lessons of a syllabus topic was extensive. This was the highlight of the three-year long teamwork; it should

augur well for valuable relationships in future between school science and the various technologies seen operating in different parts of the country.

Applications

Applications were included at different stages of each lesson to help learners develop the habit of tackling tasks that require their ability to select and apply their scientific knowledge to solve problems. Workplace activities, both rural and urban, that could be readily used in establishing and using particular scientific ideas served as valuable reference points for this component.

Investigations

Each lesson proceeded along an investigative route to help learners use a variety of inquiry skills and develop the capacity to design valid tests. These were laid out as a logical sequence of activities that started with the problem posed initially in the given context.

Throughout each lesson, learner participation, either individually or in groups, was encouraged through a wide variety of interactive teaching methods such as practical work, role-playing, model-making, discussion, creative writing, class or take-home exercises.

Main strengths and weaknesses of the approach

A sample of teachers who had not participated in constructing the materials were randomly selected from the country's four regions and asked to use the revised LISSIT material in their classrooms. They were informed that their role was to evaluate the effectiveness of the modified curriculum, especially on two aspects that reflected the desired reform. The first was on the ease or difficulty of handling LISSIT, with respect to the teaching and learning approach and the materials used. The second evaluation aspect was to be on pupils' abilities, skills and attitudes, with respect to classroom participation, cognitive activity, and attitudes to work and to people.

Teachers were asked to record their experiences and views in a daily diary and then summarise all views at a workshop.

Handling LISSIT in classrooms

A common theme running through teachers' descriptions of the teaching and learning approach was that it was challenging for most teachers because they were compelled to learn about technological operations that are a familiar sight in the environment, but which they had not previously concerned themselves about, such as a conveyor belt, a crane or a weighbridge included in the Force Unit. Teachers felt challenged to think of ways to help maintain a balance between the classroom fun aroused by an interesting context or local application used in the lesson and the orthodox science concept that had to be learnt. Further, it was not easy getting pupils to use the lesson's inquiry modes in order to think for themselves, or to convert their interesting practical observations into scientific explanations.

Finally, on the approach, teachers stated that the lessons successfully engaged pupils' interest, kept them working for most of the time and the various short- and long-term projects encouraged pupils' creativity, but the latter were problematic because they took too much time and effort to complete. With respect to the teaching and learning materials, it was generally agreed that these were easy to follow because of the guidance provided in the teachers notes and the answers to questions asked in the pupils workbook activities. The instructions written for pupils were said to be precise and simple to follow for most learners. The difficulties described were not just about weaknesses of the LISSIT approach and its materials, but were mostly those inherent in all S&T activity. For instance, teachers and pupils were disadvantaged in some lessons requiring electricity and/or technological equipment, such as video, that is not available in some schools. Also, pupils in schools that are far from modern technological activities could not begin to tackle lessons that required the modelling of ideas from observed action. However, rural pupils related well and easily executed work based on familiar contexts, such as the lessons on maize and on local housing structures.

Pupils abilities, skills and attitudes
Important observations were made on pupils' classroom participation. Teachers noted that the desire to participate increased noticeably as compared to pre-LISSIT classes. This change was evidenced by the fact that more pupils actually tried out the group practical work activities and the rate of collecting specified material from home in readiness for practical work improved. It was concluded that these inclinations to participate increased pupils' sense of responsibility for the success of their lessons.

However, there was dissatisfaction with some aspects of the material where the demands were said to be above the scope of learners. For instance, the intricacies of the weighbridge diagram 'do not encourage understanding'. Also, the inclusion of decimals for calculating proportions of animal skeletons to their body weight created difficulties. Teachers' statements on cognitive and other skills were also telling and the main theme running through their responses was that all lessons were thought to be provoking for learners. Cognitive growth was indicated by improved levels of discussion, such as when interpreting occurrences. The development of various investigative and creative skills, including the accurate observation of events, making models of tools for executing a task and perseverance, were encouraged, especially by the practical work requirements of short- and long-term projects. In addition, teachers noted an increase in the number of pupils able to tackle questions requiring the 'handling of information and applications' in monthly tests, rather than those of knowledge and understanding only.

On attitudes to science, work and people, teachers thought that the general feeling about science being abstract or difficult to understand was blunted as 'they started to realise that most of the things we do in our everyday activities involve science'. There was almost total agreement that 'pupils enjoyed most of the lessons' and their 'interest was greatly aroused' by classroom opportunities to share their personal experiences, their reasoning or appreciating one another's input. Teachers stated that this seemed to improve their disposition to apply themselves and this new orientation towards work was shown by the fact that 'most pupils did well in their continuous assessment marks of the third term, compared to the other two school terms' prior to LISSIT.

Another new feature emerging within the usual group work format was a new spirit of competition in 'producing the best model or to finish within the stated time'. Also 'some pupils considered academically weak became appreciated [by peers] for their out-of-school experiences, or their superior abilities in some practicals and group projects'. On the whole, the teachers' descriptions of their experience with the LISSIT material were what a curriculum developer would hope to achieve. Regrettably, current research on the effect of the contextualised approach indicates little success as regards the goal of cultivating enduring scientific reasoning abilities among learners (Campbell *et al.*, 2000). However, it must be noted that assessments of pupils are based on the outcomes of trials from extremely brief projects such as LISSIT. Nonetheless, the three elements titled contexts, applications and investigations described above are worth including in the S&T curriculum efforts of other African countries.

The Way Forward

The African Forum for Children's Literacy in Science and Technology has been a tireless source of inspiration for ideas and material support to a large group of individuals and institutions in many parts of the continent. AFCLIST has continuously forged ahead into new levels of action aimed at engendering a fresh resoluteness among African S&T educators to collaborate in eliminating the perennial factors that adversely affect the continent's quality of education, which, in turn, inhibits its ability to benefit materially from years of input to education. To this end, AFCLIST has established centres or nodes in different countries whose task is to stimulate developments likely to ameliorate identified qualitative problems of S&T education. Currently, Swaziland collaborates with Ghana in taking charge of the node on 'Linking School Science and Technology' with that on the 'Community and Workplace'. The centres established in these two countries are referred to as sub-node and node, respectively, and they are keen on attracting the participation of other African countries in node activities. The main factor that motivates the node's existence is the development of Africa's human resources in a way that is imbued with crucial scientific and technological values and skills needed for the continent's socio-economic development. The node expects to achieve this goal through reformed approaches to school science teaching and learning and reconstructed materials to reflect realities that are within the learner's grasp. This reformulation has to be rooted on a firm research base. Hence, among the variety of activities thought to be critical for effecting beneficial changes in S&T education is research into the various S&T features in African communities, both indigenous and modern, that have been ignored by school science over the decades. Inevitably, these changes will affect the country's education policies and must occur in partnership with all parties interested in popularising science and technology.

Conclusion

One of the greatest challenges facing many African nations is their ultimate ability to extricate themselves from an excessive dependence on Western nations for ideas and material support for the basic survival of its peoples. The apparent inability to work out practical ideas and action co-operatively for the benefit of the nation as a whole has been a characteristic feature of many decades of post-independent Africa. This incapacity can be readily associated with indolent states of mind cultivated over many years of dependence on instruction for action, through home and school education, as against questioning and tackling issues intellectually as they occur. This incapacity is contrary to the nature of science which is associated with rational thinking. There is need for a bold declaration on a school science agenda that focuses specifically on the development of rational thinking abilities among school leavers.

Information on the potential for attaining beneficial levels of economic development from the continent's plentiful natural resources is well documented. Unfortunately, the science and technology intricacies of this data remain unknown or unused as one of the curriculum strategies for nurturing pupil's cognitive and other critical skills that encourage a positive interest in African affairs. Conversely, the dissemination of information on the creative abilities of ordinary local citizens, as evidenced by the productive activities in the informal sector of the economy that closely relates to the everyday needs of the majority, is inadequate. The challenge to all those responsible for the country's advance, such as policy-makers and educators, is to be proactive in identifying and celebrating the creativity of ordinary people in the workplace. These abilities and products must also be regarded as vital national assets to be studied and improved upon. This could be one way of boosting the nation's self-esteem.

Each African country will achieve desirable levels of socio-economic development through the efforts of its own people, rather than those of donors. Hence, the government must work use its own national expertise in the search for and analysis of valuable human assets and S&T activities as part of the solution to existing 'poverty' problems. In this regard, continual research and reliance on its outcomes for making policies and effecting them will be crucial because African nations cannot escape the intensive competition for high-quality products imposed by the current 'globalisation' phenomenon. In this context, it is imperative for each developing country to identify its own human strengths that can be harnessed and genuinely incorporated into a strategy for developing an S&T culture and abilities that could transform the majority of its people from a consumption mentality towards a productive reality.

15. The Contribution of Applied Science to the Popularisation of Science and Technology: A Ghanaian Case

Professor Jophus Anamuah-Mensah
University College of Education of Winneba, Winneba, Ghana

Background

This chapter reports on science and technology projects aimed at broadening the knowledge base of junior and senior secondary school students and their teachers by linking school science and technology to industry. The projects are based on the principle that the popularisation of science and technology can best be accomplished through teaching the application of science, thereby generating meaning and relevance.

Some consider that applied science consists of 'those processes through which man has successfully interacted with their environment, and used natural resources to construct their world'. For Mukhurane and Kahn (1999), applied science is that which 'enables people to add value to their resources, is itself problem solving in its execution, and blurs distinctions between science, technology and on occasion sociology.'

The chapter looks at previous attempts to introduce applied science into science and technology education. It is argued that though the formal educational system provides opportunities for students in schools to learn science and technology, this has not been successful in making all of them science and technology literate. This is partly due to the purely academic and elitist orientation of the science and technology curriculum, as well as to its neglect of the socio-cultural environment of the learners.

Introduction

The education of Africans during the pre-colonial era has been described as relevant, practical and work-oriented and was aimed at making every citizen useful in the society. According to Brock-Utne (1999), education during this period was linked to practical reality. There was a clear link between education and productive activities, between education and social life, and between education and the culture of the people. Education at the time was therefore relevant, embracing the totality of the people's culture. The extraction and smelting of iron, blacksmithing, bead making and kente weaving were some of the productive activities carried out.

This indigenous, practical-oriented, applied science was lost during the colonial era. The introduction of Western education alienated students from the indigenous activities of the community as a result of the marginalisation of ancestral knowledge and know-how, which was seen as a counter system.

The Western science bequeathed to African countries was in general an academic and elitist training given to only a few to provide the services needed by the colonial masters. The orientation was therefore more towards satisfying the colonising countries' thirst for power than to addressing development issues raised either directly or indirectly by Africans themselves.

At the time of independence of most sub-Saharan African countries, which incidentally coincided with the curriculum reform movements of the UK and USA, science education was still elitist and academic, even though the curriculum promoted the empiricist perspective.

In Ghana, with the expansion of the economy immediately after independence through the establishment of industries in rural and urban areas, there was a realisation that the white collar jobs which used to be readily available to school leavers were no longer available. The school system became increasingly dysfunctional as it turned out school leavers who had no marketable skills. According to Dzobo (1987), 'these school leavers could see no bright future for themselves and they constitute a veritable economic and social problem for our society to solve'. People were disillusioned about the education they were receiving.

It is interesting that the dissatisfaction with the academic lopsidedness of formal education was not new. As far back as 1847, Africans and colonial administrators in Ghana recognised this, but it was not until the 1920s that the first technical school for agriculture was established as a result of the Phelps-Stokes report.

The major criticisms were that science education was not relevant to the needs of the economy and that it considered the culture of the people to be primitive with Western science being the superior culture that should replace the indigenous culture. It therefore projected the Western world view as the only legitimate view (Jegede, 1997).

In 1967 there was a shift in government policy which favoured the introduction of vocational technical education in the form of continuation schools. This was a welcome innovation at the time since it offered an alternative path for pupils who were not able to gain admission to the grammar-type secondary schools through the common entrance examination. This examination was designed to select pupils in Forms 1 and 2 of middle schools and Class 6 of preparatory schools for secondary schools.

The Continuation Day Schools in Ghana

Prior to the formation of continuation schools, the following issues characterised the education system. Pre-university school education followed a single path with everyone expected to move through six years primary, four years middle, five years secondary and two years sixth form education. No provision was made to cater for the special abilities of students.

- The common entrance examination system cut off 80 per cent of middle school leavers from continuing their education (Bishop, 1986).

- Middle school leavers were not equipped for the world of work or to create jobs for themselves.

- The public had a negative attitude to manual work, preferring white-collar jobs to practical vocations

- There was a constant stream of school leavers from the rural areas to urban towns resulting in underdevelopment of rural communities.

The two-year continuation day schools were introduced to address these conditions by bringing practical work into what was described at the time as a traditional, examination-oriented academic curriculum. The work of the school was designed to relate to what school leavers would face after school in their communities. The existing middle schools were converted into continuation schools that devoted a third of their time to practical activities that helped pupils to develop productive skills and techniques as well as to produce objects with an economic value. Village craftsmen were used as paid specialist teachers to share their expertise with the pupils. Activities covered in the curriculum included animal rearing, crop and vegetable production, kente weaving, production of sandals, baking and cooking, and needlework (Bishop, 1986).

The introduction of the continuation schools initially met with some resistance because 'farming parents did not want an education that would bind their children to a life of toil on the soil: they preferred time honoured academic education' (Bishop, 1986). However, with the embracing of the government's 'Operation Feed Yourself' philosophy, community support increased to the extent that by 1973–74 the number of continuation schools increased about 2600 per cent from the initial 18 trial schools to 467. This was, therefore, a very successful innovation that introduced applied science in the form of technical and vocational subjects into the curriculum although it did not cater for all students.

The continuation schools were phased out in 1980–81 when they were fully incorporated into the experimental junior secondary schools concept of making education both terminal and continuing. This was to ensure that all pupils were predisposed to vocational and technical skills.

Alternative Approaches

Other innovative strategies to introduce applied science into the academic curricula of schools are the village polytechnics in Kenya and the brigade movement in Botswana. The village polytechnics were established to overcome the growing unemployment of primary school leavers and the drift from rural to urban centres in search of a better quality of life. The village polytechnics were community vocational schools that were built, staffed and managed by the community to provide vocational training for primary school leavers for two years. Both academic education and practical training were offered, based on local needs and including subjects such as agriculture and commerce. The ultimate aim was to make the graduates self-employed. Parents and the public, however, saw the village polytechnics as offering second or third class education.

The brigade movement in Botswana was set up in 1963 to address the perennial unemployment problems of primary school leavers. It provided a three-year vocational, technical training that combined work and learning. Depending on the nature of the craft to be learned, a number of brigades were set up. Examples are the builders' brigade that involved putting up structures and carpenters' brigade that involved the making of desks, beds and so on. The training programme consisted of a period of production work and 'on-the-job' training, classroom instruction in vocational subjects and classroom instruction in academic subjects. Even though the brigades provided an alternative route to secondary level education, they were considered as second-rate education for those who failed to get into the regular secondary schools.

Although the continuation schools system was generally a success, a number of criticisms were made of it.

- It encountered negative reactions from the public. Many parents of children in the public school system, especially educated ones, forced their children to sit for the common entrance examination to escape going to continuation schools. This was attributed to the undue emphasis the education system placed on mental work, which unintentionally fostered the development of unhealthy attitudes towards manual work and non-academic subjects.

- It was seen as a tool for separating academically oriented pupils who entered the grammar type of secondary schools from the less academically oriented who received vocational skills and were perceived as dropouts and 'uneducables' (Dzobo, 1994).

- The continuation schools did not provide adequate training to enable the pupils to become self-employed after graduation.

- There were no avenues for further training in the vocational areas chosen by the pupils except in privately run apprenticeship programmes.

- The schools did not give an opportunity for all pupils to be exposed to practical skills.

- It is clear, however, that these efforts to introduce vocational and technical subjects into existing theoretically-based educational systems provided opportunities for a reasonable number of people to be exposed to some form of technology education.

Genesis of the STAG Project

The emergence of the Science and Technology Action in Ghana (STAG) project can only be understood in the context of the 1987 educational reforms which brought about major structural changes and mental adjustments. The reforms became necessary as a result of concerns raised about the educational system at the time. The concerns expressed about science and technology education were as follows:

- Science education at the secondary level was elitist, academic and theoretical;

- Science and technology education portrayed only the modern Western view of science and technology and was therefore not related to the environment and culture of the learners. It was therefore seen as alien and irrelevant;

- Science was perceived as a culture-free activity, which can be taught to all regardless of the receiving culture (Turner and Turner, 1987);

- Many pupils who failed to gain admission to secondary schools did not have the opportunity to develop their minds and were therefore disadvantaged for life;

- Foreign textbooks used in the schools transmitted Western 'socio-political values, not just openly but also by omission with a biased presentation of facts' or indirectly when the values are hidden in an exercise or task (Goldstein, 1978);

- There was a lack of political will to implement the recommendations of the reports of the Educational Advisory Committee (1972), also referred to as the Dzobo Committee, set up to review the educational system;

- Increasing numbers of unemployed school leavers lacked practical skills and were ill-equipped to fit into the economy;

- The teaching of science lacked the applications of science in and around the environment of the learner and especially in industry.

As mentioned above, these and other factors culminated in the educational reform movement in 1987. The reform:

- Introduced a 6-3-3-4 system of education, that is, 6 years primary, 3 years junior secondary school (JSS), 3 years senior secondary schools (SSS) and 4 years tertiary education;

- Echoed the continuation school concept of providing pre-vocational and pre-technical education for JSS students, thereby introducing practical work into the traditionally academic curriculum of schools;

- Introduced a multiple trajectory system at the SSS level through diversification of the curriculum which now enables students to pursue either a purely academic curriculum in science or applied science programmes such as agriculture and technology in the same senior secondary school;

- Included topics on science, industry and the environment in the science curriculum at the senior secondary and recently at the junior secondary levels;

- Advocated a shift in orientation from 'euro-academic excellence' with its emphasis on European standards to socio-cultural relevance with its emphasis on the culture of the people and work-oriented skills;

The STAG project originated in 1987 at the University of Cape Coast (now being hosted at UCEW) in response to the need to bridge the growing gap between school and community science and technology. It also sought to provide industry related materials that were needed to teach the science-industry-environment topics in the new syllabuses. It has currently produced materials for 15–18-year-old senior secondary school students.

What Science and Technology?

Our earlier discussion indicates that pre-colonial education of Africans was designed to be responsive to communities' practical needs and covered the totality of their social and economic life. The productive activities of African societies featured prominently in their education that was therefore application-oriented. The advent of Western education during the colonial era changed the focus by giving emphasis to academic orientation and the marginalisation of the applied nature of the indigenous science and technology education. This practice has continued to the post-independent era with vocational and technical education still not recognised as a first-rate education in our schools.

For a long time there has been concern that science taught in schools does not enable students to use their knowledge to solve problems in their homes and communities. It was theoretically oriented and driven by external examinations. It is said that, for example, many graduates of the school system found it difficult to change blown fuses in electrical plugs. However, critical observations indicate that in the community, home, farm and workplace, science manifests itself as science-in-use or science-in-reality, that is, as applied science. This is in contrast to the school, which generally promotes science as theoretical and mythic (Smolicz and Nunan, 1975). This creates a gap between the applied science in the community and the pure science view of school. The STAG project promotes an applied science view and therefore brings aspects of the community, especially industry, to the science classroom in some form. For example, the concept of flotation is presented as it is applied in the gold industry.

Whose Science and Technology?

The adoption or adaptation of Western science by post-independent African countries was accompanied by the culture, that is the values, norms and customs, of the country of origin. This culture shaped the thought, feelings and actions, and the world view of students. Culture has been described as the webs of significance people spin for themselves and in which they are suspended (Geertz, 1973). The webs include the values, norms, indigenous technologies and their links to school science and technology and 'out-of school living' (Solomon, 1996).

If culture is an important variable in science education (Ogunniyi *et al.*, 1995; Jegede and Okebukola, 1988; Ogawa, 1986; Ogunniyi, 1987, 1988), then community culture and knowledge should determine the science education content and delivery in our schools (Jegede and Solomon, 1999).

The STAG project promotes science and technology which are derived from Ghanaian culture. The industries in the country served as the base for this. For the first time, industries were asked to help determine the curricular content. Industries in Ghana were recognised as the locus of applied knowledge while science teachers were deemed to be the custodians of pedagogical knowledge and skills. That is, the teachers' role was to consider how to make the applied knowledge of industry meaningful to themselves and their students.

The account of the industries presented in STAG materials is the result of a distillation process that saw the removal of highly technical terms and complex illustrations and yet produced authentic accounts. The essence was to make the applied science located in industries available to students.

Science and Technology for What?

According to Skilbeck (1984), any educational discipline such as science education has three fundamentally different purposes – cultural transmission of knowledge, vocational needs and societal reconstruction.

The first purpose requires that the accumulated knowledge of science and technology is passed on to the next generation of research scientists who will help to push back the frontiers of knowledge. This is what Makhurane and Kahn (1998) have alluded to as high science.

The second purpose, preparation to meet vocational needs, although important for the development of developing countries, is hard to find in school science education. This requires that students are given core transferable skills that will enable them to secure jobs as middle-level manpower. Such skills necessarily include familiarity with science as practised in industry, a positive attitude to science and the desire to learn about industry. The 1992 industrial policy of Ghana states that industrial development requires human resources with scientific skills as well as 'appropriate general skills and the motivation to acquire and develop specific skills on-the-job' (Republic of Ghana, 1992). This vocational purpose of science education is related to Makhurane and Khan's (1998) low science. The lack of this vocational orientation of science education has contributed in no small way to the underdevelopment of most African nations.

The third purpose, reconstruction of society, involves inculcating what is variously called 'scientific culture', 'scientific and technological literacy' and 'public understanding of science' in the population. In this era of great scientific and technological achievements that impinge on the day-to-day lives of every citizen, it is the democratic right of every citizen to be fully involved in the scientific and technological culture. Every individual should be provided with an understanding and appreciation of science and technology concepts as they relate to their daily lives. They should also develop a positive attitude to science and technology and should find them enjoyable. Issues such as deforestation, irradiated food, trade in human organs, ozone layer depletion and *in vitro* fertilisation require informed decisions based on science and technology. We need to help youth to engage in discussions of such issues.

Public support for science and technology education and research will depend on the culture of science and technology created in society. The STAG project has attempted to provide a vocational orientation as well as creating the platform for a scientific and technological culture. This has been achieved by introducing both teachers and their students to applications of science in indigenous and modern industries operating in the country. Materials for 18 industries, including steel, gold, petroleum refining, cement, aluminium, wood, textiles, beer, cocoa and soap, have been developed to expose students to applied science. These constitute the economic backbone of the community and also provide employment opportunities for a large percentage of the country's school leavers (Towse and Anamuah-Mensah, 1991).

Many senior secondary schools are using the STAG materials to help them interpret the 'Science, Industry and Society' section of the science syllabus. The students' workbook provides practical investigative activities (projects), as well as games, case studies and role-plays that enable students to engage in discussions and debates about issues related to industry, such as pollution and improvement of an industrial product. Activities are provided to enable students to construct an environmental impact profile (ecoprofile) for each industry.

The project has produced a resource book for science teachers, a students' workbook and video clips on some industries. The last two will soon be available on the market.

The resource book, *Science in Action: A Resource book for Science Teachers*, consists of 20 chapters, 18 of which discuss specific industries. The other two chapters are on broader issues that concern all industries. Each industry is presented according to the following sub-headings: introduction, highlights on industry, production or manufacture of a specific product, raw materials, production processes, quality control, uses, safety and future development.

The students' workbook is organised according to the chapters in the teachers' resource book. For each chapter there are games, case studies, role-plays, projects and an ecoprofile. They have been developed to engage students in investigative activities, provide fun through the games and engage in discussion of social issues relating to the industries through role-plays and case studies.

Role Play: Potassium Bromate in Bread Making

Introduction

Potassium bromate is commonly added to improve the quality of flour. It acts as both an oxidizing and bleaching agent and is reduced to potassium bromide (KBr). This is toxic and harmful when excess potassium bromide is produced. Ascorbic acid that is not harmful may be used as a substitute for potassium bromate.

The Role Play

Recently bakers in the bread industry have been disturbed over poor sales because of the publicity about potassium bromate ($KBrO_3$) in the flour. During their Fifth Annual Congress, the President of the Bakers' Association sent a memo to the following inviting them for a discussion on "Potassium Bromate in the Bread Industry":

The President of the Ghana Chemical Society whose concerns include the harmful effects of bromate and the advantages of ascorbic acid;

The Director of the Ghana Standards Board concerned about certification of ascorbic acid in flour and sanctions that might be meted out to defaulters;

The Chairman of the Flour Millers' Association who is sensitive to the public's reluctance to buy bread and other bakery products;

The Chairman of the Consumers Association which fears cancer and is aware of a possible need to destroy any foodstuff containing bromate.

Instructions

Write appropriate memos as: a) the President of the Ghana Chemical Society, b) the Director of the Ghana Standards Board, c) The Chairman of the Flour Millers' Association, and d) the Chairman of the Consumers Association.

Lessons Learned

A major problem the project encountered was to ensure that the materials reflected a truly Ghanaian setting and did not just present these processes in a culturally neutral way. This became a thorny issue for some time. It was, however, addressed by incorporating indigenous technologies, socio-economic issues and other situation-specific information.

Contextualising the presentation posed difficulties in publishing the materials. It is noteworthy that two multinational publishers rejected the final manuscript of the resource book as being 'too Ghanaian'. A Ghanaian publisher, after reading the manuscript, decided to publish the book.

The interaction between industrialists and teachers provided an opportunity for shared meanings. There was openness in these interactions and bonds of friendship were established, making it easier for the project team to have access to industrialists' knowledge and their factories.

The involvement of industry as curriculum partners has created a larger community of knowledge producers and transformers. In the past, teachers were regarded as the sole producers of classroom knowledge, probably because they are deemed as possessing pragmatically-validated knowledge about teaching, learning and school organisation (Richardson, 1994). However, with the emergence of what Gibbons (1998) refers to as the 'global distributed knowledge production-system', that considers production of knowledge by other groups such as industrialists, the inclusion of industry in the project broadened the sources of classroom knowledge.

The involvement of industry and the general enthusiasm generated has encouraged several industries to make financial contributions for reprints of the books.

Industrialists seemed more willing to respond to reviews drafts of their industries than to produce drafts themselves.

The discussions, reviews and re-writing served to reduce the technical information, yet provided an authentic portrayal of the industries.

The STAG materials constitute the first set of locally produced resource material available to science teachers. Hitherto, the textbook has been the main source of information for science teaching and learning. It is believed that more than 95 per cent of science teachers use the science textbook more than 95 per cent of the time as the source of notes, practical activities and assignments.

Fig 15.1. Major areas of study at SACOST

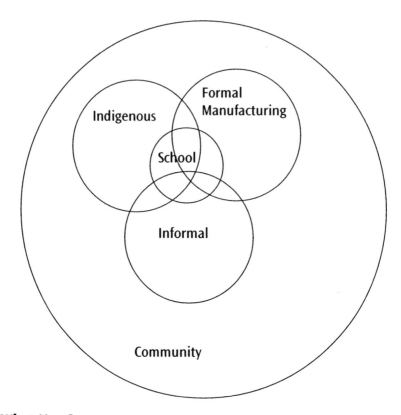

What Next?

With STAG materials now being used in science classrooms, the next activity is to evaluate their use in schools. Observation instruments and other industry-based test instruments will be developed for this purpose. How the science teacher uses the materials will be of great interest to the project. The project intends to develop industry-oriented examination items and other authentic assessment tools. Already some items in the external examinations conducted by the West African Examination Council for junior secondary schools have an industrial bias; this will be encouraged through discussion with the Ministry of Education. The project intends to maximise the good relations it has developed with industries to establish a partnership between industry and schools and universities. This will involve, among other activities, the use of industrialists as guest lecturers and part-time teachers. The partnership should allow for short industrial attachments for students during the long vacation and assist students to develop industry-based projects. The formation of a Centre for School and Community Science and Technology Studies (SACOST), a node of excellence for bridging school and community science and technology at the University College of Education of Winneba, Ghana, will help to co-ordinate all the above activities. The centre will spearhead studies leading to the development of teaching and learning materials on activities in the informal and indigenous sectors of the economy as well as adding value to those sectors, and will be a reference centre for studies in these areas. Figure 15.1 gives the major areas of study at the centre. It is envisaged that these activities will lead to increased access to science and technology for all pupils in schools and for those in adult education irrespective of gender.

16. Promoting the Public Understanding of Science and Technology: The South African Case

Dr Botlhale Tema
Department of Arts, Culture, Science and Technology, South Africa

Kebogile Dilotsotlhe
Department of Arts, Culture, Science and Technology, South Africa

Professor Jaap Kuiper
University of the North, South Africa

Introduction

1994 saw the election of South Africa's first democratic government. This had immediate consequences for the development of social programmes in general and for science and technology policies in particular. The Public Understanding of Science, Engineering and Technology (PUSET) has become an important issue. Extensive national and international research has been carried out to develop up-to-date and globally inspired and competitive policies on science and technology PUSET.

The Department of Arts, Culture, Science and Technology (DACST) of the South African government is responsible for the formulation and overseeing of the implementation of science and technology policies, including those of PUSET. A specific 'Directorate for Science and Society' has been created within DACST that shows the commitment and importance given to PUSET in South Africa. Indeed, the South African government is well aware of '... the importance of science and technology to modern societies and the role of a technologically educated population in promoting economic and social development. The complex relationship between the economy, society, the environment and scientific knowledge makes a multidisciplinary approach to the development of society essential and calls for skilled communicators, able to address technological issues' (DACST, 2000b).

This chapter will first discuss DACST's White Paper on Science and Technology that is fundamental to all issues related to science and technology in South Africa. From this White Paper, the need for PUSET and consequently for a Directorate for Science and Society became clear. The Directorate for Science and Society has developed a draft strategy for PUSET that will also be discussed in this chapter. Following this, a number of specific initiatives on PUSET in South Africa will be briefly described, and lastly the future focuses on how a new body, the Foundation for Education, Science and Technology, has been created by DACST to further the aims of PUSET will be outlined.

South Africa's Policy on Science and Technology

In 1996 the 'White Paper on Science and Technology: Preparing for the 21st Century' was published (DACST, 1996). This White Paper, forming the base of all further policy formulation and implementation, points out that 'innovation' is a crucial aspect when pursuing the well-being and prosperity of a country. Innovation must be based on a framework for social and economic policy that maximises possibilities for all parts of the system to interact for the benefit of individual stakeholders or groups of stakeholders, as well as for the advancement of national goals. The White Paper, therefore, provides a National System of Innovation (NSI) with science and technology at its core. This is based on the following considerations:

♦ Promoting competitiveness and employment creation

♦ Enhancing the quality of life

♦ Developing human resources

♦ Working towards environmental sustainability

♦ Promoting an information society

♦ The importance of knowledge creation

♦ The role of human sciences in innovation

♦ Finance, management and performance.

The National System of Innovation based on the above issues has six sets of functions that are outlined below according to their being 'Government' or 'Shared' functions (DACST, 1996):

Government Functions: Policy formulation and resources allocation at national level

Regulatory policy-making

Shared Functions:	Performance-level financing of innovation-related activities
	Performance of innovation-related activities
	Human resource development and capacity building
	Provision of infrastructure

The functions show that government not only considers policy formulation. It also considers that implementation of policy, appropriate resource allocation and the stimulation of innovative activities are crucial. Furthermore, government pays explicit attention to the development of human capital, capacity building and appropriate infrastructure. In all, the White Paper provides a clear and comprehensive framework for the promotion and development of science and technology for economic development, social innovation and an uplifting of all people of South Africa. Indeed, the White Paper states that: 'The stimulation of a national system of innovation will be central to the empowerment of all South Africans as they seek to achieve social, political, economic and environmental goals. The development of innovative ideas, products, institutional arrangements and processes will enable the country to address more effectively the needs and aspirations of its citizens. [...] A well managed and properly functioning national system of innovation will make it possible for all South Africans to enjoy the economic, socio-political and intellectual benefits of science and technology' (DACST, 1996).

Rationale and Strategy for PUSET

In the White Paper particular attention is given to PUSET. Government promotes the recognition, understanding, use and benefits of science and technology both through initiatives in the formal education sector and through special programmes. The White Paper argues that: 'Access to information is empowering, enabling people to monitor, lobby, learn, collaborate, campaign and react to proposed legislation ... The democratisation of society and elimination of poverty can only occur if people have equal access to the services and resources they need to perform their productive tasks' (DACST, 1996). The White Paper continues: 'For the national system of innovation to become effective and successful all South Africans should participate. This requires a society that understands and values science, engineering and technology and their critical role in ensuring national prosperity and sustainable development'.

The White Paper stresses the need for development of a public understanding of science, engineering and technology and outlines a campaign that has two elements: promoting the power of science, engineering and technology (SET), and literacy in these fields. This is done through programmes that include:

♦ Increasing people's familiarity with the natural world;

♦ Promoting understanding of some key concepts and principles of science and technology;

♦ Demonstrating that science, engineering and technology are social tools;

♦ Fostering an ability to use science and technology knowledge in ways that enhance personal goals, as well as economic and community development.

These points show a clear recognition that PUSET is critical if South Africa is to continue to develop as a functioning democracy. To participate more fully in democratic processes, South Africa's peoples must understand, rather than fear, science and technology; and since poverty is recognised as an obstacle to effective democracy, all our people must use science and technology to contribute to its eradication.

The Directorate for Science and Society within DACST has published a document entitled *Towards a Strategy for Public Understanding of Science, Engineering and Technology* (DACST, 2000b). The document highlights the importance DACST and the South African government give to developing a society that is comfortable with science and technology, competent in its proper use and capable of contributing to its development. The document particularly identifies women and rural populations as requiring particular attention. It also advocates an appropriate recognition of local and traditional practices and their effective use, as well as the more prevalent use of 'mainstream' science.

The Strategy Document explains that the Science and Society Directorate will develop a PUSET model to implement and interact with the formal education system. From an awareness that South Africa does not rank highly in international comparisons on an understanding of science and technology, a need arose to develop a concerted effort to improve PUSET for the country. Indeed, the strategy is based on the recognition that there is a need to:

♦ Revisit the current approach of 'Taking SET to the people' and to develop it into an implementable strategy that recognises the inputs at all levels of society and incorporates them into the conceptualisation, design, implementation, monitoring, evaluation, funding and communication of PUSET programmes at the National Level;

♦ Create a PUSET model for South Africa that by 2005 will constitute the realisation of Vision 2005 of the Directorate: Science and Society.

Aims of the draft strategy include:

- Generating a public interest in science, engineering and technology;

- Making society aware of the everyday use of science and technology;

- Encouraging the scientific community to become more transparent to society by communicating more appropriately with the public through media such as television, newspapers, radio and e-mail;

- Creating partnerships with scientific institutions, business, communities, NGOs, Institutes of Higher Education and other government departments;

- Improving scientific and technological education to enrich the lives of people without negatively affecting local culture;

- Stimulating the production of new resources that harmoniously combine mainstream scientific knowledge with traditional knowledge;

- Raising the scientific and technological literacy of women.

The strategy strives to integrate stakeholders in a public understanding of science, engineering and technology and make it a concern of national importance to which all can and must contribute. There is explicit reference to other government departments, business, schooling, the scientific community, the media and women. The strategy makes a clear move towards integrating the many role players that are active in PUSET and to develop a co-ordinated approach where resources, skills and capacity are fully used in a complementary and supportive rather than in a competitive manner.

A last document that is important to PUSET is the Report from the Foresight Project initiated by DACST (DACST, 1999). The National Research and Technology Foresight Project is one of a number of initiatives being undertaken by the Department of Arts, Culture, Science and Technology as part of its mission to review and reform South Africa's science and technology system. The outcomes of the Foresight Project, along with other policy initiatives, will contribute to new directions for science and technology in South Africa. The aim of the project is to help identify those sector-specific technologies and technology trends that will best improve the quality of life of all South Africans over the next 10–20 years. The project encompasses technologies that impact on social issues and wealth creation through product or process development. In particular the Foresight Project seeks to:

- Identify those technologies and possible market opportunities that are most likely to generate benefits for South Africa;

- Develop consensus on future priorities amongst the different stakeholders in sectors such as the industrial, socio-economic or service sectors;

- Co-ordinate research efforts between different players within selected sectors;

- Reach agreement on those actions that are needed in different sectors to take full advantage of existing and future technologies.

As important as these outcomes is the foresight process itself that will bring together government departments, industry, science councils, higher education, organised labour, professional organisations and other stakeholders who previously related to each other in a highly fragmented way. This is the start of a process that will see a long-term strategic approach to science and technology within South Africa, and greater focus on the role that technology has to play in the country's development.

In the Foresight Report (DACST, 1999) the development of human resources is identified as a crosscutting element in all the foresight areas that range from agriculture to information technology, mining and environmental issues. In this respect, a public understanding of science, engineering and technology is again identified as an important element of South Africa's plans for development of the competitive science and technology needed for the country to become an equal player in the global market.

PUSET Initiatives

DACST, and particularly the Directorate for Science and Society, has been instrumental in developing many initiatives related to PUSET. Some of these initiatives as well as some of those developed with partners are briefly outlined below:

Year of Science and Technology, 1998
South Africa proclaimed 1998 the Year of Science and Technology (YEAST). Each of the nine provinces held a week-long festival where they invited the general public, and specifically school children, to come to view and actively participate in a science and technology fair. Business, schools, universities and research institutes, both national and international, developed a 'road-show' that travelled to all provinces. More than 200,000 people were reached through YEAST. The initiative appeared to be a big success, particularly where good partnerships were created between business, government, research councils, education NGOs and formal institutes. YEAST also gave an enormous boost to PUSET.

National Science and Technology Girls' Camps

The first National Science and Technology Girls' Camp was held in 1998. Its objectives were to develop a better understanding of science and technology amongst the girls participating; to make them more aware of and able to deal with gender issues; and to alert them to the HIV/AIDS scourge. Through involving role models, businesses, and VIP and other visitors the status and accessibility of science and technology for the girls was enhanced. In 2000, three more girls' camps were held in which over 250 girls from all nine provinces participated.

National Science, Engineering and Technology Week

Building on the success of YEAST, a yearly week on science, engineering and technology is being held from 2000–2002. Each year, three provinces have been selected to host a 'Science, Engineering and Technology Week'. The public, particularly school pupils, have been invited to attend seminars, workshop displays and demonstrations designed by science councils, universities, business and other interested parties.

Women in SET Reference Group

Recently DACST initiated a Reference Group for Women in SET. The Reference Group sees its task as enhancing: a) the contributions from senior women scientists; b) career pathing for women; c) access for women to SET institutions; d) access and participation in school science and technology education; and e) use of science and technology as a tool for rural development and poverty eradication.

Science Journalism Awards

DACST recognises the important role played by the media in the public understanding of science, engineering and technology. To stimulate active and constructive media participation, DACST initiated Science Journalism Awards identifying seven categories. Some universities in South Africa have started to offer modules on Science Communication and Journalism.

Science Centres

Over a dozen science centres operate in South Africa. Typically they are based at a university, government education department or museum. Some centres target the public while others provide support for teachers and learners in their endeavour to understand more about science and technology. Some are interactive and others are more oriented towards displays. These science centres often have outreach programmes especially for rural schools.

Grahamstown Science Festival

The yearly Grahamstown Science Festival, SciFest, is another initiative that explicitly aims at developing PUSET. Yearly, since before 1998, between 30,000 and 40,000 people visit SciFest where in a similar way to the Year of Science and Technology, national and international research groups, businesses, universities, schools and others display and involve the public in the latest and most topical science and technology developments.

Research into PUSET

The National Research Foundation (NRF) funds a number of university-based research projects into PUSET that are related to topics such as the implementation of the new curriculum, C2005; the use of indigenous knowledge in the school curriculum; and the development of scientific literacy, and rural science and technology learning.

Conferences on PUSET

DACST has hosted two conferences on PUSET where national and international researchers presented their research findings. Specific attention was given to the evaluation of YEAST and other PUSET activities and to mapping a way forward.

Solar Eclipse Project

In 2001 a 75 per cent solar eclipse could be observed in Southern Africa, and 2002 will see another. DACST developed materials and stimulated other initiatives for school children and the public that use the national media and other channels to make people more aware of the eclipse and its significance.

The new National Curriculum for Formal Schooling

The South African government has developed a new curriculum for Grades 1–9 (DoE, 2001) that sets out to contribute to the public understanding of science, engineering and technology. The new curriculum, called Curriculum 2005 (C2005), is based on outcomes-based education where clear end goals are formulated towards which all learning must contribute. The critical outcomes to which all education in South Africa is striving are to:

♦ Communicate effectively using visual, mathematical and language skills;

♦ Identify and solve problems using creative and critical thinking;

♦ Organise and manage activities responsibly and effectively;

♦ Work effectively with others in a team, group, organisation and community;

♦ Collect, analyse, organise and critically evaluate information;

♦ Use science and technology effectively and critically, showing responsibility towards the environment and the health of others;

♦ Understand that the world is a set of related systems.

These outcomes are achieved through learning in eight learning areas, namely language, mathematics, natural sciences, technology, social sciences, arts and culture, economics and life orientation. These critical outcomes clearly show a goal of learning that develops learners into citizens with an ability to understand and use science and technology in their lives and have an understanding of the world as a complex set of related environmental systems. This curriculum is a clear departure from traditional curricula that focus on the static reproduction of academic knowledge. The curriculum is ambitious and issues of teacher preparedness, development of appropriate learning resources, and learner and parent expectations are problematic. However, the government has recently simplified C2005, making it more user-friendly, and will support teachers and learners in a more effective way than it did in the first version of C2005. It is therefore likely to contribute to South Africans' understanding of science, engineering and technology.

In all, it can be seen that there are many initiatives in the area of PUSET in South Africa. Indeed, when seen in the broader African context, South Africa has a relatively well-developed infrastructure, technology-based industry and formal education system up to tertiary level. All these greatly assist in identifying a variety of stakeholders who are interested in PUSET and can contribute to it. A number of large businesses, research councils, universities and the media all are able and willing to play their part in the development of PUSET. However, at times perhaps the initiatives are somewhat disparate and fragmented. It is with this realisation in mind that DACST has taken a new initiative, setting up a Foundation for Engineering, Science and Technology (FEST).

The Future: Integrating PUSET through FEST

The Foundation for Engineering, Science and Technology was recently set up to ensure a better co-operation, mutual awareness and beneficial cross-fertilisation of ideas and initiatives to improve the public understanding of science, engineering and technology. The rationale for FEST is that DACST felt a need to better co-ordinate activities for the public understanding of science, engineering and technology, as well as to have a facilitating body to concentrate on implementation of policies for PUSET. DACST develops policy, while FEST will become a body which facilitates the disbursing of funds, identification of stakeholder groups, and co-ordination of proposals and other implementation issues. It is envisaged that FEST, through the representation of all major stakeholder groups in society, will enhance the contribution of society to PUSET. The public understanding of science, engineering and technology is seen as requiring a facilitating body to ensure that the policies that have been generated over the past few years will be implemented widely and that this process becomes an integral part of the public domain. As such, it is seen as essential that FEST effectively performs a bridging function between DACST and South African society. Through systematic planning, networking, evaluation, tendering, generating and disbursement of funds, PUSET will then become an integral part of development for and by society.

17. Indigenous Technology as a Basis for Science, Mathematics and Technology Education at the Junior Secondary School Level: A Sierra Leonean Case Study

Dr Sonia Spencer
British Council, Sierra Leone

Introduction

Sierra Leone, a small developing country with a population of about 4.2 million people, lies on the West African Coast between 7 and 10 degrees north of the equator. From north to south the greatest distance is around 190 miles (320 km) and from east to west about 175 miles (290 km). Yet there is geographical diversity, with a variety of ecosystems – coastal beaches and mangrove swamps, savanna woodlands and tropical forest.

The country is divided into four regions, the western area on the Atlantic Coast, where the capital Freetown is located, and eastern, northern and southern provinces. There is considerable ethnic variety. The major ethnic groups are:

- Krios – Western area
- Themnes and Limbas – northern province
- Mendes and Konos – eastern province
- Mendes and Sherbros – southern province.

Sierra Leone is not a highly industrialised country but it can boast of a large variety of indigenous and traditional technologies that are sometimes referred to as 'cottage industries'. Each ethnic group has its own indigenous technologies although some are now common to more than one region, as shown in Table 17.1.

Table 17.1: Indigenous Technologies by Region

Western Area	Eastern Province	Northern Province	Southern Province
Foofoo/Ogirie processing	Country cloth weaving	Palmwine tapping	Garri processing
Fish processing	Extraction of vegetable oil	Gara dyeing	Fishing
Charcoal processing	Metal works	Soda-soap making	Distillation of local gin
Gara dyeing	Food preservation	Rice parboiling	Canoe and trap building
Soda-soap making	Hunting	Foofoo processing	Thatch house construction
Metal works	Fish farming	Thatch house construction	Extraction of vegetable oil

The New Education Structure

The new structure of schooling is a three-tier system that started in the 1993/94 academic session. This system consists of six years of primary education, then three years of Junior Secondary Schooling (JSS), and finally three years of Senior Secondary Schooling (SSS). In brief, it is 6-3-3-4. The 4 is for four years of tertiary education. It replaces the old system which consisted of 7 years of primary schooling and 5–7 years of secondary, followed by tertiary education.

Junior secondary school

At the end of primary schooling, pupils take the external National Primary School Certificate Examination (NPSCE), which helps placement at the JSS, at the end of which they take the Basic Education Certificate Examination (BECE). This, together with students' continuous assessment score and their profile put together by guidance counsellors, determines placement in SSS or another educational option. The JSS curriculum consists of nine core subjects – English Language, Mathematics, Integrated Science, Social Studies, Physical and Health Education, French, Agricultural Science, a Sierra Leonean Language, Religious and Moral Education. These are compulsory for all students.

Pre-vocational electives

The vocational subjects are Introductory Technology, Electronics, Local Crafts, Home Economics and Business Studies. Two non-vocational subjects are Arabic and Creative Arts. For BECE, a candidate must take all nine core subjects and three others, of which at least two must be pre-vocational subjects.

Senior secondary school

The curriculum of the SSS is wider in scope. It consists of six core subjects and a whole list of electives to be offered according to the provision in the school and the needs of the students. The compulsory core subjects are: English Language, Mathematics, a science subject, Agriculture or a vocational or technical subject, Sierra Leone Studies and a Sierra Leonean language. Nearly all the subjects now offered in the 'O' and 'A' levels are in the list of electives. For a pass in the International Senior School Certificate Examination a candidate must offer the six core subjects and two or three electives.

Science Education: A Brief History

In the past 30 years or so, science teaching in developing countries captured the attention of educationalists of many countries. Initially, attention was focused on developing elementary science education programmes. The aim was to introduce young learners to science and also prepare them for formal science teaching at the secondary level. Consideration was given to the possibility of developing junior secondary science programmes utilising indigenous cultural materials such as toys and games and natural phenomena experienced by the individual pupil.

The first major attempt at science curriculum development in Africa in which Sierra Leone participated was conceived in 1960. During the International Conference on Science in the Advancement of New States held at Rehovoth, Israel in 1960, a series of conversations was held between Rev. Solomon Caulker of Fourah Bay College, Sierra Leone and Professor Jerrold R. Zacharias of the Massachusetts Institute of Technology (MIT). These conversations led to a mutual agreement to explore the potential application of modern curriculum development techniques to the educational needs of Africa.

The Caulker-Zacharias conversations led to an initial conference held in MIT's Endicott House in July 1961 out of which evolved the African Primary Science Programme (APSP). The APSP prepared appropriate materials for teaching primary science in the Anglophone African countries that participated in the programme. Local materials such as bamboo sticks and discarded items such as empty tins, jars, bottles and bottle tops were used in developing improvised equipment for primary pupils to experiment with. Teachers' guides were also developed for approximately 50 units, all of them emphasising the use of local materials and natural processes in the environment.

The ripple that APSP generated was felt throughout the English-speaking African countries. By the time APSP metamorphosed into the Science Education Programme for Africa (SEPA), a critical mass of science educators in Africa had been developed. Extensive revision of science education policies with clearly defined goals started emerging in many African countries.

In 1976, the Government of Sierra Leone committed itself to the diversification of the secondary school curriculum. This led to the development of the Core Course Integrated Science (CCIS) for the junior secondary school level. Bockarie (1982) found out that because there was no government policy making the use of CCIS mandatory in all secondary schools, the majority did not use it. Hence it lasted only five years.

In 1983, when the 6-3-3-4 system of education was being planned for all English-speaking West African countries, the Ministry of Education delegated responsibility for developing a national curriculum to the Institute of Education (the arm of the university responsible for curriculum development activities). After a series of meetings, the subject areas agreed on included Language Arts, Science, Social Studies, Mathematics, Home Economics, Agriculture, French and Technical Subjects. The science curriculum proposed was not high technology driven because Sierra Leone was, and still is, not sufficiently economically strong to develop and maintain such a curriculum. Besides, Sierra Leonean children need to be taught science relevant to their situation.

The State of Play

For the past three decades or so, Sierra Leone has been in a state of severe economic depression. This has led to very low teacher morale and the steady deterioration of the standard of science teaching in the country. Teachers do not commit themselves fully to their work in a system that seems to care very little about education. Added to this, many of those who are still left in the system are inexperienced, unqualified and have to deal with overcrowded classes of indisciplined pupils. It is not surprising that their classroom style is one of survival characterised by dependence on the textbook or dictated notes. Teachers have clung tightly to this didactic approach of teaching because it seems the easiest (though not the best) method, given the present circumstances.

Spencer (1993) outlined the problems affecting science education in a declining economy at secondary school level which she observed during four years of teaching practice supervision and informal discussions with student teachers and regular science teachers in different parts of the country. The problems were:

- Lack of adequate textbooks;

- Reading difficulty of the available textbooks;

- Lack of funds to purchase equipment, chemicals and for improvisation of some simple apparatus;

- Overcrowded classrooms, laboratories and timetables;

- Shortage of qualified and trained teachers;

- Pressure of external certificate examinations;

- Lack of co-operation between government and school administrators;

- Lack of motivation among teachers with very low morale and status;

- The use of archaic teaching methods and materials foreign to pupils background;

- Poor attitude of pupils to academic work;

- Prevalence of superstitious beliefs and the general lack of a reinforcing home environment.

If the education system is to fulfill its aim of producing well-rounded Sierra Leoneans capable of successfully interacting and integrating with their physical and social environment, then it is obvious that something needs to be done. The use of indigenous technology in teaching science is one way of solving some of the problems identified. The Sierra Leonean environment is rich in local resources which could be used to teach science, maths and technology in a meaningful way. This chapter is an attempt to draw attention to this and show how our indigenous materials and technologies can be used for this purpose effectively.

Indigenous technology
What is it?
Indigenous technology has been defined as the traditional methods and skills concerned with the production processes which transform locally available materials into products. These products are either for sale or for domestic consumption or use (Amara, 1987).

Makhubu (1988) pointed out that in contemporary literature, indigenous technology is referred to as the techniques and practical skills and crafts which are rooted in local traditions and customs passed on from one generation to another. In this discussion, the expression 'indigenous technology' is used to denote the traditional methods and skills used in the production processes in cottage industries in Sierra Leone.

A survey of rural technology by Cole and Hamilton (1978) revealed that in Sierra Leone there is a vast array of rural technologies. Among other things, this survey identified the range of available indigenous technologies that could be employed in attempting to develop new science curricula for primary and secondary schools and also showed that children (school-going or not) are involved in carrying them out. These indigenous technologies have been organised into the following classification:

Food Technology – fish, oil, salt, foofoo and so on;

Clothing Technology – country cloth wearing, gara, and ronko dyeing;

Household Technology – soap, charcoal processing and so on;

Metal Technology – such as coal pots and farm implements;

Trap Technology – wild animals, fishing;

Bamboo Cane Technology – furniture;

Construction Technology – thatch house and bamboo fronds woven into sheets.

This classification has been based upon the most important materials used in the technology, or the use that is made of the technology. For the purpose of curriculum development, these technologies are classified according to the scientific processes they exemplify.

Technologies exhibiting chemical processes are: extraction of vegetable oils and salt; manufacture of soap, lubi, snuff, dyes and dyeing; and charcoal processing and metal working.

Technologies exhibiting physical processes are exhibited in construction processes – house-building, canoe and trap building – and in hunting, fishing, weaving and drawing water.

Technologies exhibiting biological processes are: foofoo (pounded fermented cassava), garri (parched, grated cassava) and ogiri (fermented sesame seeds) processing; palm wine tapping and distillation of local spirits; fish farming and fish preservation; and rice parboiling.

Technologies exhibiting mathematical concepts are: measurements of weights and volumes in chemical processes; lengths in physical processes; and time and statistical data in biological processes.

Why Indigenous Technology?

It is certain that the world will eventually be dominated by modern technology and therefore it would appear to be a retrograde step to be advocating the use of indigenous technology in the new millennium for teaching mathematics, science and technology. Nevertheless, indigenous technology is still widely used in Sierra Leone and therefore constitutes an important part of a large majority of the students' (both rural and urban) environment and lifestyle. It is important to introduce at an early age the idea that what is indigenous is not static but can be modified in order to improve its efficiency and productivity. If our schools are to impart basic, relevant and usable knowledge, this area cannot be ignored because with indigenous technology, the starting points for learning are real, everyday activities and problems that have science and technology components, instead of starting with abstract concepts and processes.

When studied by students, indigenous technology will exemplify scientific, mathematical and technological principles and processes. Although questions have been raised regarding the fact that some of the chemical and biochemical processes involved with local materials and processes will be too complex and not understood by 12–14-year-old students, the usefulness of such materials for instructional purposes have been investigated by Cole (1979) and Spencer (1993). In the modules on energy based on the 'coalpot' (a locally constructed charcoal metal stove) and 'Gara', Spencer showed how indigenous technology deals with issues that are relevant to society in addition to science and technology concepts. For example, in the module on energy, pupils leaned about:

- Science concepts, such as forms and sources of energy, heat transfer and loss, and energy transformation;

- Mathematical concepts, such as measurements of time, volume and weight, percentages and the need for accurate repetition;

- Technology processes, such as determining the efficiency of various models of coalpots, and the design and construction of an energy-saving model;

- Environmental concepts, such as the effects of tree-cutting and burning on the environment and wildlife, and the efficient use of energy and fuels.

She further revealed the potential for further development of these indigenous materials as a base for industrial exploitation. The elementary treatment of these local technologies and materials will motivate both the primary and secondary pupil in learning the sciences, mathematics and introductory technology because indigenous technology can provide pupils with opportunities to:

- Identify problems with local interest and impact;
- Use local resources (human and material) to provide information that can be used to solve problems;
- Extend their learning beyond lesson time, classroom and the school to their communities;
- Develop a certain amount of autonomy in their learning, particularly as they identify individual issues.

This approach is therefore a conscious attempt to allow pupils to become actively involved in the process of learning, instead of passively receiving the teacher's flow of information.

Supporting the inclusion of indigenous technology in both the formal and informal education programmes, Chaytor (1991), a well-known Sierra Leonean scientist and science educator, said:

At the base of every indigenous technology, there is a science, the proper understanding of which permits the mastery, adaptation and improvement of the technology. Education should promote the understanding of the relevant science so as to nurture ingenuity, innovation and improvisation.

There is no doubt that indigenous technology, by providing settings and opportunities for considering basic science, technology (reinforcing mathematical) concepts and processes at the same time, has the potential to help pupils develop the necessary scientific and intellectual skills that they have been deprived of in the traditional teacher-dominated learning situations that usually lead to rote learning.

Finally, the value of using indigenous technology can also be seen in the light of current trends in science education. Thus it links science with technology; it places science in a social context and provides opportunities to introduce issue-based studies. And by associating pupils' conceptual development in science with their commonplace understanding, it enables the values of a constructivist approach to teaching to be exploited.

Indigenous Technology and Science and Maths Teaching

How does indigenous technology fit into all this? The familiarity and the local nature of the materials and processes being explored will enable children to understand elementary scientific, mathematical and technological principles which would be difficult to comprehend if they were foreign to their experience or merely elaborated for direct delivery in the traditional teaching manner.

Maruping (1976) taught reactions of acids and bases to groups of secondary school pupils in Bo and Taiama in Sierra Leone using potassium hydroxide and Sierra Leone 'lubi' (a vegetable-derived material) as bases. She concluded that although lubi was a local material with apparently more impurities than the imported laboratory reagent, the effectiveness of the reactions was the same for both substances. Lubi had all the properties of a base and the quality of conceptualisation by the pupils was high compared with that achieved when imported materials were used.

The use of indigenous technology and materials to study science, mathematics and technology offers pupils an opportunity to carry out the scientific processes of observation, data collection and recording, computing and making generalisations. In terms of acquisition of scientific knowledge, pupils do not miss out on anything they should know at a particular level. In Forms 1, 2 and 3, some of the concepts specified in their science and mathematics syllabuses can be taught using the indigenous technologies set out in Table 17.2.

Table 17.2: Indigenous Technology and the Various Concepts Involved

Indigenous Technology
'Omole' (local gin) production
Salt and oil extractions
Extracting and drying materials
Food production ('foofoo', 'ogirie', 'ogi', fish processing)
Gara dyeing
Coal pot – construction and use
Charcoal processing

Scientific Concepts/Processes
Distillation solutes, solvents solubility and solutions
Density
Evaporation, filtration
Fermentation, osmosis, microbiological actions – bacterial, enzymatic, fungal
Colours, oxidation, solar energy, rainbow
Properties of metals, energy, heat transfer/loss
Fuel and burning in a limited supply of air
– co
– co^2

Mathematical Concepts/Processes
Measurement – weight
Volume, time
Length,
Temperature, quantities, ratios
Proportions
Geometrical shapes
Percentages, statistical analysis

Technology Concepts/Processes
Technology process
Efficiency of system
Structures, strength of materials
Conservation
Recycling – compost production and use (organic farming)

Environmental Educational Concepts
Pollution
Deforestation – erosion

In Form 3 (JSS 3), pupils can be taught fermentation, microbiological action and oxidation. Pupils can carry out small-scale investigations on the suitability of materials used, and ways of improving conditions and processes. Measurements and tests can be done in all instances and data recorded for analyses and where appropriate reagent tests can be done in impure and purified materials to determine reactions with reagents and changes that take place with purification.

For each indigenous technology listed in Table 17.2, concepts can be taught from science, mathematics, technology and environmental education. Take 'Omole' (local gin) production, for example. A teacher can teach about distillation, vaporisation and condensation, measurement of volume and temperature, efficiency of the production system, cost-effectiveness, fuel types and their use, pollution and the effects of deforestation.

On the whole, the table shows that indigenous technology is not about single concepts, as science and mathematics are. It is about multiple concepts, including a combination of science concepts and concepts from other disciplines.

Indigenous Technology and Technology Teaching

In this discussion, technology is seen as any method, thought process or idea (however small) that leads to a better state of affairs. The focus is not so much on the invention of new machinery and equipment, but on the skills, abilities, knowledge, system and processes necessary to make things happen. The technology used in indigenous technology has been evolved by people in their particular locality to solve their own problems.

The introduction of technology as a subject into the general education system in Sierra Leone has been hampered by such things as lack of qualified staff, facilities, the necessary policy and time-tabling difficulties in the system itself. Nevertheless, indigenous technology and the rich collection of cultural objects with scientific bases could serve as valuable starting points for the introduction of technological skills. The technology used in the indigenous practice being studied should be identified and understood before pupils are given an opportunity (in the form of projects or problems) to see what improvements can be made.

From the indigenous technologies that involve construction of devices, pupils will learn to recognise common patterns of structure and interactions and attempt to explain such patterns. Hypotheses will be formulated and tested and experiments will be performed through actual pupil activities using indigenous materials, thus linking what is familiar in the child's environment with the new scientific or technological knowledge and understanding that is to be acquired. These objects and processes can also, by themselves, serve as problems for investigation.

The design and construction of artefacts should be studied as and when the need arises. The following questions could be used as guides for pupils:

Is the construction of an artefact necessary? What should be constructed? How is it to be made? How does it or will it work? This aspect of the work has two dimensions: an intellectual aspect that involves the design of the artefact, which calls for creativity; and a practical aspect that calls for imagination, initiative, manual dexterity and form and detail recognition, as well as planning and organisation. Technology, whatever its form, has basically these two dimensions.

Introducing Indigenous Technology into the Syllabus

Two approaches can be used. The first is the inclusion of indigenous technology as a subject, as is currently being done at the Young Women's

Christian Association (YWCA) Vocational Institute in Freetown. The second is to integrate it into the science syllabus.

In Sierra Leone, because the science syllabus is organised on the following themes – science and society, matter, energy, universe, continuity and change – the latter approach is likely to be favoured. After examination of the five themes, the author concluded that only continuity and change was not suitable for integrating indigenous technology. Integrating indigenous technology into the current science syllabus will allow co-ordination between themes, make cross-curricular and interdisciplinary approaches more meaningful, and will also provide opportunities for understanding the role that science and technology can play in helping to identify and resolve local problems.

Teaching methodologies

The recommended teaching strategies are child-oriented and activity-based and can be achieved through projects, follow-up activities, field trips and the involvement of non-teaching resource persons from the community. Guided discovery method is advocated with suggestions for (learning) activities to be done in the classroom, laboratory, outdoor and in the community. Teachers are encouraged to adapt the materials to the needs and abilities of their pupils. It is also worth noting that for this level (Forms 1–3), no elaborate or sophisticated laboratory facilities are needed. Pupils will look at ways of applying scientific, mathematical and technological principles to solving problems from their homes, local community and hopefully from the nation as well.

The roles of the teacher in indigenous technology

The majority of Sierra Leonean children are familiar with some aspects of indigenous technology. Rural children and a majority of their urban counterparts are familiar with both the processes and the products. However, a majority of urban children are more familiar with the products than the processes. This means that the children already have ideas about the subject and this may have a major influence on learning. Teachers should, therefore, devise a methodology to ascertain the particular ideas children hold. In this way the teacher assumes the role of a 'diagnostician'. Freyberg and Osborne (1985) explain that, in order to diagnose children's existing knowledge, teachers must provide plenty of opportunities for pupils to express their ideas, whether in small groups or whole class settings. But this alone is not enough. Teachers need to ensure a classroom climate where children's ideas are valued and listened to. The teacher can also diagnose pupils' framework of ideas by analysing not only their incorrect answers to questions in class and examinations but also their reports on laboratory work based on indigenous technology or devices.

In addition, the teacher must take on the role of a guide to enable pupils to link their experiences with indigenous technology to accepted scientific ideas. The teacher as a guide should provide pupils with many examples and applications of science to indigenous technological processes and materials. The teacher should also encourage further elaboration of the idea by having pupils consider it from a number of points of view, both as individuals and in small groups.

Assessment

Assessment is an issue that is bound to raise questions in relation to the inclusion of indigenous technology in the curriculum. This is because teachers and pupils alike recognise that assessment procedures reflect the goals of teachers and school, and that many pupils put their best efforts into activities that will be rewarded. In addition, from the kinds of activities involved in different indigenous technologies, some people may find it easy to assess in the psychomotor domain only and may have difficulty determining how overall assessment can be done.

However, through the work of Cole (1979) and Spencer (1993) who used achievement tests, laboratory performance tests and project reports, it can be seen that in assessing pupils' cognitive achievement, it will be necessary to determine their:

◆ Recognition of different classes of materials, their interactions with other substances and the products of such interactions;

◆ Applications of scientific principles in certain situations involving indigenous technological processes;

◆ Ability to solve problems related to indigenous technology processes.

In the domain of affective behaviour it will be necessary to ascertain:

◆ The level of pupils' interest in science as shown by the readiness to discuss scientific matters related to local technology, environmental conservation and topics of local or international relevance;

◆ Pupils' enjoyment and willingness to carry out activities related to the course;

◆ Pupils' recognition of problems of scientific interest out of school, at home or in interaction with peers;

♦ Pupils' increasing understanding and pride in indigenous technology and cultural practices.

Conclusion

Some teachers and educationalists see indigenous technology as progressive, while others see it as an irrelevant and retrogressive approach to learning science. However, there is no doubt that work and studies done by researchers such as Cole (1979), Makhubu (1988) and Spencer (1993) show that pupils enjoy it and have been able to understand certain scientific, mathematical and technological concepts better. Indigenous technology has been found not only to enrich teaching by providing variety in what would have been 'chalk and talk' lessons, but also to enhance teacher-pupil relationships.

Every country has its own indigenous technology that can be researched and used in the classroom as a basis for the teaching of science, mathematics and technology, using the Sierra Leonean mode. This will not only be a step in demystifying science, mathematics and technology, but will add to the preservation of the country's cultural heritage. In this way, society is brought into the classroom in ways that will subsequently make learning more relevant to the everyday experience of the child.

To achieve this, teachers should be provided not only with the necessary teaching materials but also be given in-service and pre-service training, because a change of approach is necessary if a good job is to be done.

18. Using Television to Promote Science and Technology

Professor Marian Addy

Department of Biochemistry, University of Ghana, Legon, Ghana

The National Science and Mathematics Quiz Programme, a weekly nationally televised quiz show in science and mathematics, debuted in 1994 and is now in its seventh consecutive year. The programme was initially intended to encourage and assist students in the country's Senior Secondary Schools (SSS) in their learning of mathematics and science. However, the audience includes practically everybody, both in and out of the formal school system. During the programme, which is approximately one hour long, two schools compete by answering questions in biology, chemistry, mathematics and physics. There are three contestants from each school and any of the contestants can answer the question put to the school.

It all started on a tennis court among members of the Legon Tennis Club. Club members discuss matters of importance to the welfare of the state when they gather after each practice for the 'second phase' of the tennis game. They also try to help one another. So when one member, now the Managing Director of Primetime Limited, producers of the televised programme, informed the club that he was starting an advertising company with education in mind, those of us who had ears to hear felt that we ought to try and help him become established. One way of helping was to come up with educational programmes that a company or a philanthropist might sponsor. But what type of educational programme and at what level? A few suggestions were made, including a quiz programme in science at the SSS level. One member of the club took upon himself to develop the concept into a programme. What we see on television now differs very little from his original design.

That the programme is sponsored by industry is worth noting because production of the programme is expensive. The title of the programme, when it was originally conceived, had the name of one of the products of the sponsor. The sponsor admitted an increase in sales of the product, even though its price kept going up. The Ministry of Education is pleased enough with the programme to send representative at the highest levels, including deputy ministers and directors of education, to recordings of the final programme. On one occasion, the Minister of Education himself came.

There are prizes for each contestant (cash and goods), and not only for those in the winning school. The teachers of the schools that enter the semi-final stage also receive prizes. The winning school and the runner-up receive handsome prizes in laboratory equipment or other supplies specified by the school and, finally, the winning school really feels proud. During the first three years of the competition, one school won twice, and the school had T-shirts printed to that effect, 'Two time winners of the Brilliant Science and Math Quiz Programme'. Old Boys or Old Girls Associations of the various secondary schools, which are often influential organisations, are eager to see their schools win and have contributed to the success of the programme.

The popularisation aspects have to do with what the out-of-school public learns from the programme, as well as what students learn. Students who do not compete also benefit. Some schools gather students around a television set, and particular students are detailed to take down certain questions and their answers so that these can be used as study guides. Of the five rounds of competition, one round is devoted to questions that relate to science in our daily lives. Viewers who are out of the formal school system appreciate this. Another round that seems to appeal to viewers out of the formal school system deals with 'riddles' during which both scientific and non-scientific clues are given, and the two schools compete as they try to be the first to come up with an answer to the riddle. This round is different because, unlike in the other rounds, the first school to come up with a solution to the riddle wins marks and the other school gets nothing. With the other rounds of competition, each school has its own questions and so the scores can be close.

Why the SSS level? We argued that primary school and JSS science was not at a level that would whip up enthusiasm among the general audience. Science at the university level was too advanced for the same general public. The choice was the second cycle of educational institutions. Many programmes were considered and the final choice was a weekly television quiz in science and mathematics.

I have always had an interest in encouraging females to excel in whatever they choose to do. I felt that this encouragement was necessary because societal pressures can easily influence their choices. If a female is interested in mathematics or science, she should be encouraged to pursue her interest in those fields. I cannot overemphasise the encouragement provided by role models of any kind. Unfortunately, there are not many female scientists to play that role in Ghana. Therefore, when I was asked to be the hostess of the programme, there was no way I could say 'no', even though I had not thought of being a television hostess.

Extracurricular activities necessarily take some of the time that I would normally devote to my work at the university, that is, teaching, and laboratory research. I cannot get away from teaching students, which is my primary responsibility, and invariably my laboratory research work suffers when I have to give up some of my time. I love the laboratory so I normally become grouchy when I am away from it. However, I have not regretted spending this time away from the laboratory because of the benefits and the success of the programme. I was not enthusiastic about being the quiz mistress. I preferred the term 'hostess', but I was ruled out and told, in no uncertain terms, that mistress was the proper terminology in these matters.

What were our expectations when we drew up the programme and finally got the 'green light' to go ahead? We did not know what to expect even after we had recorded all the contests for the first competition for schools in the southern sector of the country. We had to see the first contest on the television screen before we became sure that it was a good thing. We were all happy with the very first contest. The programme aimed to encourage the study of science by institutionalising a healthy competition between schools. We were also thinking of a type of programme that would educate the general public and help promote a public understanding of mathematics and science. We, that is the people involved in putting together the programme, were hoping that it would be successful. However, I must confess that the success of the programme has exceeded our expectations. Everybody watches it. By 'everybody' I mean scientists and non-scientists, the young and the old, the well-educated and not-so-well-educated, men and women, primary school boys and girls, and those out of school.

How do I know that everybody is watching? I am amazed at the number of school children in school uniform who point at me and shout or whisper to their friends, 'There goes Professor Ewurama Addy'. In the first year of the programme, I walked into my hairdresser's salon one day and one of the trainees there exclaimed, 'I was right after all. As soon as I saw her, I said to myself "our salon created this hairstyle"'.

My own colleagues in the university sometimes stop me, congratulate me and point out some imperfections when they do occur. I am reminded of the time when a physics colleague stopped me to let me know that I had given a raw deal to one of the schools in a contest. The answer the contestant had given was correct but because I was not familiar with the units that he used, I thought the answer was wrong and had passed the question on to the other school that used the units with which I was familiar. The situation was analogous to my saying 'no' to an answer of 36 inches and 'yes' to one of 3 feet! Unfortunately, my physics consultant was not present to help me. Fortunately, the contest was so one-sided that there was no argument as to who should have won. Such comments are extremely helpful as they help improve the quality of the programme. We cannot afford to give incorrect answers.

I have been stopped many times by people I do not know saying 'I know you from somewhere'. I ask them if they watch television and they congratulate me, bless me and ask for the good work to continue. Of course, there are those who stop me to tell me that I was responsible for their school losing a particular contest, but these are friends and therefore I do not think I need a danger allowance from the producers and sponsors of the programme. There have been occasions when people have approached me requesting that I help them to find a job because I have been urging them to stay in science, they have done so, they have obtained degrees and need science-based jobs. One student wanted me to be his guardian in school which meant commenting on his school report and helping him make progress. I was delighted at that request but not at another request from a student who wanted to be my son and was transferring to come and live with me (his parents had already approved his move, he wrote). I cannot even begin to write about the nature of the letters that I have received and the various sources from which they come.

Some lessons have come from the reactions of the public to the programme and my own observations. What are these?

People want their children to be educated. They want their children to learn mathematics and science. Students want to learn and to excel. The old boys and girls are very proud of their alma mater when their schools win or do well.

Some students are so bright that you cannot help but feel good when you are with them. So what do we do for the outstanding students? One of our sponsors has a programme that accepts students into any of its industrial establishments during the holiday period. Perhaps it would not be a bad idea for the Ministry of Education to think of mounting a programme that would challenge the brightest and the best of our youth during the school holidays.

Throughout the competition, the schools balloted for their opponents, as well as the order in which they would appear in the competition. They even balloted for which side of the quiz mistress they would sit. During the first year of competition, a woman stopped to tell me of her 7-year-old daughter's prediction of who was going to win a contest. The girl had noticed that winning schools were the ones that sat on my left! Actually, for the first seven contests during the first year of competition, the schools on my left won consecutively. I guess the 'spell' was broken because the young girl talked about it. She should have kept the information to herself! The following week, the school on my right won.

Some schools won or lost because of their opponents; they could have lost or won if they had a different opponent. But that is life! Sometimes things appear to be unfair. Sometimes, I am accused of being biased and intentionally giving easy questions to contestants from some schools. I could not do that even if I wanted to, which is out of the question. All the questions for the competition are set before we start the competition. The questions for a contest are collated, enveloped and labelled with the number of the contest. We keep this arrangement so strictly that should a school not compete for whatever reason and we miss a contest, that envelope of questions is not used. There is no way that I, or anybody else, would know which questions are to go to which school. The comments from some of my schoolmates when my own school lost miserably were the most interesting: 'Marian, you mean you sat there and mediated a contest in which St. Monica lost so terribly? How could you? You mean you couldn't do ANYTHING about it? Come on!' No, I couldn't do anything about it. Even if I could, I would not. This programme is planned as a healthy competition to encourage our students to learn and stay with mathematics and science. Honesty is essential. There will be no unfairness and no cheating, and certainly not from any of the people responsible for putting together the meat of the competition for as long as we are associated with the programme.

The audience probably does not notice that the contestants argue with me when they have lost a point or two. I do not dismiss their claim to being right. I merely go over the question and answer, and explain to them why they are wrong, if they are wrong. A few times it has been my mistake, in which case I make the necessary correction. I have to be sure of what I am saying and the basis for my argument when I argue with contestants. So yes, for every contest I know the answers to all the questions and not only that, I know how the answers were arrived at. This is the only way that I can explain to students why they are wrong when they are wrong. It has been a lot of work but it has paid off because those young people out there are not merely going to accept that they are wrong because I say so. I think that is a good stand to take. I have to show them why I am right and they are wrong. Science has nothing to do with age; you should be able to show that your professor is wrong, if (s)he is wrong. In the same vein, I have to have a good reason for giving a school one or two out of three instead of the full mark.

It is interesting to note a few of the incredible things that some schools would go through just to win. Here is a confession from a headmaster who told me that he, together with some students and masters, were not present to cheer the contestants from their school in a final contest. Where were they? In 'prayer cells' during the whole period that their school was competing – they prayed for their school to win. Well, his school won that particular contest, but as to whether the victory was by divine intervention or the preparedness of the contestants, I will leave to the reader to decide. If I am asked, the God that I know will not let me win over someone who has been studying harder and is better prepared for an encounter than I am, merely because I pray and (s)he does not. We must keep body and soul together and not develop one at the expense of the other.

Overall, boys were much more confident than girls, and it did not matter to them who their opponents were. I remember our first competition for the northern sector schools. The very first contest was between Prempeh College, which won the national championship that year, and my old school, Saint Monica's Secondary School. The girls from Saint Monica's lost the contest even before it began, simply because they lacked confidence. As soon as they realised that they were going against the boys from Prempeh College, they gave up. They would not even put their fingers on the bell to try and ring it when they felt they knew the answers to the riddle! The boys from Prempeh just rolled over them. At the end of the contest I had to talk to them about being confident. The girls would probably have lost anyway, but at least, they should have put up a fight. Saint Louis Secondary School, a different girls' school, appeared to have a lot of confidence the first time we went to Kumasi, but it could be because they were certain that they would beat the school they were competing against.

That boys have more confidence than girls is nothing new. However, if we are to encourage all to excel in their chosen fields, then we may have to have programmes geared at building the confidence of girls who would like to pursue the sciences. Somehow, we have to let them know that they can do it, because they can do it. We need to develop the capabilities of all, including the females, to the fullest for the nation to derive maximum benefit from the expenditure on education. As has been pointed out, women are among the leading new forces on the international scene and the prospect of their full participation in society at all levels is one of the main hopes for a better order in world affairs. If we do not find ways for their full participation, we will be wasting close to 50 per cent of the human ingenuity that we require for our development.

Schools that participated in the programme were selected according to their performance in mathematics and science and in the examinations set by the West African Examination Council in the recent past, taking into consideration regional representation and gender balance.

The programme has done what it set out to do, arousing interest in mathematics and science and urging the students to learn. Students have been motivated to study and excel in mathematics and the sciences, but to what end? What good is it to have students studying and excelling in mathematics and science? Should we even encourage students to study the subjects?

Everybody recognises that economic growth and development depend on science and technology. This science and technology-led development requires innovation that is related to the local environment in such a way that value is added to what already exists. The time is past when economic growth and development depended on natural resources, or capital, or sheer numbers of an unskilled workforce. In today's world, technological innovation and economic growth are determined by the quality of human resources. Capacity building in mathematics and science will provide this quality in personnel that we require. We need qualified personnel for all our industries, small, medium and large scale, if we are to make any advances.

For every discipline, there are a critical number of people required to allow for the necessary interaction and benefit accruing from studying that discipline. We just do not have that critical number in mathematics and the sciences. We need to build capacity to benefit from it. As we enter the twenty-first century, especially now that the Cold War has ended, the distinction is no longer between first, second and third world countries. It is between countries that have science and technology (S&T) and those that do not. The gap between the haves and the have-nots keeps widening since the have-not countries have not put in place the necessary structures for capacity building in S&T locally.

It is important that capacity building is local because that is the only way to have peculiarities in both human and material resource development, peculiarities that give comparative advantage, another important rung in the ladder of development. Without trained personnel available locally, foreign investors, who are coming in through the 'globalisation' door, may come and establish their business but they will bring the skilled labour with them. If the only thing we can provide is unskilled labour in large numbers, we will not achieve development. Our people will still be at the bottom of the social structure. Let me stress again that it is human ingenuity that is important for the development of a country, and not large amounts of unskilled labour, capital or even natural resources.

Putting the necessary structures in place is only one of the requirements for successful solutions to problems of capacity building and the development of our S&T. The other requirements are that scientists must be employed and paid well so that they have job satisfaction and stay in the job. Poorer remuneration compared to that of colleagues in other sectors is what compels science students to leave the sciences. They switch because they see their colleagues in other institutions in the service sector doing far better financially than themselves. We cannot blame them when they leave. We must use our scientists and pay them well.

But what should we use our scientists for? We need scientists for the development of improved ways of doing things in industry, as well as in the service sector. We need them in health care delivery, in nutrition and in agriculture. Development of a country may be measured by the quality of its goods and services. When quality assurance is part of an industrial establishment, the products are better and they sell, locally and abroad. Let us make it a part of our culture to employ scientists as quality control managers or consultants who demand quality products. We may also engage scientists in research and development to improve our products, be it increased production, new products, new processing technique, use of a different material base and even for basic science from which new ideas can proceed. We simply cannot continue to do things the way we have always done them and merely hope that one day we will develop.

The use of scientists should proceed in two ways in opposite directions. Industries and other organisations and institutions should be able to go to the scientists with their problems, potential problems or desire for improvements and request that these be addressed. The necessary resources must be put in place. On the other hand, scientists should be able to approach industry and similar organisations and institutions and present them with proposals about what they can do to help. Of course, the proposal must be of direct benefit to these organisations that are there primarily to make money. The relationship may start on a small scale and lead to better and bigger things for both parties.

In developing countries, scientists who are engaged in local industries ought to regard themselves as pioneers or ambassadors. They should therefore do their best to gain the trust and confidence of the few local organisations that can use scientists. If this happens, these organisations will feel confident about entrusting their research and development to local people instead of having it done outside the country. The potential problem is that, because of the poor state of our laboratories, we tend to request quite substantial amounts from these potential funding sources. This tends to push the organisations into thinking that we only want money from them. There is, therefore, a need for our laboratories to be adequately equipped so that the request to these organisations will be of a supplementary nature, at least at the beginning of the relationship.

The National Science and Mathematics Quiz Programme is currently presented on Saturday mornings at 11am GMT. The television station claims that that is the best time for students. I have had quite a number of people complaining to me that they have many chores to do on Saturday mornings, not to mention funerals and weddings, and therefore miss the programme. The original time scheduled was on Wednesday at about 7.30pm – primetime. Since the programme also helps promote a public understanding of science, many viewers are not students. For the adult population, especially women, Saturday mornings are busy periods and many cannot reorganise their weekend programme. The time slot is an important issue to resolve.

Several schools send me word that they would like to participate in the competition. In order to accommodate as many schools as possible, we have made it a policy not to invite schools that lost during the preliminary rounds unless they did very well and lost with high marks, thus creating room for schools that have not participated to be able to do so. So many schools are keen to participate, not realising that it may not be as easy as it seems to score high marks on the programme. The only school from my home town to participate had no points at the end of the first round of their contest. I am sure the school is not in any hurry to come back to the television screen. You may think it is easy when you are sitting in the comfort of your home watching the programme. My people have a saying: 'annko bi a, ese woanko' ('because you were not among the fighters, you are saying they did not fight gallantly').

The success of the programme has been due to a number of reasons. I very much appreciate the togetherness, the co-operation, team spirit and keenness shown by my team of consultants. Any woman would welcome working with these respectful and respectable men. We have worked hard together and have had so much fun doing so. My seamstress and hairdresser should also be commended for making me appear in such fashion that some people watch the programme only to find out what the quiz mistress is wearing on her body or on her head. We want people to watch, for whatever reason. They will improve their scientific knowledge and be better for it.

Analysis

Though I have written a personal account of my part in the television competition, I think that there are more general lessons to learn. From our experience, nothing has been more important than the part played by those of us who participated in putting the programmes together. I could talk about our dedication and other worthy motives, but the truth is that we all have enormous fun doing it. I am not sure how others who want to replicate our project could ensure this fun, but it will be impossible to take mathematicians and scientists away from their research because of dedication alone, since we already feel that our research has the greatest importance to national development. However, contrary to popular belief, researchers love having fun. Whether in other situations the initiative for such programmes comes from academics who then persuade the media, or whether the initiative comes from the media who then persuade the academics, will depend on country contexts, but the appeal must include having fun.

Originally, we thought of students as the target audience. Luckily for us we realised early on that the programme had an enormous potential to promote an understanding of mathematics and science among a much larger audience. On reflection, I believe that this is another important underlying principle to which others desiring to replicate this use of television should adhere – that is, to use students to reach a much wider audience. Of course, I can think of no reason why radio producers who reach a much wider audience than television cannot use the same programme format.

It takes a long time to put a series of programmes together. A general principle that I wish that our production staff had adhered to was providing us with a comfortable retreat for a few days far from the reach of our offices and families so that we could work in peace.

Finally, I am not sure why we have not encouraged other firms to sponsor my coiffure, clothing and beauty products, and be acknowledged in the programme's end titles. Distasteful as I might find doing this at a personal level, just as I agreed to be 'mistress', so I would agree to be exploited in this way if it brought the programme more money. Then, perhaps, they would agree to send us on retreats, increase the prize money, even donate some funds to the Ghana Association of Science Teachers that conducts some excellent projects but are always short of funds.

PART IV

19. A Synthesis

Prem Naidoo
African Forum for Children's Literacy in Science and Technology
University of Durban-Westville, South Africa

Introduction

Science and technology are recognised as key drivers for soci-economic development and Commonwealth countries have recognised the need for their popularisation. This chapter critically re-examines why this need exists; the current state of popularising science and technology in different Commonwealth countries; and the arguments for Commonwealth governments to co-operate and initiate a systemic and effective approach to popularising science and technology in their respective countries.

The Growing Need – Why Popularise Science and Technology?

It is widely acknowledged that science and technology play an important role in the development of a country's economy, environment and social relations. An understanding of S&T is essential for coping with facts, principles, material technologies and practices, and social forces that shape our world. These factors help to define the circumstances of individuals and communities, and eventually determine their possibilities for further development. Development theorists often cite orientation towards a scientific and technological way of life as one of the main indicators of sustainable modernisation and development. Moreover, advances in science and technology have dictated the pace of development, degree of inequality, and change within and across countries, and continue to do so.

In the coming years, the pace of change will quicken. Change will impinge on all citizens, young and old and rich and poor, and much of the change will involve new technologies that will influence living conditions and the environment. To adjust to such change, a new flexible science education will be required to enable coming generations to deal with social decisions that relate to issues concerned with technology and science. Citizens are faced, more than ever before, with decisions about issues of public policy – food and health security, nuclear energy and the disposal of waste, invasive medical technologies, gender identification of embryos, care for the environment, AIDS, organ donation, the list is endless. Without some familiarity with the scientific concepts that underlie such issues and how science views evidence, it is impossible for citizens of a democratic regime to take part in its decisions.

Denying them this right to participate in government, and to determine the future developments of their country and that of the Commonwealth, negates the current plan of action on the Jomtien Declaration of Education for All. Hence there is a need for all citizens to be scientifically and technologically literate through all stages of their lives. Following the Jomtien Declaration in 1995, UNESCO has endorsed the call for *science and technology literacy for all*. However, few citizens within the Commonwealth are scientifically and technologically literate. Thus, popularising science and technology will help the realisation of this central need and aspiration. Here popularisation carries several meanings. It means the spread of scientific and technological knowledge to the masses, the acquisition of new science and technology for improving one's social and economic life, and the sceptical, questioning, problem solving frame of mind characteristic of science and technology.

The Growing Gap – The Current State of Popularising S&T

The Commonwealth is made up of both industrialised and developing countries. It includes 13 of the world's fastest growing economies and 14 of the world's poorest, with a high degree of correlation between the state of the of these countries economies and the level of science and technology development. In the past all Commonwealth countries used formal education structures to popularise science and technology.

Great progress has been made in these formal education systems through curriculum reform and with innovative ways of presenting S&T. However, formal scientific and technological knowledge in most developing countries remains beyond the public domain, particularly for girls and women, and it is largely the preserve of elites. Indeed the expansion of S&T has been such that even amongst the educated elites of industrialised countries, specialisation means they can only lay claim to certain facets of S&T knowledge. Consequently, the majority of human beings in the world continue to live in relative ignorance about the forces, principles, phenomena and technologies that shape their lives. As important, few have received an education that familiarises them with the rules of evidence so central to the practice and understanding of science and technology that are essential to making appropriate decisions and judgments.

The issue then is how far formal education in S&T can influence the everyday thinking and actions of the general population. Can we cultivate a genuine popular scientific and technological culture by changing the school curriculum and the way in which we present S&T to learners? Do we need to combine this approach with other strategies for success or are we simply barking up the wrong tree?

In the last two decades science and technology have become increasingly popularised through non-formal and informal structures. In the last decade this has accelerated in industrialised countries, with scattered efforts in developing countries including. Commonwealth countries. However, the capacity to popularise science and technology, that ironically is key to narrowing the wealth gap with industrialised countries, is more limited in developing countries.

Developing countries recognise the role of informal structures and many have committed considerable resources to the development of their science and technology, and their educational systems. In the early 1960s, immediately after independence, most African Commonwealth countries promoted capacity building in science and technology by sending scholars for training in universities in industrialised countries, while offering science and technology as subjects in their primary and secondary schools. Some invested heavily in development of infrastructure such as national laboratories, and university and school science departments. Similar patterns were followed in many other developing countries in the Commonwealth.

Despite such investment, these countries continue to rely on agrarian and extractive sectors and, in some cases, tourism. The agrarian sector largely consists of subsistence farmers and pastoralists who often cannot produce sufficient excess to meet national needs and exports of cash crops such as coffee, tea and horticultural products. Tourism is dependent on adequate infrastructures and stability, itself dependent on good governance.

Numerous theories are used to explain the underdevelopment of these countries, including a lack of science and technology infrastructures. I argue that much science and technology, and science and technology education, is irrelevant or dysfunctional to the developmental needs of these countries, and that their failing can be ascribed to a lack of understanding of what and whose science and technology system was introduced and promoted. The first assumption made when science and technology was 'introduced' was that no science and technology was practised in developing countries and that the knowledge base and tools for science and technology had to be imported and transplanted. Most scientists were trained in industrialised countries with rich resource infrastructures for research that focused largely on fundamental problems within the scientific disciplines. As a result, scientists and technologists trained in the metropolitan centres could not continue their research when they returned home, and many could not contextualise their research within their country's development needs. Within the industrial sector, little scientific research is conducted because most industries are multinationals that conduct research in the parent companies located in the mother country. Thus development and practice of science and technology is the state's responsibility, and is largely confined to education and training. Over the past decades, economic decline has contributed to a deterioration of government infrastructures for science and technology, promoting a flight of many of the best scientists to developed countries. Furthermore, training of scientists at school and university levels is based on irrelevant curricula that are decontextualised from societal problems and indigenous, informal, and formal sector science and technology practices. Such science is alien to indigenous society; an alienation that is further promoted by rote learning that does not embed science and technology in everyday practice and culture. Thus science and technology are seen as alien, Western bodies of facts that must be memorised and that have no bearing on the improvement of the everyday existence of indigenous people.

For such reasons, I argue that science and technology have not realised their full potential for improving the quality of life for most people in developing countries, though they have contributed, for example, to reducing the incidence of infectious disease, improving agricultural production and better communication and transportation. However, these and other benefits have been better capitalised on in developed countries and will continue to contribute to an accelerated pace of improvement, hence further widening the gap between rich and poor countries. Indeed, developed countries have launched major programmes on 'Science for All' to popularise science in their countries. They have recognised that scientific and technological literacy is a major precondition for continued modernisation, wealth generation and development of a democratic society. They argue that a science and technology culture addresses the need for innovation and problem solving, acquisition of transferable skills, a capacity to think and act rationally in response to new experiences, appreciation of new technological developments and the ethical issues involved in active participation in modern democracies. This renewed interest in science and technology in industrialised countries recognises the role of the local community, state and private sectors in promoting, developing and sustaining a science and technology culture, as well as the comparative edge it gives in the global economy.

Although, to date, science and technology, and science and technology education, have failed developing countries, I emphasise that this has been a science and technology that stresses memorising facts rather than problem solving. To narrow the gap, developing countries also must recognise the need to promote, develop and sustain a culturally sympathetic, problem-solving science and technology culture. Formal education on its own has so far demonstrated its inadequacy (some would even say inappropriateness) to enable S&T to take root in the local cultures of non-Western societies and become an integral part of everyday thinking and action. This has given rise to experimentation with alternative ways of presenting S&T, which resonate with local cultures. A major challenge for non-industrialised Commonwealth countries, therefore, is to develop strategies for promoting an S&T acculturation that enables individuals to realise their own potential, while playing diverse roles in the development of society. This challenge becomes increasingly urgent in the quest to close the development gap.

A recent study by Sjoberg and others (2000) has revealed some interesting trends. A survey undertaken in 22 countries showed that children in developing countries see scientists as caring people who try to solve society's problems, while in developed countries children see scientists as cruel, uncaring people. The study also showed that there is a greater interest among children (both boys and girls) in developing than developed countries in the study of science or in following science careers. The inferences one can draw from this are that:

◆ Popularising S&T among children in developing countries will be easier;

◆ Developed countries have a huge challenge in attracting the next generation to S&T and will need to develop special programmes to target children – otherwise they will lose the gains they have made through the development of S&T.

Increasing strategies to popularise S&T.

Recently, there has been a dramatic increase in the number of strategies to promote S&T, particularly outside formal education and government. I have identified five important sectors that use a variety of strategies to promote S&T, namely government, academy and professional associations, business and labour, civil society and NGOS. I will delineate some of the more significant strategies these sectors use.

Government policy

Almost all Commonwealth countries have developed policies for science and technology, within which the popularising of science and technology is seen as a priority.

Formal education

All governments use formal education, particularly at primary school levels, to popularise S&T and some have initiated programmes at pre-school levels. The formative years of children's development are important in shaping views, attitudes and aptitudes towards science and technology. Some governments are making it compulsory to study some S&T at secondary school level, while some universities have compulsory courses on public understanding of science for all graduates.

Science councils
In Britain, Canada, Australia, New Zealand, India, Malaysia and South Africa, government-sponsored councils that fund and engage in S&T research are obliged to promote popularisation. Some have made it compulsory for researchers to participate in programmes that promote the public understanding of S&T. In South Africa, for example, researchers funded by the National Research Foundation are expected to develop a plan that promotes a public understanding of the science that is integrated with their research project. Some councils have actively participated in science fairs and promoted science competitions and campaigns.

Museums
Most countries use museums as vehicles to popularise S&T. The common strategies they use include permanent, temporary and travelling exhibits; special events; school programmes; workshops and demonstrations; publications and loans; conferences and lectures; expert advice; and joint action with other museums and organisations with similar goals. In some countries, such as Canada, a special Science and Technology Museum has been established. The mission of this museum is to help the public to understand the ongoing relationships between science, technology and Canadian society.

Science centres
Some countries have established science centres that provide opportunities for the public and schools to gain hands-on experience of science. Such centres design exhibits that encourage participants to explore and solve problems. Models show the operation of technology and live demonstrations show natural phenomena. These centres have proved to be popular among adults and children alike.

Events, programmes, competitions and campaigns
The South African government declared 1999 a year of science and technology and planned an extensive campaign to popularise S&T. Together with other stakeholders, the government developed and operationalised an extensive programme that covered both rural and urban areas. The campaign certainly heightened awareness of S&T within the country. For the last ten years, Ghana has run a week-long science camp for girls to popularise S&T

among girls and encourage them to pursue S&T-related careers. Singapore runs a competition for youth to encourage new technological inventions. The Indian government runs a National Children's Science Congress during which children write research papers that are presented to their peers and evaluated by eminent scientists. Many countries sponsor radio and television programmes to popularise S&T. Most government departments run extensive related campaigns, such as the Ugandan health department's campaign on AIDS. In Kenya, the government family planning department has used strategies such as song, dance, poetry, drama and story telling to popularise family planning which has proved effective, since they appeal to the rich oral tradition of most African societies.

Other initiatives
In India, the National Council for Science and Technology Communication (NCSTC) is a national apex body for communication and popularisation. The government Department of Science and Technology set up NCSTC with two broad objectives – to orchestrate and co-ordinate popularisation, and to promote the development of science communicators in the various Indian languages.

Academy and professional associations
In the 1980s, the Royal Society of Scientists in Britain realised they had to become more involved in popularising S&T. Under the leadership of John Ziman, the society embarked on an extensive research and development programme on public understanding of S&T. The British Association for the Advancement of Science organises the successful National Week of Science or the Science Festival. An average of 3000 events are held during this week that draw audiences of up to 2 million and approximately 60 million through a BBC TV special.

Today, in most Commonwealth countries, academy and professional associations such as the Trinidad and Tobago Scientific Association are actively involved in popularising S&T. Generally, the academy and professional associations use similar strategies to those outlined above, including writing for the media and giving public lectures. In some countries, such as Australia, Britain and Canada, scientists are actively encouraged to demystify their research and make it accessible to the general public and to attend special courses that help them develop such skills. Science journalism has become a degree course and career option in some countries. However, the academy should also play another role to evaluate current strategies and develop more effective strategies to popularise S&T. This area has been grossly neglected in most Commonwealth countries and needs urgent attention.

Business and labour

Many industries in the developed countries of the Commonwealth play an active role in popularising S&T. In the main they provide financial resources to sponsor popularisation programmes. More recently, some have developed programmes about the science and technology that is involved in their industries. In Ghana, for example, industrialists work with science educators to produce multimedia curriculum materials that bridge school science and industrial science and technology. Some industries are open for school tours that demystify the science and technology.

In South Africa, the biggest trade union has recognised the role of science and technology within the workplace and has developed education programmes to help workers understand the science and technology behind industrial processes. Similar efforts are planned in Zimbabwe, particularly around AIDS awareness. The potential for labour unions to promote popularisation among workers is an underutilised strategy.

Mass media

Most countries use the mass media to popularise S&T. In developing countries radio is the most accessible media and is being used extensively. Developed countries use TV and the Internet. Dave Chalk's TV Computer Show, for example, is beamed weekly across several countries, including Canada, the USA, Philippines, India, Singapore and Australia, to 70 million viewers. In an entertaining and informative manner, viewers are introduced to the latest hardware and software.

Civil society

Self-initiated interest groups are societies or clubs of individuals that have a mutual interest in a particular area such as bird clubs. These clubs can be made up of individuals from a wide range of occupations and can develop a sophisticated understanding of birds and their environment.

Self-initiated need groups are informal groups of individuals who have the need to understand and cope with a particular issue that affects their friends or family, for example parents of children with Downs Syndrome. These individuals develop a good scientific understanding of Downs Syndrome and in addition develop a good practical understanding of how to care for Downs Syndrome children. They integrate their everyday practices and scientific knowledge so that they optimise their care for their children. In addition, they share experiences with each other and provide mutual emotional support.

Social movements for action and change involve a group of interested or affected persons who try to initiate action for change. Examples of such movements include Greenpeace in Canada and Kerala Sastra Sahitya Parihat (KSSP) in India. Greenpeace is an activist group that uses scientific understanding to prevent the further destruction of the environment. On the other hand, KSSP, with the slogan, 'Science for Social Revolution', is an organisation with diverse activities that cover social services, environmental protection, woman's development, educational reform and scientific methods in agriculture. This group uses scientific knowledge to promote people's empowerment and development. These movements go against the grain of traditional thinking within the scientific community that science is information taught to a group of scientific illiterates. It is interesting to note that more such groups are emerging. The scientific community, governments and business need to take note of this development.

NGOs and other organisations

International NGOs operate in many countries including the Commonwealth. An example of such an NGO is the Wildlife Society that effectively popularises environmental and conservation using a variety of strategies.

Continental organisations operate on a continent and within Commonwealth countries on that continent. An example of such an organisation is the African Forum for Children's Literacy in Science and Technology. AFCLIST's mission is to popularise S&T among children and young people in sub-Saharan Africa. Approximately 70 projects have been initiated in 15 African countries. Projects range from using traditional toys to science camps for girls.

Country organisations operate within a particular country. An example is the NGO Eklavya in India, which has activity centres where children can conduct science experiments, origami, clay modelling, painting and other activities. These clubs spread across a network set up for children. They organise children's fairs, exhibitions, quiz competitions and street theatre.

Towards a Coherent Strategy to Popularise S&T

Commonwealth co-operation

The gap between developing and developed countries within the Commonwealth is widening. S&T is key to decreasing this gap. The development of S&T capability is dependent on popularisation of S&T. Countries within the Commonwealth have evolved a host of effective strategies to popularise S&T and it is important that they learn from each other. It is therefore recommended that the Commonwealth Secretariat should launch a co-operative plan to help all countries popularise S&T.

The corporate plan should include a cataloguing of all effective popularising strategies; publishing and disseminating good practices; providing professional and technical assistance to assist countries develop their plans; training programmes for professionals involved in popularising S&T; and organising workshops and conferences to share experiences on popularising S&T.

National plans

Formal education is no longer the only vehicle to popularise S&T. Increasingly many countries use a variety of strategies and agencies. Although this new development increases the ability to popularise S&T it does not always increase effectiveness. Effectiveness will only increase if all popularising strategies and agencies work within a coherent and co-ordinated framework. Hence there is a need to develop a national plan. Governments must take the initiative and develop plans with the participation of major agencies and stakeholders. These plans must be flexible so that they allow for regional needs and cultural diversity. They should be implemented in a reflexive manner with continuous evaluation and allowance for appropriate implementation adjustments.

Conclusion

The popularisation of S&T in the Commonwealth is key for the development of Commonwealth nations. A variety of strategies and agencies can be used. Their effectiveness is dependent on their fitness and purpose. When one develops strategies for popularising S&T, one has to consider why, how and for which target audience. I have not explored these ideas, but they will need careful consideration. Because there is a need to popularise S&T in all Commonwealth countries, the Commonwealth Secretariat should develop a plan to assist them. However, individual countries need to develop and implement their own national plans in order to optimise the effectiveness of popularising S&T.

20. Towards a Theory of Change: A Postscript for Policy-Makers

Mike Savage
African Forum for Children's Literacy in Science and Technology
University of Durban-Westville, South Africa

Introduction

Do our educational systems continue as they do by design or out of inertia?
I would suggest that the answer is a bit of both. Some of the reasons for this
are financial. Throughout Africa, despite the fact that a significant percentage
of recurrent budgets is spent on education, schooling becomes increasingly
inadequate with the rising demand on available funds. One must then ask why
we continue to support a style of schooling that is demonstrably failing and
that we cannot sustain. Yet education in Africa has seen wave after wave of
attempts to reform the curriculum but they have not had the desired impact.
Perhaps this is because they have been initiated and implemented either by
donor organisations that cannot be expected to fully understand conditions in
Africa and whose professional reference point is international, or by
politicians whose motives are to ensure that they are re-elected. Neither are
adequate motivations.

We must, however, be convinced of the validity of the type of science and
technology, and science and technology education, that we wish to promote.
Chapters 1 and 2 address these issue directly and all the other chapters do so
indirectly. They suggest that from the furthest village to the sophisticated
laboratories in the capital, Africa must become a continent of knowledge
producers rather than consumers. Chapter 3 suggests criteria that the countries
of sub-Saharan Africa could use to develop relevant and productive science
and technology and science and technology education programmes. Africa
needs scientists and technologists working at the most sophisticated level to
solve her economic problems, in the way that Fabiano, Mshigeni and
Mwandemele describe in their account of the establishment of a cassava starch
industry in Malawi (Chapter 4). Africa needs her best technological minds to
work with artisans and village women to transform their practices as described
in the account of projects in Ghana (Chapters 5 and 6). We must question
why educational systems (formal and non-formal) in the countries of sub-Saharan

Africa continue to promote science as a body of knowledge to be taught using non-existent expensive equipment, that is to be memorised and that cannot be used to solve everyday problems. Chapters 11–17 have argued, with detailed anecdotal evidence, that a problem-orientated science and technology can have a deep impact not only on the lives of learners, but also on those of the local community. Does traditional science teaching lead to village households with energy-conserving stoves, evaporation-driven coolers and a better understanding of household medicine as described in Chapter 13? Chapters 4–6 have eloquently demonstrated that this approach to science and technology can contribute significantly to the formal and non-formal sectors of the economy. Chapters 4 (on informal sector consultancy services), 11 (on museums, press and radio) and 18 (on television) have shown that structures other than schools can effectively promote an inquiry approach to science. Chapters 15 (Ghana) and 16 (South Africa) have shown how policy can initiate and support change and a better public understanding of science and technology. AFCLIST is convinced of the benefits which an appropriate science and technology and science and technology education can bring to our continent. Convinced of this, and based on its experience with more than 100 projects in 15 countries over 12 years, AFCLIST has developed a theory of educational change to enable it and others to participate more effectively in the process.

The Theory

The African Forum for Children's Literacy in Science and Technology is committed to educational transformation and feels it has a responsibility to reflect on its 12 years of experience in order to develop a theory or hypothesis of systemic educational change for consideration by educational policy-makers and activists. To effect sustainable educational change and development, AFCLIST considers the following to be critical:

♦ Identification and nurture of innovators

♦ Adding value to innovators and innovation

♦ Extracting value from innovation and innovators

♦ Institutionalising innovation

♦ Providing the catalyst for system-wide change.

Identification and Nurture of Innovators

Africa has enough problems; we see bad teaching at all levels of education and in the informal, as well as the formal, educational system. Perhaps we would be better off looking for the good rather than the bad. Not all teachers will be as talented as the Malawian primary school teacher or the secondary school teacher who established the village environmental centre in Zanzibar (Chapter 12), but without doubt talent there are talented teachers, from those in Chilambo's environmental education project in Malawi (Chapter 13), to the inventive scientists and technologists that have done so much to energise the informal sector in Ghana (Chapters 5 and 6), to the ingenious authors and publishers in far-off Kagera in Tanzania (Chapter 11). Previous chapters in this book have been a litany of praise to Africa's innovators.

We must not, however, expect to find innovation fully formed. We must learn to recognise innovation even when it is a seed. Every innovator described in previous chapters, indeed every author in this publication, began in the smallest way. We and they have grown and developed because we have been professionally nurtured. Whether we are pre-school teachers, university professors or cabinet ministers, how well do we look for and nurture innovation?

An aspect of professional support that AFCLIST encourages is that provided by grantees' colleagues. Though input provided by us 'experts' may be invaluable, we are lucky if we can visit innovators even once a year yet colleagues are met daily. AFCLIST fosters such co-operation with colleagues whenever possible, funding groups rather than individuals. Some school systems, such as that in Zanzibar, have institutionalised such support by establishing appropriate networks of teachers' centres and encouraging professional associations.

As more than one chapter recounting experiences in Ghana, as well as the case study from Swaziland, reported, professionals in the formal and informal sectors of the economy can, when approached properly, provide substantial professional and financial support to innovators at all levels of the educational system. Such support was outstanding in the starch project described by Fabiano. Yet throughout Africa, in-service teacher developers consistently overlook such nurturers of innovation, either calling on their professionalism too late to provide them with an opportunity to mould projects or asking only for financial support. Such sectors are the future employers of school-leavers, have constructive ideas concerning school learning and are frequently more committed to supporting good schooling than they are given credit for.

Perhaps the most important, and certainly the most permanent, group of stakeholders in the ongoing development of schools is the local community, especially the parent body. Certainly gender projects that AFCLIST has supported in Ghana and Zanzibar have demonstrated that lasting impact is achieved only when the local school community is involved, unlike the fleeting impact made by 'girls only' projects such as science clinics. Findings by Naidoo in an unpublished PhD thesis confirm that though outstanding principals or teachers can temporarily change a school's culture, it is only when the culture has been institutionalised by the local community that a culture of innovation become long-lasting.

Adding Value to Innovators and Innovation

Nurturing innovation is, of course, adding value. However, since AFCLIST's experience is that the innovators drive change, their impact will be more significant and lasting the more dedicated, skilled and professional they become. AFCLIST uses a variety of approaches to broaden identified innovators' professionalism and to strengthen their dedication.

One of the strategies AFCLIST uses to add value to innovators is to support a variety of networking activities. These include sponsoring individuals engaged in similar work to make working visits to each other. The Science and Technology in Action in Ghana (STAG) project in Ghana (Chapter 15) and the Linking School Science with Local Industry and Technology (LISSIT) project in Swaziland (Chapter 14) both grew as a result of such visits. Work in mainland Tanzania, Eritrea and in selected island states in the Indian Ocean has similarly been stimulated. Constant encounters with like-minded colleagues from other countries at meetings sponsored by AFCLIST to add value to innovators have further strengthened innovation. AFCLIST has added to the competencies of many of the educators responsible for the projects described above through convening special skills workshops in areas such as print materials production, proposal writing and action-research methodologies that are always task-orientated. AFCLIST considers that the high quality of publications such as those produced by STAG, LISSIT and others described above fully justifies their investment.

Extracting Value from Innovators and Innovation

One invests to receive a return in the future and one must anticipate how to use one's return. AFCLIST deliberately plans how to extract and apply the investment it makes in innovators and innovation and does so even before it makes a grant.

Though AFCLIST's policy when making grants is reactive rather than proactive, it hopes that the work it supports will, at some time in the future, affect national educational systems. By encouraging proposals from teams that represent key institutions, such as curriculum centres, advisory services and examinations councils, AFCLIST's intention is to foster feelings of ownership and increase the likelihood of projects having a national influence. Thus AFCLIST attempts to anticipate the day when it will extract value from its original support for innovation as projects go national. AFCLIST has found that it is critical that all stakeholders are involved in change as early as possible. STAG in Ghana and LISSIT in Swaziland provide examples of such stakeholder involvement.

AFCLIST must also, however, extract value from projects it supports in ways that benefit the African continent and not only their country of origin. Ways that AFCLIST has used to extract value from its investment in innovation include:

♦ Sponsoring project team members to give presentations at key regional and international meetings such as GASAT9 and IOSTE9 during 1999. Cross-country professional connections made at such meetings frequently lead to follow-up work such as the project involving the Malawian primary school teacher described in Chapter 12 and educators from Cameroon, Nigeria and Togo that grew from professional links made at GASAT9.

♦ Strongly encouraging and technically supporting grantees to publish so that others can become familiar with their work. A spin-off benefit of this policy is that writing motivates grantees to become more reflective and analytical about their work. AFCLIST's support has led to many forms of communication by projects from single-page broadsheets targeted at teachers, to sophisticated web sites, to scholarly articles in journals, to seminal books such as ASTE95 and manuals such as that on proposal writing.

Institutionalising Innovation

Although educational systems in the countries of sub-Saharan Africa are almost constantly in a state of change, usually the repeated changes are in response to political or donor insistence. Reform is usually hurried and is a response to some perceived crisis; more often than not a fresh curriculum team ushers in the new curriculum. Regardless of any qualities, good or bad, of previous curricula, the most recent team of educational experts must initiate a 'new fix'. A culture of crisis, rather than innovation, has become the norm in educational circles in Africa. Ministry of Education officials, as one donor pointed out, are usually too busy maintaining the status quo to engage in innovation, which they leave to the donors. Furthermore, curriculum development and change in Africa rests with Ministry of Education bodies who usually have little contact with universities, which are the institutions charged with the responsibility for exploring the frontiers of new knowledge and for transmitting this knowledge and the techniques of knowledge production to subsequent generations. As a result, too often in Africa educational innovation literally means starting all over again. Rarely is there even an institutional memory of earlier reforms, or a knowledge of what has been tried in countries with similar circumstances. Instead, more often than not a team of high-powered educationalists will visit and advise approaches used in, for example, Canada or Australia. In the absence of an established culture of educational innovation, the countries of sub-Saharan Africa will forever continue to be dependent on such foreign expertise.

Professor Jophus Anamuah-Mensah is the Principal of Winneba College of Education and Director of SACOST. As described in Chapter 15, SACOST was deliberately established in 2000, with help from AFCLIST, to institutionalise a culture of educational innovation with specific reference to linking school science and technology with that of the community and workplace. As Professor Anamuah-Mensah describes, SACOST has already established vibrant formal and professional relationships with appropriate institutions in the Ministry of Education and the Ministry of Science and Technology, many major industries, other universities and professional teachers' associations, as well as key parastatal institutions such as Ghana Regional Appropriate Technology Industrial Science (GRATIS) and the National Board for Small Scale Industries. SACOST sponsors undergraduate, graduate, PhD and postgraduate research, involving scholars at other universities as well as practising teachers. Often this work is supported by local industries which, for example, sponsored a Winneba researcher to attend a major international meeting held in Hawaii in the summer of 2001 on indigenous science. SACOST has been selected by the Ministries of Education and of Science and Technology to be the secretariat of a major government commission on science and technology education. In short, in a brief length of time, SACOST has become a national and international focal point for linking school science with that in the community and workplace.

We have described SACOST in some detail. With similar assistance from AFCLIST, a sister centre to SACOST has been established at the University of Swaziland, as well as centres at the University College of Science and Technology Education in Zimbabwe and Venda University in South Africa, that address issues of teaching science in large, under-resourced classrooms. Centres in Malawi and Zanzibar address issues of environmental education in much the same way.

AFCLIST intends to help create other centres of excellence in different countries of sub-Saharan Africa and has taken steps to do so in the critical fields of examinations and teacher education. Without such institutions, as far as science and technology education is concerned, Africa can never have a past; without a past it is difficult to envisage a future.

Providing the Catalyst for System-wide Change

Rarely do the stakeholders in education have an opportunity to meet in a relaxed atmosphere to discuss schooling. During 2000 and 2001, AFCLIST facilitated such gatherings in Zanzibar, Ghana and Malawi. Each meeting followed a similar pattern. Grassroots representatives attended the first day of the meetings, namely representatives of students, teachers, parents, small-scale business people, and religious and political leaders. Short presentations of the science and technology projects in their respective countries were followed by discussion. Then participants observed a class of primary school children being taught by an experienced teacher – in Zanzibar this became known as the 'bang' lesson. The general response can be summed up by a remark made by a local sheikh when he exclaimed that nobody in their right mind would ask someone to prepare a body for burial who had learned how to do so only from books. He added that he did not understand the minds of the Ministry of Education. After discussion in the 'bang' lesson, participants broke into groups; parents met together, teachers met together and so on, and they were given the task of discussing what each group would do on their return home, using their own resources, to promote that style of science teaching. At all meetings these groups worked late into the night.

On the following day participants were representatives of college-based and school-based teacher development institutions with the most articulate of the representatives from the first day remaining behind. The pattern for the second day was similar to that of the first day except that the teacher educators listened to the action plans of the grassroots representatives.

On the third day, senior Ministry of Education officials were represented, such as staff from the advisory service, curriculum centre and examination council, and they too listened to action plans, observed a 'bang' lesson and in turn developed their own action plans. By this stage of the meetings, in the relaxed atmosphere provided by the meeting facilitators, everybody had the confidence to express themselves openly. Indeed, the primary school students participated in all meeting sessions, presenting their views with confidence and determination.

There was no 'bang' lesson on the fourth and closing day. Instead, participants spent the half day listening to the action plans of all the groups from the previous three days and the first group to present their plan were the children, who held participants fascinated. On the fourth day the participants were ministers, principal secretaries and directors from relevant ministries such as education, science and technology, and foreign affairs; representatives of the formal sector and the donor community; and representatives of the media. Deliberately, no requests were made of these groups other than that they participate in discussion and respond to what they heard reported. In all three countries the unsolicited responses were almost frighteningly enthusiastic, and in all three countries follow-up by all parties is showing signs that an integrated approach to change in the popularisation of science and technology is now underway.

Summary

We have described AFCLIST's theory of systemic educational change in some detail. We have done so in the hope that some of it may resonate with the thinking of some policy-makers and activists. Our message is simple and optimistic. Provided they are given an appropriate environment, African children are capable of amazing creativity and focused work. And, most important, the appropriate environment can be provided using our own human, cultural, physical and economic resource base. What educational systems in Africa perhaps need most of all is vision, determination and an absence of expecting miracles by decree.

References

Chapter 1

Makhurane, P. M. and Kahn, M. (1998). 'The role of science and technology in development'. In Naidoo, P. and Savage M. (eds). *African Science and Technology Education into the New Millennium: Practice, Policy and Priorities*, Kenwyn, Juta.

Naidoo, P. and Savage, M. (1998) (eds). 'Into the new millennium'. In Naidoo, P. and Savage, M. (eds). *African Science and Technology Education into the New Millennium: Practice, Policy and Priorities*, Kenwyn, Juta.

Chapter 2

Dahl, R.A. (1998). *On Democracy*, Yale University Press.

Fabiano, E. (1998). 'Resourcing science and technology education'. In Naidoo, P. and Savage, M. (eds). *African Science and Technology Education into the New Millennium: Practice, Policy and Priorities*, Kenwyn, Juta.

Harris, Mary (1999). *Gender Sensitivity in Primary School Mathematics in India*. Commonwealth Secretariat, London.

Hochschild, A. *King Leopold's Ghost: A Story of Greed, Terror, and Heroism in Colonial Africa*. Houghton Mifflin Company.

Jegede, O.J. (1998). 'The knowledge base for learning in science and technology'. In Naidoo, P. and Savage, M. (eds). *African Science and Technology Education into the New Millennium: Practice, Policy and Priorities*, Kenwyn, Juta.

Makhurane, P.M. and Kahn, M. (1998). 'The role of science and technology in development'. In Naidoo, P. and Savage M. (eds). *African Science and Technology Education into the New Millennium: Practice, Policy and Priorities*, Kenwyn, Juta.

Mazower, M. (1998). *Dark Continent*, Alfred A. Kopf, New York.

Mbano, N. (1999). 'Change of school culture can improve the performance of learners: experience of a cognitive acceleration intervention'. In Reddy, V. (ed.). *Gender, Science, Technology and Education: Sustaining Participation*. University of Durban-Westville, South Africa.

Naidoo, P. and Savage, M. (1998) (eds). 'Into the new millennium'. In Naidoo, P. and Savage, M. (eds). *African Science and Technology Education into the New Millennium: Practice, Policy and Priorities*, Kenwyn, Juta.

Okebukola, P. (1995). 'Organization and conditions of secondary science education in Nigeria'. Submitted to *Planning science education at the secondary level*. Johannesburg: IIEP and CEPD.

Reddy, V. (1998). 'Relevance and the promotion of equity'. In Naidoo, P. and Savage, M. (eds). *African Science and Technology Education into the New Millennium: Practice, Policy and Priorities*, Kenwyn, Juta.

Rollnick, M. (1998). 'Relevance in science and technology education'. In Naidoo, P. and Savage, M. (eds). *African Science and Technology Education into the New Millennium: Practice, Policy and Priorities*, Kenwyn, Juta.

Savage, M. (1998). 'Curriculum innovations and their impact on the teaching of science and technology'. In Naidoo, P. and Savage, M. (eds). *African Science and Technology Education into the New Millennium: Practice, Policy and Priorities*, Kenwyn, Juta.

Yoloye, E.A. (1998). 'Historical perspectives and their relevance to present and future practice'. In Naidoo, P. and Savage, M. (eds). *African Science and Technology Education into the New Millennium: Practice, Policy and Priorities*, Kenwyn, Juta.

Chapter 3

Australian Research Council (2000). *Science and industry linkages*. http://www.arc.gov.au

Department of Arts, Culture, Science and Technology (South Africa) (1999). *Loss of Skills from the Public Sector*.

Department of Arts, Culture, Science and Technology (South Africa) (2000). *Survey of resources allocated to research development*.

Department of Arts, Culture, Science and Technology (South Africa) (1998). *System-wide review*.

Department of Trade and Industry (UK) (1998). *Forward Look*.

Narin, F., Hamilton, K.S. and Olivastro, D. (1997). *Research Policy* 26:317–330.

Sara, V. (2000). *National Investment in Research, Benchmarking Industry-Science Relationships*, Berlin, in press. http:www.industry-science-berlin 2000.de

Stewart, W. (1995). Invited talk, FRD Policy Lunch Club, 1 March 1995

Chapter 4

Molloy, F.J., Critchley, A.T., Mshigeni, K.E., Rotmann, K.W.G. and Chang, S.T. (1999). 'Turning Seaweed and brewery industry waste into valuable oyster mushroom crop', *Discovery and Innovation* 11:1–7.

Mshigeni, K.E. (2000). 'Highlights on Africa's Natural Resources Heritage'. In Mshigeni *et al.* (eds). *Revitalising Science and Technology Focus in Africa: A New Hope for Liberating the Continent from the Poverty Trap*, University of Namibia, Windhoek.

Mshigeni, K.E., Critchley, A., Mwandemele, O.D. and Molloy, F. (2000). 'Unrealized Wealth in Africa's Aquatic Resources with Special Reference to the Development of Marine Centre of Excellence in Henties Bay, Namibia'. In Mshigeni *et al.* (eds). *Revitalising Science and Technology Focus in Africa: A New Hope for Liberating the Continent from the Poverty Trap*, University of Namibia, Windhoek.

Chapter 6

Department of Housing and Planning Research (Ghana) (1971). *Social and Economic Survey of Suame Magazine*. University of Science and Technology, Kumasi.

Gratis Foundation Corporate Profile. Tema, Ghana.

Powell, J. (1995). *The Intermediate Technology Transfer Unit – A Handbook on Operations*, KNUST, Kumasi.

Chapter 7

Marimba, A. (1994). *Yuguru, Africa*, Eritrea, World Press.

Bio-Diversity Campaign News (1996). Internet.

Christofferson, N., Campbell and Bruce, Du Toit, J. (eds) (1996). *Communities and Sustainable Use: Pan-African Perspective*, ICUN, Zimbabwe.

Convention on Biological Diversity (1992).

Dipholo, D.K. *Agricultural Resource Board*, Botswana.

Gashe, B.A. and Mphuchane, S.F. (1996). *Phane: Proceedings of the First Multidisciplinary Symposium on Phane*, Botswana.

Hoppers, O.C. and Makhele Mahlangu, P. (1998). *A Comparative Study of the Development, Integration and Protection of Indigenous Knowledge Systems in the Third World, An Analytical Framework Document*, HSRC, p.5.

Hountondji (1997). *Endogenous Knowledge and Research Trials*, Dekar, CODESR.

Kaya, H.O. and Maleka, S. (1996). 'Building on indigenous'. *Journal of African Studies* 10 (1), Pula, Botswana.

Kgathi, D.L. (1987). *The Grapple Plant Project – Aspects of Grapple Trade*. NIR Research Notes No. 24, University of Botswana, Gaborone.

Lalonde, André and Morin-Labatut, Giséle (1993). 'Indigenous Knowledge and Innovation: Its Contribution to Sustainable and Equitable Development', paper presented at the 1993 Annual Meeting of the African Studies Association, Boston, Mass.

Larsen, J. (1998). *Perspectives on Indigenous Knowledge Systems in Southern Africa*, Environment Group Africa Region, The World Bank.

Materechera, S.M., Hansen-Quartey, J.H. and Nyamapsene, K. (1998). 'Soil properties as influenced by cultivation of the aromatic shrub, artemisia afra, South Africa'. *Plant Ground* (15) 1.

Matowanyika, J.J., Garibaldi, V. and Musiwa, E. (1994). *Indigenous Knowledge Systems and National Resources Management in Southern Africa*, Workshop Report, 20–22 April, Harare, ICUN, Zimbabwe.

Mazrui, A. (1990). *Cultural Forces in World Politics*, James Curry, London.

Mmegi/Reporter, 22 August 1997.

Moruakgomo, M.B.M. (1996). *Commercial Utilization of Botswana's Veld Product*, Thusano Lefatshe, Gaborone, Botswana.

Mushita, T.A. (1995). 'Indigenous Knowledge Systems in Southern Africa', conference paper, 24–28 April.

Ntsoane, O. (2000a). *Implications of Intellectual Property Rights on Indigenous Knowledge Systems Southern Africa: A Comparative Study of Selected Rural Communities In Botswana and South Africa*, unpublished Master's thesis, North-West University, South Africa.

Ntsoane, O. (2000b). 'Towards a Definition of Indigenous Knowledge Systems', unpublished article.

Pula (1996). *Botswana Journal of African Studies*, Vol. 10, No. 1, 60–70.

Quin, P.J. (1995). *Foods and Feeding Habits of the Pedi*, Witwatersrand University Press, Johannesburg.

Sacks, R.K. (1997). *Baseline Socio-Economic Survey: Community Based Management of Indigenous Forest Project in Motokwe, Khekhenye and Tshwaane, Kweng West Sub-district, South Central, Botswana , Veld Products Research*.

Sekhwela, M.B. and Ntseane, P.G. (1994). *Development Grapple Plant (Hapogophytum Procumbens, D.C.) Management Strategies in Botswana: Peoples' Agenda for Effective and Sustainable Natural Resources Utilization and Management*, University of Botswana, NIT.

Senghor, L. (1965). *On African Socialism*, Stanford.

Sing, N.G. (1996). 'Biodiversity, Community Rights, Trade and International Law: Legal and Practical Options for Developing Countries', paper presented at OAU, Ethiopia, 11 June.

Thusano Lefatsheng (1994). *Studies in Kang Region*, Botswana.

Todaro, M. (1985). *Economic Development in the Third World*. Longman, London.

Van der Vlueten, J. (1998). *Community-based monitoring of non-timber forest products*. Veld Products Research, Gaborone, Botswana.

Chapter 8

Dzama, E.N.N. and Osborne, J.F. (1999). 'Poor performance in science among African students: an alternative explanation to the African worldview thesis'. *Journal of Research in Science Teaching* 36(3): 387–405.

Lewin, K.M. (1993). *Science Education in Developing Countries: Issues and Perspectives for Planners*. IIEP, Paris.

Mshigeni, K. *et al.* (1994). Study on Science and Technology (mimeo). SADC, Gaborone.

Ogbu, O.M., Oyeyinka, B.O. and Mlawa, H.M. (1995). *Technology Policy in Africa*. IDRC, Ottawa.

Ogunniyi, M.O. (1996). 'Improving science and mathematics curriculum in African schools: a synopsis'. In Stoll, C., de Feiter, L., Vonk, H. and den Akker, I. (eds). *Improving Science and Mathematics Teaching in Africa*. V U Press, Amsterdam.

Southern African Development Community (SADC) (1998). *Protocol on Education and Training*. SADC, Gaborone.

Chapter 9

George, J. (1999). 'Contextualised science teaching in developing countries: positives and dilemmas'. In *Proceedings of the 7th Southern African Association for Research in Mathematics and Science Education (SAARMSE)*. Harare, Zimbabwe.

Massaquoi, J.G.M. (1997). 'Regional cooperation for human resources development in science and technology: a case for networking', UNESCO Nairobi Office Bulletin, 32 (1).

Massaquoi, J.G.M. (1998). 'Regional cooperation in the dissemination of scientific information from African universities – the case for ANSTI', UNESCO Nairobi Office Bulletin, 33 (1)

Ramsden, J.M. (1992). 'If it's enjoyable, is it science? Pupils' reactions to context- and activity-based science'. *School Science Review* 73: 65–71.

http://www.cgiar.org

http://www.cgiar.org/ilri/

http://www.cgiar.org/warda/

http://www.cgiar.org/icraf/

AFCLIST (1999). *The African Forum for Children's Literacy in Science and Technology*, brochure and information sheets.

Bot, M., (1997). *Baseline Study: Education 2000 Plus Macro Indicators, 1991–1996*, report commissioned by the Centre for Education Policy Development, Evaluation and Management, CEPD.

Bude, U. and Wippich, M. (1999). *Science and Agriculture Primary School Leaving Examination Papers 1998 (Eastern and Southern Africa)*. Bonn, Education, Science and Documentation Centre (ZED).

Bude, U. and Lewin, K. (1997). *Improving Test Design: Vol. 1 – Constructing Test Instruments, Analysing Results and Improving Assessment Quality in Primary Schools in Africa*. Bonn, Education, Science and Documentation Centre (ZED).

Bude, U. and Lewin, K. (1997). *Improving Test Design: Vol. 2 – Assessment of Science and Agriculture in Primary Schools in Africa, 12 Country Cases Reviewed*. Bonn, Education, Science and Documentation Centre (ZED).

Commonwealth and the Association for the Development of Education in Africa (1998). Newsletter, *TMS News*, January.

DAE Newsletter (1995). Vol. 7(3): 8–10, July–September.

Dorsey, B.J. (1996). *Gender Inequalities in Education in the Southern Africa Region: An Analysis of Intervention Strategies*, pp. 80–83, LTNESCO Sub-Regional Office for Southern Africa

Dyankov, A. (1996). *UNEVOC Studies in Technical and Vocational Education – 8: Current Issues and Trends in Technical and Vocational Education*. UNEVOC-International Project on Technical and Vocational Education.

Enjiku, D.B. (1977). *Who's Who in Science And Technology Education in Africa*. African Network for Research and Development in Science and Technology Education (ANRDSTE).

Fabiano, E., Naidoo, P. and Savage, M. (1997). *Building Partnerships for the Future*. AFCLIST Monograph 1, an occasional paper, Durban, South Africa.

Female Education in Mathematics and Science in Africa (FEMSA) (1997). *Country reports*. Nairobi, Kenya

Harris, A. (1996). 'The Improving Education Quality Project: The Role of Assessment in the Rhythms of Reform', paper presented at the Comparative and International Education Society Meeting, Williamsburg, VA, March.

Januario, F.M. and Mariano da Jasso, C. (1997). 'Promotion of the Equal Access of Girls to Science Education and Technical/Vocational Education in Africa', paper presented to the UNESCO Sub-Regional Meeting for English Speaking Countries on Scientific, Technical and Vocational Education for Girls in Africa, 8–12 September.

Levy, S. (1994). *Projects speak for themselves*. 2nd ed. Houghton, Sharon Levy.

Malpede, D. (1997). 'Women in Science Education in English Speaking African Countries', paper presented to the UNESCO Sub-Regional Meeting for English Speaking Countries on Scientific, Technical and Vocational Education for Girls in Africa, 8–12 September.

Mannathoko, C. (1997). 'Strategies for Mainstreaming and Institutionalising Gender

Equity into Science Education and Vocational Training – The Case of Botswana', paper presented to the LTNESCO Sub-Regional Meeting for English Speaking Countries on Scientific, Technical and Vocational Education for Girls in Africa, 8–12 September.

Mulemwa, J.N. (1999a). *Scientific, Technical and Vocational Education of Girls in Africa: Guidelines for Programme Planning*, booklet commissioned and published by UNESCO, Education Sector.

Mulemwa, J.N. (1999b). 'The State and Challenges of Gender Equity in Science Education in Africa'. In Savage, M. and Naidoo, P (eds.) *Using the Local Resource Base to Teach Science and Technology: Lessons from Africa*, pp. 19–53, University of Durban-Westville, South Africa.

Mulemwa, J.N. (1998). 'Science Education in a New Uganda', paper presented to a science education seminar, University of Oslo, Norway, 18–19 May.

Mulemwa, J.N. (1997). *Female Education in Mathematics and Science in Africa FEMSA: The Uganda Country Profile Report*.

Munene, J.C. et al. (1997). *Teachers' Work Experience and Pupils' Schooling Experience as Determinants of Achievement in Primary School*. Uganda IEQ Project Phase 2 Research.

O'Connor, J. (1997). 'Towards sustainable Development though Gender Equity in Science and Technology. The FEMSA View', paper presented to the UNESCO Consultative Meeting on Girls and Women in Science and Technology in Africa: Challenges and Opportunities for the 21st Century, Arusha, Tanzania, 17–19 September.

Odhiambo, T.R. (1997). 'Popularization of Science and Technology and Promotion of a Culture of Science: The Experience of CHISCI', paper presented to the UNESCO Consultative Meeting on Girls and Women in Science and Technology in Africa: Challenges and Opportunities for the 21st Century, Arusha, Tanzania, 17–20 October.

SAARMSE (1998). *Proceedings of the Southern African Association for Research in Mathematics and Science Education (SAARMSE)*.

Savage, M. (1995). 'Curriculum Innovations and their Impact on Teaching of Science and Technology', paper presented to the ASTE '95 Conference on African Science and Technology Education into the New Millenium: Practice, Policy and Priorities, held at the University of Durban-Westville, Durban, South Africa, December.

Savage, M and Naidoo, P. (eds) (1997). *Improving girls' participation and performance in science education in Africa*. University of Durban-Westville, South Africa.

Schubert, J.G. (1996). 'The Improving Education Quality Project: A Snapshot of IEQ', paper presented at the Comparative and International Education Society Meeting, Williamsburg, VA, March.

Simelane, N.O. (1997). 'Participation of Women and Girls in Science-Based Occupations in Southern Africa', paper presented to the UNESCO Sub-Regional Meeting for English Speaking Countries on Scientific, Technical and Vocational Education for Girls in Africa, 12 September.

Sjoberg, S. (1997). 'The Access of Girls to Science and Technology', an invited paper to the Conference on Public Understanding of Science and Technology, University of Western Cape, South Africa, 4–7 December 1996.

Sjoberg, S., Mehta, A.J. and Mnemwa, J. (1996). SAS: *Science and Scientists – A Cross-Cultural Comparison of Children's Experiences, Attitudes and Perceptions that may be of Relevance for Learning Science, with particular Reference to Gender Aspects*, Oslo University, working documents and questionnaire.

South African Magazine. *The Year of Science and Technology: Calendar 1998*.

Takundwa, M.G. (1997). 'Viable Alternatives in Science Education and Vocational Training for Girls: Zimbabwean Experience', paper presented to the UNESCO Sub-Regional Meeting for English Speaking Countries on Scientific, Technical and Vocational Education for Girls in Africa, 8–12 September 1997.

UN Gender Work Group (1995). *Science and Technology for Sustainable Human Development: Gender Dimension*, The Gender Working Group of the UN Commission on Science and Technology for Development, May,

UNESCO (1996). *Practical Guide For the Development of Instructional Materials For EPD in Africa South of the Sahara*, UNESCO Regional Office, Dakar.

UNESCO, Project 2000+, POPSTAFRIC Sub-Regional Workshop, Harare 17–21 October 1994, Final Report, UNESCO Regional Office, Dakar.

UNESCO (1993). *Better Education Today for a Better World Tomorrow: World-wide Action in Education*.

Whittle, P., Gray, B. Hodzi, R. and Manana, L. (1993). *The Harare Generator. 12 Innovative Ideas and Techniques for Science Educators in Africa*, ICSU, Zimbabwe.

Yoloye, E.A. (1995). 'Historical Perspectives and their Relevance to Present and Future Practice', paper presented to the ASTE'95 Conference on African Science and Technology Education into the New Millenium Practice, Policy and Priorities, held at the University of Durban-Westville, South Africa, December.

Chapter 14

Ajeyalemi, D. (1990). 'Science and technology in perspective'. In Ajeyalemi, D. *Science and Technology in Africa*.

American National Academy of Sciences (1996). No other details are available as this document was read in a library in Kenya when the author was there on sabbatical.

Anamuah-Mensah, J. (1999). 'Science and Technology in Ghana', occasional paper, University College of Education of Winneba, Ghana.

Black, P. and Harrison, G. (1985). *In Place of Confusion: Technology and Science in the School Curriculum*, Nuffield-Chelsea Curriculum Trust and National Centre for School Technology, Newgate Press, London.

Bloom, B.S. (ed.) (1956). *Taxonomy of educational objectives. The classification of educational goals. Handbook 1: Cognitive domain*. Mckay, New York.

Campbell, B., Lubben, F. and Dlamini, Z. (2000). 'Learning science through contexts: helping pupils to make sense of everyday issues', *International Journal of Science Education* 22(3): 239–252.

Clark, N. and Juma, C. (1991). *Biotechnology for Sustainable Development: Policy Options for Developing Countries*, African Centre for Technology Studies, ACTS Press, Nairobi.

George, J. (1999). *Contextualised Science Teaching in Developing Countries: Positives and Dilemmas*. In Proceedings of the 7th Southern African Association for Research in Mathematics and Science Education (SAARMSE), Harare.

Horton, R. (1967). 'African traditional thought and Western science'. In Young, M.F.D. (ed.). *Knowledge and Control*. Collier MacMillan, London.

Hountondji, P. (ed.) (1997). *Endogenous Knowledge: Research Trails*, Council for the Development of Social Science Research in Africa (CODESTRIA), Dakar.

Irvine, D. (ed.) (1985). 'Problems of science popularization in the Caribbean', opening address in S. Laurent, seminar/workshop, Caribbean Industrial Research Institute.

Lubben, F., Campbell, B. and Dlamini, B. (1995) 'In-service support for a technological approach to science education', Education Research Papers, serial, no. 16, Department of International Education, London.

Lubben, F., Campbell, B., Maphalala T. and Putsoa, B. (1998). 'Science curriculum material development through a teacher-industrialist partnership: industrialists' perception of their role', *Research in Science and Technological Education* 16 (2): 217–230

Makhurane, P. and Kahn, M. (1998). 'The Role of Science and Technology in Development'. In Naidoo, P. and Savage M. (eds). *African Science and Technology Education into the New Millennium: Practice, Policy and Priorities*, Kenwyn, Juta.

National Research Council (1996). *National Science Education Standards*, National Academy Press, Washington, DC.

Ogunniyi, M.B. (1996). 'Policy Issues in Science Education. The African Scene'. In Yandila, C. and Charakupa, R. (eds). BOLESWA *Mathematics and Science*, Regional Conference, Gaborone.

Putsoa, B. (1992). Investigating the ability to apply scientific knowledge, through process skills, among high school leavers in Swaziland. Unpublished D.Phil thesis, University of York.

Putsoa, B. (1999). 'Bridging School Science with that of the Community and Workplace'. In Savage, M. and Naidoo, P. (eds). *Using the Local Resource Base to Teach Science and Technology: Lessons from Africa*, University of Durban-Westville, South Africa.

Ramsden, J.M. (1992). 'If it's enjoyable, is it science? Pupils' reactions to context- and activity-based science', *School Science Review* 73: 65–71.

Roberts, D.A. (1982). 'Developing the concept of 'Curriculum Emphases' in science education', *Science Education* 66: 234–259.

Solomon, J. and Aikenhead, G. (eds) (1994). *Science, Technology and Science Education: International Perspectives on Reform*, Teachers College Press, New York.

Tsuma, O.G.K. (1998). *Science and Technology in the African Context*, Jomo Kenyatta Foundation Publishers, Nairobi.

UNESCO (1972). *Survey of the present position of the promotion of public understanding of science and technology in Africa*, Unesco, Paris.

UNESCO (1983). *Science and technology education and national development*, Unesco, Paris.

Wellington, J. (ed.) (1989). *Skills and Processes in Science Education: A Critical Analysis*. Routledge, London.

Wright, C. (1999). 'Concepts, Issues and Strategies'. In Ramanathan, S. (ed.). *Popularising Science and Technology: Some Asian Case Studies*, Singapore, AMIC/Commonwealth Secretariat.

Yager, R.E. (1990). 'STS as a Development in Science Education', *Science Education International Journal* 1(4): 24–27.

Chapter 15

Anamuah-Mensah, J. (1999). 'STAG: An Innovative Science Project Linking School Science and Industry in Ghana', *Journal of Science and Mathematics Education*, 2 (1): 88–93.

Anamuah-Mensah, J., Brown-Acquaye, H., Quaye, E.C. and Towse, P. (1999). *Science in Action: A Resource Book for Science Teachers*, Adwinsa Publications, Accra.

Bishop, G (1986). *Innovation in Education*, Macmillan, London.

Brock-Utne, B. (1999). 'African Universities and the African', *International Review of Education* 45 (1): 87–104.

Dzobo, N.K. (1987). *Report of the Educational Advisory Committee on the Proposed Structure and Content of Education for Ghana*, Ministry of Education, Accra.

Geertz, C. (1973). *The Interpretation of Cultures*, Basic Books, New York.

Gibbons, M. (1998). *Higher Education Relevance in the 21st Century*, The World Bank, Washington.

Goldstein, P. (1978). *Changing the American Textbook*, Lexington, Massachusetts. P.1: D. C. Heath.

Jegede, O.J. (1997). 'School Science and the Development of Scientific Culture: A Review of Contemporary Science Education in African', *International Journal of Science Education* 19 (17): 1–20.

Jegede, O.J. and Okebukola, P. (1988). 'The Ecology of Socio-cultural Factors in Science Classrooms', *International Journal of Educology* 2: 93–107.

Jegede, O. and Solomon, J. (1999). 'Promoting a popular science and technology culture'. In Ramanathan, S. (ed.) *Popularizing Science and Technology: Some Asian Case Studies*, Singapore, AMIC/Commonwealth Secretariat.

Krugly-Smolska, E. (1995). 'Cultural influences in science education', *International Journal of Science Education* 17 (1): 45–58.

Makhurane, P. and Kahn, M. (1998). 'The Role of Science and Technology in Development'. In Naidoo, P. and Savage M. (eds). *African Science and Technology Education into the New Millennium: Practice, Policy and Priorities*, Kenwyn, Juta.

Ogawa, M. (1986). 'Toward a new rationale of science education in a non-western society', *European Journal of Science Education* 8: 113–119.

Ogunniyi, M.B., Jegede, O.J., Ogawa, M. and Yandilla, C. (1995). 'World views projected by science teachers in Nigeria, Japan, Botswana, Indonesia and the Philippines'. *Journal of Research in Science Teaching* (no other details available).

Ogunniyi, M.B. (1988). 'Adapting western science to traditional African culture', *International Journal of Science Education* 10: 1–9.

Ogunniyi, M.B. (1987). 'Conceptions of traditional cosmological ideas among literate and non-literate Nigerians', *Journal of Research in Science Teaching* 24: 107–117.

Republic of Ghana (1992). *Industrial Policy Statement: A Strategy for Industrial Regeneration*, Ministry of Industry, Science and Technology, Accra

Republic of Ghana (1999). *National Education Forum: A Decade of Educational Reforms – Preparation for the Challenges of a New Millennium*, Ministry of Education, Accra.

Republic of Ghana (1974). *The New Structure and Content of Education for Ghana*, Tema, Ghana Publishing Corp., Accra.

Richardson, V. (1994). 'Conducting Research on Practice', *Educational Research* 23 (5): 5–10.

Skilbeck, M. (1984). *School-based Curriculum Development*, Harper, London.

Smolicz, J.J. and Nunan, E.E. (1975). 'The philosophical and sociological foundations of Science Education: the demythologizing of school science', *Studies in Science Education* 2: 101–143.

Solomon, J. (1996). 'Societal Impact', *Castme Journal* 16 (1): 5–7.

Towse, P. and Anamuah-Mensah, J. (1991). 'Science and Technology in Action in Ghana', *Science Educational International* 31–34.

Turner, S. and Turner, T. (1987). 'Multicultural education in the initial training of science teachers', *Research in Science and Technology Education* 5 (1): 25–35.

Chapter 16

Department of Arts, Culture, Science and Technology (1996). *White Paper on Science and Technology: Preparing for the 21st Century*, Pretoria.

Department of Arts, Culture, Science and Technology (1999). *Report from the National Research and Technology Foresight Project*, Pretoria.

Department of Arts, Culture, Science and Technology (2000a). *Directorate for Science and Society: Towards a Strategy for Public Understanding of Science, Engineering and Technology*, first draft, Pretoria.

Department of Arts, Culture, Science and Technology (2000b). *The Year of Science and Technology, Project Year-End Report*, Pretoria.

Department of Education (2001). New 2005/draft revised national curriculum http://education.pwv.gov.za/DoE_Sites/Curriculum/

Chapter 17

Amara, J. (1987). 'Indigenous Technology of Sierra Leone and the Science Education of Girls', *International Journal of Science Education* 9(3): 317–324.

Anon (1980). 'Indigenous Technology', unpublished paper.

Anon (1994). 'Module on Gara', prepared for the Do-it-Herself Exhibition organised by the British Council, Freetown, Sierra Leone.

Bockarie, S.A. (1982). *Placed Authority and Transactions with Innovations: A Study of the Diffusion of the CCIS into Sierra Leonean Schools*, unpublished Ph.D thesis, University of London.

Chaytor, D.E.B. (1991). 'Training of Future Science and Technology Operators in Sierra Leone', speech delivered to the Freetown Dinner Club at the British Council, Freetown, 31 August.

Cole, M.J.A. (1979). 'Development of Foundation Course in Science Based upon Indigenous Technology', unpublished paper prepared for the YWCA Vocational School, Freetown.

Cole, M.J.A. and Hamilton, D.B. (1978). 'Survey of Rural Technologies in Sierra Leone', ECA/SL Ministry of Social Welfare Project, Atlantic Printers, Freetown.

Freyberg, R. and Osborne, P. (1985). *Learning in Science*. Heineman, Auckland.

Makhubu, L.A. (1988). 'The Introduction of Indigenous Technology into the Curriculum of Schools in Africa. Objectives and Modalities', paper presented at the

UNESCO Consultative Committee on the Renewal of Science and Technology Teaching in Africa.

Maruping, E. (1976). *'Lubi' as a Chemical Reagent*, unpublished dissertation submitted for the partial fulfillment of the degree of B.Sc ED, University of Sierra Leone.

Spencer, S.M.A (1993). *Indigenous Technology as a Basis for Science and Technology Education at the Junior Secondary School: A Sierra Leonean Case Study*, unpublished doctoral thesis, University of Southampton.

Chapter 19

Commonwealth Secretariat (1997). 13th Conference of Commonwealth Education Ministers, Gaborone, Botswana, 28 July–1 August.

Castells, M. (1996). *The Rise of the Network Society*, Blackwell, Malden, Mass.

Hendrix, A. (Comp)(1996). *Southern African Conference: public understanding science and technology, draft proceedings*, 4–7 December 1996, Western Cape, South Africa

IMPULS, Science and Technology Center (1994). *Prototyping for the 21st Century*, Amsterdam.

IOSTE (1999). 9th Symposium of the International Organization for Science and Technology, Proceedings, 26 June–2 July, Durban, South Africa.

Ming, C.K. and Fong, L.K (eds) (1989). Popularization of science and technology : what informal and non-formal education can do. Proceedings, 4–9 September, Hong Kong.

Naidoo, P. and Savage, M. (eds) (1998). *African Science and Technology Education into the New Millennium: Practice, Policy and Priorities*, Kenwyn, Juta.

Nelson, G.D. (1999). 'Science Literacy for All in the 21st Century', *Educational Leadership* 57 (2) October.

Ntsoane, O. (2000). 'Indigenous knowledge systems and their economic potential in South Africa: A Case Study, paper.

Ramanathan, S (1999). *Popularising Science and Technology: Some Asian Case Studies*, Commonwealth Secretariat, London.

Sjoberg, S. (2000). *Science and Scientists: The SAS-study*, Blindern, Oslo.

Suid-Afrikaanse Akademie vir Wetenskap en Kuns. *The popularisation of science and technology and the creation of wider scientific and technological literacy in South African society.*

UNESCO (1999). *Connect* 24 (4), 1999.

UNESCO (1998). *World Science Report*, UNESCO, Paris.

World Conference on Science, Budapest, Hungary, UNESCO 25 June–1 July 1999.